The business of birth control

Manchester University Press

The business of birth control

Contraception and commerce in Britain before the sexual revolution

CLAIRE L. JONES

Manchester University Press

Copyright © Claire L. Jones 2020

The right of Claire L. Jones to be identified as the author of this work has been asserted by her in accordance with the Copyright, Designs and Patents Act 1988.

Published by Manchester University Press
Oxford Road, Manchester M13 9PL
www.manchesteruniversitypress.co.uk

British Library Cataloguing-in-Publication Data
A catalogue record for this book is available from the British Library

ISBN 978 1 5261 3628 2 hardback
ISBN 978 1 5261 8232 6 paperback

First published 2020

The publisher has no responsibility for the persistence or accuracy of URLs for any external or third-party internet websites referred to in this book, and does not guarantee that any content on such websites is, or will remain, accurate or appropriate.

Typeset by
Servis Filmsetting Ltd, Stockport, Cheshire

For John – with all my love

Contents

	List of figures	*page* viii
	Acknowledgements	xi
	Introduction: contraceptive commercialisation before the Pill	1
1	The dynamics of production: contraceptive manufacturing	31
2	Shaping markets: packaging, brands and trademarks	63
3	The print culture of contraceptives: advertising and the circulation of birth control knowledge	98
4	'As honest as business permits': medical practitioners, birth control clinics and contraceptive efficacy	134
5	Over the counter and on the high street: contraceptive retailing in the urban landscape	172
	Epilogue	205
	Appendix	215
	Bibliography	223
	Index	239

Figures

1 'The factory test'. Condom testing by air inflation and visual inspection at Prentif's latex manufactory, St Mary Cray, Kent, c.1937. Reproduced with permission from the Wellcome Library (SA/FPA/A7/101, Prentif, *Contraceptive Practice*, 2 (February 1938), 4). page 46

2 Condom testing by elongation at LRC's latex manufactory, Shore Road, Hackney, 1938. Reproduced with permission from Vestry House Museum, London Borough of Waltham Forest (LRC album P1, N11 577). 47

3 'One of the workrooms where "Lam-butt" contraceptive appliances are made', Lamberts Prorace Ltd, *Latest Price List of Approved Contraceptive Appliances* (1941), p. 1. Reproduced with permission from Museum of Contraception and Abortion, Vienna. 49

4 Women manually dipping and drying condoms, LRC, Chingford, c.1940. Reproduced with permission from Vestry House Museum, London Borough of Waltham Forest (LRC album P1, N11 418). 54

5 Girl testing condom by air inflation, LRC, Chingford, c.1950. Reproduced with permission from Vestry House Museum, London Borough of Waltham Forest (LRC album 2, 1994.80.231). 54

6 W. J. Rendell's 'Wife's Friend' Soluble Pessaries, Rendal's Surgical Store, *Catalogue* (c.1935), p. 19. Reproduced with permission from the Thackray Medical Museum, Leeds. 66

7 H. A. Allbutt's *The Wife's Handbook*, promoting Rendell's 'Wife's Friend', H. A. Allbutt, *The Wife's Handbook*

LIST OF FIGURES

	(London: R. Forder, 1894). Reproduced with permission from the Thackray Medical Museum, Leeds.	68
8	E. Lambert and Son, 'Pro-Race' cervical cap, England, 1915–25. Credit: Science Museum, London, under Creative Commons Licence.	70
9	E. Lambert and Son, *Revised List* (London: E. Lambert and Son, 1897), p. 29. Reproduced with permission from the Thackray Medical Museum, Leeds.	74
10	E. Lambert and Son, *Special List of Domestic and Surgical Specialties* (London: E. Lambert and Son, 1900), front cover. Credit: Wellcome Library, under Creative Commons Licence.	101
11	Chemical pessaries are promoted next to rubber bandages. Charles and Co., *Price List of Surgical Appliances and Rubber Goods* (London: Charles and Co., 1910), p. 15. Reproduced with permission from the Thackray Medical Museum, Leeds.	102
12	Contraceptives advertised in the *Illustrated Police News* (30 October 1897), p. 11. Reproduced with permission from the British Newspaper Archive (www.britishnewspaperarchive.co.uk). Newspaper image © The British Library Board.	104
13	Company catalogues disguised as birth control manuals. Dr St Clair Maurice, *Advice to Married Women* (London: The Medical and Surgical Supply Co., 1938); Dr Oster Mann, *Birth Control* (London: The Hygienic Stores, 1938); D. R. Payne, *Private Words to Women* (London: The Hygienic Stores, 1934). Image and catalogues are author's own.	113
14	Lamberts' clinic – 'A Consulting-Fitting Room at the Birth Control Advisory Bureau', Lamberts (Dalston) Ltd, *Latest Price List of Approved Contraceptive Appliances* (London: Lamberts (Dalston) Ltd, c.1950), p. 5. Reproduced with permission from the Wellcome Library (SA/FPA/A7/68, Lamberts (Dalston) Ltd).	144
15	The Hygienic Surgical Store, 95 Charing Cross Road. The Hygienic Stores Ltd., *Revised Catalogue of Birth Control and Surgical Rubber Goods* (London: The Hygienic Stores, c.1936), p. 19. Image and catalogue are author's own.	177

16 A slot machine vending condoms outside Dunsby's Chemists, Leeds, 1932. Reproduced with permission from the Wellcome Library (PP/BED/B.2, Lord Dawson population and birth control, 1932–34). 180

Acknowledgements

There are many people who have helped me in the long journey to getting this book published. Numerous temporary and short-term employment contracts in universities and in museums has meant that this book has been ten years in the making. I began to think about the commercialisation of contraceptives during my PhD research on medical trade catalogues where I came across numerous advertisements and catalogues promoting condoms, pessaries and other contraceptive goods. I had the opportunity to develop these thoughts in a postdoctoral project at the University of Warwick in 2010 and 2011 and would like to thank the Department of History for supporting my work during that year. Particular thanks go to Professors Hilary Marland and Roberta Bivins for their unwavering support and kindness during my first foray into postdoctoral life and for making my experience so positive. I was then fortunate enough to be able to engage public audiences with my early research at the Infirmary Museum, Worcester, and would like to thank Catriona Wilson for giving me that opportunity. My research continued when I returned to the University of Leeds in 2012 and I would like to thank the staff in the Centre for the History and Philosophy of Science and Alan Humphries at the Thackray Medical Museum for their enthusiasm and guidance on this project. The project moved with me to King's College London in 2014 and it was here that I began to shape my research into a book. I would like to thank colleagues in the Department of History at King's College; the Centre for the History and Philosophy of Science, University of Cambridge; the London School of Hygiene and Tropical Medicine; the Centre for the History of Medicine at the University of Birmingham and participants in the 1920s and 1930s Network for hosting presentations of my research and for insightful comments from the audiences. I finally had the time and space to write the book during my lectureship, my first permanent post, at the University of Kent from 2016 and I would like to thank all colleagues in the School of History for their support in allowing me to finish this project. Beyond Kent, a number of colleagues were keen to see my work on this topic appear in book form and I would particularly like to thank Jesse Olszynko-Gryn, Jessica Borge, Laura Kelly and Caroline Rusterholz for convincing me that this book would be something people would be interested in reading. I hope that remains the case and the book meets expectations. Thanks too to Emma Brennan and the team at Manchester University Press, who have been a pleasure to work with. Huge thanks are also due to Dr Dominic Berry, Professor Chris Lawrence and Dr Emily Manktelow, who generously offered their time and expertise to read through the manuscript in its various drafts; their input has been invaluable. Finally, I would like to thank my family, friends and my husband for their unending love and support. Without them, this book would not have been completed.

Introduction: contraceptive commercialisation before the Pill

> The problem of the modern conscienceless commercialisation of the sale and advertisement of contraceptives is a different matter from that of birth control per se.
>
> Alison Neilans, 'Exploitation of vice',
> *Edinburgh Evening Dispatch* (20 February 1937)

In 1937, Alison Neilans (1884–1942), social reformer, suffragist and secretary of the Association for Moral and Social Hygiene, reported her views on birth control in the British press. As secretary of an association long concerned with curbing moral vice, Neilans was all too aware of the volume and diversity of contraceptive goods that had become widely commercially available since the First World War.[1] Indeed, the interwar period was a pivotal moment in the unfettered growth of markets for rubber caps, chemical pessaries, spermicidal foams, liquids and lotions, enemas, douches, reusable rubber sheaths and disposable latex condoms. Alongside a rise in general consumerism, a liberalisation in social attitudes towards birth control had resulted in new contraceptive consumer cultures. Promoted and distributed by a plethora of entrepreneurs, mail-order firms, retailers and birth control clinics, contraceptive goods were being transformed by modern business practices from disguised and niche semi-medical appliances to visible commercial products.

Neilans made her comments not only in light of this prolific trade and the changing commercial status of contraceptives but also amid a political response to the industry's growth. The Contraceptives (Regulation) Bill was presented to the House of Lords in 1934 by Bertrand Dawson (1864–1945), royal physician and birth control advocate, before being read in the House of Commons in 1938.[2] The

Bill, the first of its kind in Britain, aimed to limit the 'conscienceless' promotion, sale and distribution of contraceptives, and thereby curtail the immoral behaviour, particularly promiscuity and sex outside of marriage, that was seen to accompany it. Unlike the United States under the Comstock Laws of the 1870s, there was no legal regulation of contraceptive sale and distribution in Britain.[3] Indeed, there was no British consensus on what constituted 'conscienceless', the degree of restriction and how restriction should and could be enforced. As both Neilans and Dawson pointed out, birth control and the commercialisation of contraceptives were two distinct issues and no legislation should restrict contraceptive access to married couples choosing to limit their family as an increasingly accepted and legitimate practice. The irresolvable nature of the debate meant that Neilans, among others, refused to support the Bill. While the outbreak of the Second World War meant that the Bill was ultimately abandoned, the tensions between the 'modern conscienceless commercialisation' of contraceptives and the provision of 'legitimate' access to birth control remained.

This book is about the interwar moment when contraceptive products first became widely available. It is this interwar tension – between the 'modern conscienceless commercialisation' of contraceptives and the provision of what was considered legitimate access to birth control – that forms its focus. As Neilans would have been aware, the Contraceptives (Regulation) Bill formed part of a mid-century 'moral panic' reminiscent of the legislative restructuring of the 1880s and 1900s centred on the censorship of obscene material; however, its explicit call to restrict the business methods of manufacturers, promotors and distributors made it distinct.[4] The Bill was also just one of many complex and often contradictory responses to the unprecedented public display, sale and promotion of contraceptives that formed part of the growing public discourse on sex and birth control in this period, another response of course being an increase in consumption. In an era when the restrictive moral values surrounding Victorian and Edwardian sexuality and the demographic and emotional consequences of the First World War co-existed with a vision of the future premised on stability wrought by science, medicine and technology, old and new ways of thinking about sex and sexual behaviour jostled uncomfortably against one another. New sexual possibilities in this era, described by Harold Perkin as that 'halfway house', included the separation of sex from reproduction, the control and planning of fertility and the reconfiguration of gender relationships around a companionate marriage, but there were clear tensions between these new possibilities and the lack of established contraceptive standards, formal sexual education and an officially sanctioned medical contraceptive supply chain.[5] The hundreds of firms that made, promoted, distributed and sold contraceptives had long been the only source of supply for such products. These firms formed an integral part of complex negotiations as the State and the medical profession sought to establish new standards; these negotiations, however, were disrupted by the outbreak of the second great war of the century.

And yet, while the history of sex and contraception in Britain has been exhaustingly, if not exhaustively, written about, the role of such firms in contraceptive supply is virtually unknown. Historians have generally acknowledged the existence of a mid-twentieth-century trade in contraceptive goods, making passing comment on growing contraceptive availability and technological innovation (particularly after the influence of Marie Carmichael Stopes (1880–1953) in the 1920s and the beginnings of latex production in the 1930s). But it is only after the 1960s, with the contraceptive Pill's revolutionary status and the monopolisation of the condom market by the London Rubber Company's (LRC) brand 'Durex', that industry's role in shaping new markets has come into full historiographical view.[6] Charitable, medical, state and, from the early twenty-first century, user voices have been privileged over commercial concerns, but, as this book will demonstrate, these voices were no more or less authoritative or revealing than those of the trade. In fact, it was not always possible to distinguish between them. All sectors faced a similar struggle in this new era, a struggle in which companies were intimately entwined. *The Business of Birth Control* draws attention to these struggles, and in so doing not only demonstrates the indispensability of the industry in shaping sexual and birth control knowledge and practice at a time when these aspects were in flux, but also sheds greater light on the ambiguities, tensions and struggles of interwar Britain more broadly. Indeed, this focus on commercial birth control in this transitionary period serves as an important reminder that business institutions were also social, cultural and medical institutions; the business and commercial aspects of birth control in Britain were at one time inseparable from the social, cultural and medical elements of the communities in which the trade and its customers were found. In this introductory chapter, I break down three elements of Neilans's opening statement: first, 'commercialisation', followed by sections on 'conscienceless' and finally 'modern'. The aim is to more fully explain the argument of this book, and in so doing, complicate and extend the meanings of contraceptives in this period in three key areas: the reliability of goods; the respectability of firms that produced them and their commercial visibility; and the sexual knowledge of consumers.

'Commercialisation': contraceptives as commodities

Since their establishment in the late nineteenth century, rubber and chemical contraceptive manufacturers, wholesale mail-order entrepreneurs and retailers sought to shape contraceptives into reliable, effective commodities that provided value for money and which consumers could recognise and trust. Contraceptive firms shaped their goods through the commercial processes of production, branding, advertising and distribution. But in characterising contraceptives before the Pill as technologies representing sexual taboo or liberation, smaller or larger families, pregnancy or non-pregnancy, and efficacy or failure, historians have commonly overlooked the meanings of these objects as goods in the marketplace. Commercial meanings have, however, been a relatively recent historiographic omission. Reflective of their own time of post-war affluence, mass consumerism and the widespread availability of contraceptives in 'the permissive society', historians of the 1960s and 1970s highlighted the importance of the nineteenth- and early twentieth-century market for contraceptive goods, including abortifacients.[7] Indeed, John Peel, sociologist and author of the most widely cited article on the historic manufacture and retailing of birth control in England, was directed not only by a scholarly interest in the trade but also his appointment as the in-house academic of LRC in 1965. At this time, LRC was Britain's largest and most successful contraceptive manufacturer and Peel was able to obtain much of the information for his article and other published work from Angus Reid, the company's director.[8]

This commercial perspective increasingly fell out of favour from the 1980s, as historical demographers, having studied trends in national and international birth rates since at least the post-Second World War era, rejected a causative link between the rising availability of artificial means of contraception and Britain's fertility decline. Within this decline, the number of live births experienced by each married woman in the population fell from an average of nearly six in 1860 to an average of just over two in 1940.[9] Demographers argued contraceptives were largely irrelevant to the decline because fertility had already begun to fall when contraceptives became more widely available during the interwar period. It was only during and following the 1930s, where fertility was at its lowest, that British couples consumed contraceptive appliances on a significant scale, and they did so alongside non-mechanical and free methods of birth control, such as abstinence, coitus interruptus (withdrawal) and the rhythm method.[10] Figures from the period vary and are frequently unreliable, but one often-cited study reported that 9 per cent of middle-class married couples used sheaths by 1930, while another reported that 18 per cent of the whole British population (or approximately nine million people) used some form of mechanical birth control appliance in 1949.[11]

Social historians, interested in family, gender and sexuality, also increasingly shifted the topic of focus to sexual behaviour, which included the adoption of contraceptives alongside the use of abstinence, abortion and withdrawal, but rarely took into account their market consumption.[12] Pervasive contraceptive appliance consumption thus only coincided with the convergence of increasing sexual knowledge among the general population, decreasing moral resistance to artificial methods of birth control and the availability of better quality latex condoms. Accordingly, the relative quantitative insignificance of the use of mechanical and chemical contraceptives before the 1960s, and certainly before the 1930s, has resulted in neglect of their historical significance. Recent exceptions to this trend have focused on the trade elsewhere – Andrea Tone, Götz Aly and Michael Sontheimer, and Joanne Richdale address America, Germany and New Zealand, respectively – while focus on the British market has largely been restricted to condoms amid the emergence of the contraceptive Pill and the consumer society of the late twentieth century.[13]

But the increasing availability and presence of contraceptives on Britain's high streets and across print media during the interwar period and the contraceptive trade's role in attempting to legitimise birth control amid growing consumerism means that the significance and status of contraceptives as commodities is worth re-evaluating, particularly with regard to the point in the fertility decline when contraceptive consumption first became pervasive. Britons began to emerge as consumer-citizens following the First World War, maturing into this dual identity as part of a larger social and cultural trend associated with an increasingly ambitious and diversified field of practices, goods and services. Many individuals were convinced that they had entered a new and unique historical era, but this new consumer-citizen identity was not embraced by all. Objections were in part related to the connection between consumer-citizenship and the Americanisation of consumer society, where jazz, cinema and shopping for mass-produced commodities were the ultimate leisure pursuits; it was felt such Americanisation debased the more civilised culture at home.[14] But objections aside, this consumer-citizen identity formed a key part of interwar modernity, and as Trent MacNamara argued in 2018 in the context of the United States, debates over modernity at this time included birth control.[15] Within the British context, viewing contraceptives as commodities – that is, objects of economic, social and cultural value governed by the laws of supply and demand and exchanged for money in a physical or metaphorical marketplace – is not only a powerful way of examining the underexplored contributions and experiences of the manufacturers, distributors, retailers and consumers that shaped public sexual discourse and private experiences in this period; it is also a way of broadening the meaning of contraceptives and their place in the modern world.[16]

Viewing contraceptives as commodities is not only important because of their role in shaping birth control before the establishment of industry standards of quality control but also because of their unusual, if not unique, position in the market. Lisa Sigel has highlighted the important relationship between sexuality and capitalism in the twentieth century, suggesting that sexuality was used as a lure for capitalism, appearing in all manner of advertisements.[17] Contraceptives, however, represented a particular form of this sexuality–capitalism relationship and were unlike most other goods. While contraceptives were produced, promoted and sold alongside other rubber and medical goods and durable household items, the form in which they were promoted, distributed and consumed required a high level of discretion. Unlike the 'conspicuous commodities' of the interwar period, contraceptives were not consumed in an attempt to aspire to a higher social status or motivated by an overwhelming desire to get the better of fellow consumers.[18] Neither were contraceptives necessities like food, or luxuries or semi-luxuries (or 'comforts', as influential early twentieth-century economist Alfred Marshall called them).[19] Contraceptives were the antithesis of status symbols and consumption was neither fashionable nor conspicuous, due to the sensibilities surrounding birth control and the social embarrassment of its adopters. Such sensibilities, as we will see, were particularly applicable to condoms, due to their association with promiscuity and venereal disease. The increasing visibility of contraceptives in public discourse, spaces and media in the interwar period provoked concern along with the emergence of new forms of entertainment such as cheap, mass-produced fiction, cinema going and dancing. But like consumers of other goods, consumers of contraceptives were still concerned about price, safety and quality. Contraceptive consumers were reliant on communicated messages of reliability, trust and authenticity in product branding and promotion. In fact, contraceptives were consumed twice after manufacture: once by intermediaries, such as retailers, doctors and birth control clinics, and then by the end user. Signs (or systems of signs, as sociologists and philosophers of consumption have long called them) of reliability, trust and authenticity had to appeal to both sets of consumers.[20]

Contraceptives in Britain thus acquired and communicated particular sets of meanings and values as they circulated the market. For firms, contraceptives meant profit or loss, enhanced or damaged reputations and technological and anatomical knowledge or ignorance. Consumers certainly did associate contraceptive commodities with sexual taboo or liberation, smaller or larger families and pregnancy or non-pregnancy, but these functional aspects of a commodified contraceptive were also shaped and influenced by company goodwill, product branding and marketing. This book's focus on commercial dynamics within the field of contraception then extends a growing revisionist historiography on sex that acknowledges the existence of multiple and co-existing discourses operating at societal and individual levels during this period. Indeed, as historians have acknowledged, there was no universal response to sex and contraception.[21] Any generalisation about contraceptives is thus readily contradictable, dependent on approach and perspective.

'Conscienceless': contraceptive reliability and trade respectability

Describing the trade as 'conscienceless', Neilans, as an advocate of birth control, was unconvinced by the efforts of companies to shape contraceptives into reliable, trustworthy and authentic commodities. Indeed, one of the key concerns surrounding the interwar trade was whether firms were respectable enough to circulate effective goods or were mere charlatans seeking to profit from tricking gullible consumers into purchasing mispriced and useless products, concerns that were not uncommon to other trades during the 1930s. Of course, trade respectability and product efficacy depended on the ability of contraceptives to prevent pregnancy, but they were also reliant on the manner in which firms conducted their business and the methods they used to communicate to consumers. Firms had to navigate cultures of morality that shunned artificial means of birth control and commercialisation throughout the period. To be sure, many of the claims that firms made about their own respectability and the efficacy of their products, as well as calling into question the reputation and business practices of others, were exaggerated, if not false, and thus formed part of their commercial methods. One of the aims of this book is to put the claims of firms under scrutiny.

Historians are yet to probe the status of firms and the motives of those who ran them and have largely gauged trade respectability and contraceptive efficacy through the testimony of those considered the interwar gatekeepers of sexual and contraceptive knowledge. These gatekeepers – which this book defines as intermediaries between firms and end consumers – include philanthropists, birth control advocates, reformers, medical professionals and scientific researchers aligned to birth control organisations who conducted or relied on medical and social research into contraceptive reliability and efficacy.[22] Gatekeepers typically privileged 'female' methods of birth control, such as the cervical cap, diaphragm and chemical spermicides, because they were ideologically invested in enabling women to control their own fertility (although they increasingly accepted the latex condom from the 1930s). At the same time, however, these gatekeepers also publicly condemned the majority of contraceptive goods on the market and the firms who profited from their sale and from the practice of birth control more broadly. As we will see, Marie Stopes, feminist, eugenicist, founder of the Society for Constructive Birth Control and Racial Progress and author of the first mass-selling books on birth control, was not only variously arrogant, irrational, uncooperative and megalomaniacal among friends and foes, as depicted by the many studies of her life, but was also particularly vocal in her condemnation of much of the trade.[23]

More recent historical work has begun to challenge this top-down medicalised view of birth control by emphasising the fact that the majority of the interwar population never saw a medical practitioner or visited a birth control clinic.[24] Indeed, the medical profession still did not have a monopoly on the nation's health more generally; its public health provision, which began to include a birth control service, was piecemeal and ad hoc and most services were paid for privately. Moreover, public health provision on contraceptive matters post-1930 would have been dependent upon the sympathies of the local Medical Officer of Health. Most people thus resorted to a range of medical and quasi-medical methods and providers, including those from the chemist and those made at home.[25] Among historians now stressing individual agency in birth control, Hera Cook has argued that women rejected contraceptives before the introduction of the Pill because they themselves found them crude, inefficient or unreliable, in spite of what birth controllers advocated.[26] Men and women obtained information about contraceptives from personal experience and from whatever source they had access to, most commonly through the circulation of various print media or through social networks.[27] But while historians have broadened their analyses to focus on the lives of men and women, there remains a reliance on intermediary testimony and the standards of efficacy they prescribed. Indeed, intermediaries wrote much of the literature that men and women read. For example, Cook's attempt to complicate the medicalisation of early twentieth-century sexuality by emphasising that the doctors who wrote sexual manuals relied on their lived, as well as their medical, experience still suggests that birth control information was owned and promoted by the medical profession.[28]

Yet, there is nothing inherently accurate about the testimony of these gatekeepers, just as there is nothing inherently inaccurate about the testimony of commercial actors. Indeed, the privileging of gatekeeper voices among historians has inadvertently resulted in a teleology that presents the late twentieth-century emergence of reliable contraceptives as a modern medical triumph, with the Pill as its emblem. But modern scientific medicine as the 'best' and 'correct' form of birth control knowledge and practice was itself a concept formulated in the interwar period with the rise of the expert, standardisation and wider societal acceptance of birth control. Before the Second World War, the medical, charitable and commercial sectors involved in birth control occupied the hinterland of respectability and the lines between business, charity work and medicine were often blurred. Indeed, contraceptive manufacturers were among only a few authoritative voices to which medical practitioners, social reformers and birth control advocates could turn in an era in which birth control knowledge, technologies and practices were in flux; while these gatekeepers possessed anatomical and physiological knowledge, manufacturers alone possessed the technical skill and know-how to make new contraceptive designs that these gatekeepers sought to prescribe. Anatomical, medical, technical and commercial knowledge surrounding birth control were each reliant on the other and together, were reliant on sexual behaviour. But as legal scholars Martha Ertman and Joan Williams have argued in relation to contemporary North America, and as Rose Holz has suggested is relevant to interwar commercial birth control clinics, there has been a 'conventional assumption of hostile worlds: that the world is bifurcated into an economic arena dominated by rational self-interest and self-interest alone (the market), and a sharply different arena of intimacy and altruism that must be protected from the kind of instrumental behaviour that is appropriate in market contexts'.[29]

This conventional assumption of hostile worlds in the context of birth control emerged in the interwar period as medical and charitable voices sought legitimacy by distancing themselves from trade and by imposing their own more restrictive definition of 'reliable' birth control methods and those that could supply them. In 1936, for example, Norman Himes, the social and medical scientist and birth control advocate, blamed the dominance of the commercial supply of contraceptives on the medical profession's long refusal to 'accept leadership in contraceptive instruction', but implied that the profession's new interest meant that supply via any means other than medicine was no longer necessary.[30] It was at this point, during the mid-1930s, that tensions between the old world of commerce that had dominated contraceptive supply and the new modern world of medicine and science came most clearly into conflict. The contraceptive trade's role in shaping contraceptive 'reliability' and 'efficacy' began to decline just at the moment contraceptive consumption was becoming quantitively significant. By the 1950s, companies became subsumed by the birth control movement. Yet, because birth controllers and chemists relied on companies for the supply of both contraceptive goods and the technical knowledge behind them, they could never break free from this marketplace connection. Many downplayed its importance and this depiction of the separate worlds of charity and commerce fed into subsequent histories.

Historians, once too accepting of the medical and charitable point of view in assessing the interwar status of contraceptives, are only just beginning to challenge the assumption that the medicalisation of birth control in the interwar period was the sole force at work. Much research still needs to be done to include other forces of power, including commercialisation and consumption. Indeed, interwar attempts to medicalise birth control and contraceptive supply occurred alongside the maturing of a consumer society and amid the interwar push for universal services, including schools and health, and a welfare state.[31] Contraceptives thus depicted as crude, inefficient, unreliable, expensive and difficult to obtain both before, during and after the interwar period were not always considered as such by those who made, distributed and consumed them. Furthermore, the categories of 'efficacy' and 'reliability' do not always accurately reflect why end consumers resorted to birth control appliances. Indeed, as Kate Fisher pointed out in 2006, reliability was not necessarily a factor in uptake of birth control practices in the 1920s and 1930s. Other factors, including comfort and sexual pleasure, could also be important, but so too could the goodwill of firms, brand loyalty and marketing. How else do we account for the women who bought the same brand of contraceptive, condemned by the interwar medical profession, for a period of over twenty years without becoming pregnant? Can we assume, as Hera Cook has, that these couples were just lucky or had low fertility? Perhaps. But infertility is certainly not a factor these women articulated and one with which they may not have been familiar; some, as we will see, certainly explicitly stated their trust in particular brands. Our picture of birth control is, therefore, incomplete without factoring in the relative influence of the market.

This book then does not aim to show how the contraceptive industry transformed from unrespectable and ineffective to respectable and effective, but instead examines how these terms were not attached to any discernible standards and thus had no fixed meaning until after the Second World War. *Perceptions* of efficacy and reliability were crucial. Interwar medical practitioners and birth control advocates attempted to fix these meanings, causing tension with companies and resulting in a rhetoric of the separation of the medical and commercial worlds. Yet such attempts did not stop medical reliance on the trade; companies were integral to the birth control world, as they are today, in spite of the efforts of medical practitioners and birth controllers.

Still 'conscienceless': sexual knowledge, commercial visibility and consumption

With contraceptive knowledge among companies and intermediaries in flux in the interwar period, it was inevitable that knowledge was similarly fractured among contraceptive purchasers, those this book will describe as end consumers. Certainly, there is no reason to assume that those who purchased contraceptives saw themselves as 'consumers'; a mass consumer identity of the kind historians of consumption are increasingly unfolding did not exist in relation to contraceptives before the emergence of the so-called consumer society of the late twentieth century.[32] Indeed, the 'consumer' is not a natural or universal category, but was the product of historical shaping where situated actors made sense of material culture against the background of their existing knowledge and wants and their social, cultural, political, moral and economic circumstances. As Frank Trentmann has argued, consumption was not an automatic response to the spread of markets; consumers had to be made.[33] But the alternative categories of 'patient', 'citizen' or 'user' have connotations; they were also historically shaped and privilege the medical, political and technological while undermining consumption as a form of agency and social conditioning. As we will see then, contraceptive consumers were being made during consumption's coming of age in the interwar period.

Terminology notwithstanding, the interwar trade presented a highly confusing picture for both intermediaries and end consumers, but it also offers a contradictory picture to us now. Contraceptives were widely available via retailers, birth control clinics and mail order, were promoted in various printed media and formed part of more open public discourse on sex and birth control than had hitherto existed. Yet they remained inaccessible to many due to sustained and widespread sexual ignorance in an era transitioning from Victorian and Edwardian moralities to modernity. This context meant that disguised and subtle promotion was not always interpreted as sexual or commercial information and nor could it be distinguished from misinformation. Recent historical work has emphasised not only the importance of ignorance for keeping contraceptive consumption relatively low among those beyond the educated middle classes into the 1950s but also the significance of interpretation.[34] As Fisher has stated, 'ignorance was as much a state of mind as a quantifiable level of understanding. Knowledge was not an objective set of facts waiting to be received'.[35] Few people were engaged in overt, self-conscious attempts to gain sexual knowledge, and still fewer endeavoured to participate in the making of it, so for many, any sexual knowledge was the product of 'a combination of blind ignorance and sordid misinformation'.[36] Sexual mystery, rather than repression, was institutionalised in society.[37]

Sustained ignorance was both real then but it was also performative. It formed a crucial part of female social status, being closely connected to women's respectability and, in particular, their avoidance of illicit sexual behaviour. Indeed, sexual cultures were segregated by gender and existed in most schooling, occupations and family life.[38] But how a growing and visible trade was able to successfully function amid high levels of ignorance has not yet been explained. This book then focuses on how consumption could take place, and a consumer identity could start to form, alongside high levels of ignorance in the interwar period and the tensions between the two. It demonstrates how contraceptives could be both simultaneously taboo and not taboo, both invisible and visible, and in so doing presents a more complex picture of contraceptive knowledge in this period. Consumers could obtain commercial information, but not necessarily interpret it as intended and this sat alongside other methods of knowledge acquisition, haphazard or otherwise.

By focusing on the trade, it becomes clear that firms were very aware not only of the co-existence of what this book will call knowing and unknowing consumers but also that they played a crucial role in perpetuating the divide between the two. Of course, contraceptive supply was, and indeed still is, dependent on demand, but firms did not simply stimulate demand by presenting consumers with information; information required consumer interpretation, which relied on some level of existing sexual knowledge. Indeed, while the long-standing unspeakable status of commodified contraceptives did not stop the trade (and neither did the law), it made manufacturers, promoters and sellers aware of the sensitivities of selling taboo products and of the difficulties in disassociating them with sex outside marriage, promiscuity and venereal disease. Contraceptive sale and promotion were carefully managed so that ignorance was maintained, while providing knowing consumers with important information. These knowing consumers not only included the archetypal married couple discussed by historians of birth control but also more difficult-to-trace non-conformist consumers, including, for example, the non-married, the adulterous and the bachelor. Marketing methods that firms adopted included branding, disguising products as other everyday goods and shaping catalogues into respectable medical books, in order to transform their commodities into reliable, medical technologies. The strategy of high pricing to denote reliability was also important, as was the use of euphemisms in advertising contraceptives as 'surgical appliances', 'scientific', 'hygienic', 'Malthusian' and 'racial'. Firms promoted contraceptives alongside other rubber medical commodities, while distancing themselves from abortion. When methods veered too far from the status quo by becoming too explicit, such as rebranding 'surgical appliances' as 'birth control requisites', displaying contraceptives in shop windows and slot machines, they were met with vocal condemnation. Disguised and euphemistic promotional and distribution methods ensured that only consumers already knowledgeable about contraceptive appliances could purchase them and use them for their intended purpose, but some viewed companies as overstepping the boundary into sex educators. For example, as we will see in Chapter 1, some married women, once exposed to contraceptive knowledge and goods through work within the factory, vowed never to purchase such goods.

Knowing how end consumers in the interwar period, either those who were able to encode commercial meanings and indeed those who were not, felt about contraceptives is of course notoriously difficult for contemporary historians. The sensitive nature of the subject matter meant that few interwar consumers were ever likely to record their thoughts and feelings about contraceptive goods. Even the general consumption of commodities was such an ingrained everyday activity for some in the interwar period that consumer responses are relatively rare.[39] Nonetheless, this book uncovers consumer responses where possible and, where such responses exist, reveals a variety of consumers and consumption patterns. These consumers included married and soon-to-be-married men and women, soldiers and adolescents. Like Fisher's oral history work, it emphasises the importance of the middle- and working-class married male as a hitherto neglected contraceptive consumer, particularly of the rubber sheath (the supposed 'male' contraceptive), but it also maintains that married middle-class women, as both the main focus of earlier birth control histories and of histories of interwar consumption, were important contraceptive consumers too.[40]

Yet, there are a wealth of consumption patterns – not only among the married but also among the non-married, the adulterous, the adolescent and the otherwise disreputable consumer – that were never recorded and the traces of which are almost impossible to identify. Indeed, the trade in condoms specifically was undoubtedly sustained in part by non-married or adulterous couples, through prostitution and other non-conforming sexual activity, despite firms' best efforts to promote them as birth control goods and themselves as birth control specialists for the married; evidence of consumption among such groups is non-existent. This book will thus extend current understandings of the interwar contraceptive market by demonstrating the importance of imagined consumers. Imagined consumers were those that firms overtly targeted. Indeed, the variety and form of print promotion (in Chapter 3), the effort firms went to in order to supply birth control clinics (Chapter 4), their retailing strategy (Chapter 5) and firms' continued use of these strategies suggests that consumers were spread across social classes, geographic locations and genders in a way that has not yet been explored in detail. Purchasing decisions could also be joint and were not necessarily dictated by gender. Uncovering firms' strategies, alongside direct testimony, suggests that some married couples made purchasing decisions together, and that men also purchased female appliances on behalf of their wives. Such findings further emphasise Fisher's suggestion that decision-making about family size was not necessarily revolutionary or calculated; just as couples could switch birth control method – both technological and non-appliance methods – with shifting degrees of regularity according to varying levels of determination, some could openly discuss the methods they purchased and consumed.[41]

But imagined consumers also included the type moralists feared the trade were encouraging to consume condoms, namely the ignorant, innocent and unmarried adolescent. As we will see, moralists feared that adolescents were inadvertently exposed to the 'modern conscienceless commercialisation' of contraceptives at work, through print promotion and on the high street. While Michael Schofield's

1965 survey on *The Sexual Behaviour of Young People* demonstrated that knowledge of birth control among young people was rudimentary and its practice rare, increasing contraceptive availability some forty years earlier meant that adolescents in urban spaces could purchase condoms without necessarily possessing sexual or birth control knowledge.[42] Indeed, in this case, contraceptive knowledge and consumption were not intimately intertwined and purchases were not necessarily about restricting family size – they could also be impulsive; certain consumers could purchase contraceptive products spontaneously without very much thought on what they were or what they did. Again, as a commodity, the form and function of a contraceptive could be reduced to secondary concerns as branding, marketing and distribution created new meanings and values for such consumers. However, with little direct testimony it is difficult to ascertain the extent to which adolescents did consume contraceptives. The moral panic surrounding the exposure of youth to contraceptive products and knowledge from which the Contraceptives (Regulation) Bill emerged may suggest that the issue was far smaller than identified and was restricted to a few isolated incidents. Yet the perception of change on the part of social conservatives is as crucial a part of this interwar period as change itself.

'Modern': sources and structure

The wide range of voices involved in the contraceptive commercialisation debate in the interwar period means that this book will draw on a wealth of new archival and overlooked source material. Of course, of key importance is material on contraceptive firms and the trade itself. While the book draws on a few extant company archives, it draws more heavily on the trade's neglected promotional output, including over one hundred mail-order catalogues (listed in the appendix) and direct advertisements in regional and national papers. The exact number of catalogue editions and copies of editions published and distributed throughout the period is difficult to establish, but every manufacturer, retailer and mail-order house issued at least one price list in pamphlet form and updated it when new products or contraceptive information were introduced, hence the increase in editions following the cement process and latex production methods. Information on the trade and individual companies is also available within the extensive archives of the Family Planning Association (and its predecessor organisations) and those of Marie Stopes and her Society for Constructive Birth Control and Racial Progress.[43] These archives not only shed light on birth controller reliance on such firms but also on the importance of the trade in widening access to contraceptives and in constructing cultural attitudes towards sex throughout this period.

Yet the interpretation of these sources is not always straightforward. Indeed, from these sources, it is not even possible to identify and trace the number of firms within the trade. The trade's secretive nature meant that companies frequently appeared and disappeared without trace; some firms made claims that cannot be verified, such as their manufacturing credentials, making it difficult to distinguish between manufacturers and wholesalers; and some changed names and launched and promoted new products under subsidiary companies, the connections to which are opaque. Indeed, merchants and agents, geared at making profits from the sale and distribution of other people's goods rather than their own, were a core part of the contraceptive trade. Of course, company assertions about, for example, manufacturing output, dominance over sectors of the market and product superiority cannot be seen as empirically literal, but are nonetheless revealing of the extent to which rhetoric, with its own layers of meaning and significance, formed part of the contraceptive trade. This book then is not only concerned with the factual truth of the shape of the contraceptive trade but also with the role rhetoric played in shaping it. All we can say with certainty is that the trade was diverse and highly adaptive to economic, social, cultural and medical circumstances.

Wide-ranging and direct responses to contraceptives from both end consumers, intermediaries and opponents to birth control and its commercialisation are contained within archival and primary material, the likes of which historians have long consulted but typically overlooked due to their commercial slant. Such material includes the records of the Family Planning Association and Marie Stopes, but also those of the Association of Moral and Social Hygiene and the Public Morality Council, parliamentary debates, and surveys, questionnaires and reports from the Mass-Observation Archive, which began to record information about sexual knowledge and behaviour amid its recording of the ordinariness of life from 1937. Letters from the Marie Stopes Collections at the British Library and the Wellcome Library – including ten thousand or so interwar letters written to Stopes by middle-, lower-middle- and working-class women and men from Britain and across the Empire asking for her help in sexual matters – are also revealing not only of consumer knowledge and ignorance but also of Stopes's own knowledge and ignorance of the contraceptive trade.

Of course, these sources do not provide anywhere near a complete picture of interwar consumption, and one person's experience is readily contradicted by another. Like the records of contraceptive firms, evidence suggesting consumption should also not be taken at face value, not least because moralists likely exaggerated the extent of a moral threat in order to challenge it.[44] Nonetheless, such fragmentary material is pieced together in order to demonstrate the prominence of discourse on contraceptive commercialisation throughout the period of study and provides important insights into regional and class differences in contraceptive consumption, particularly from the 1920s onwards. Such records not only point towards evidence of consumption but also indicate the varying views on the extent to which commercialisation should form part of modern sex and marriage in this period. Indeed, Stopes, members of the medical profession, the chemists' profession, the Association of Moral and Social Hygiene, the Public Morality Council and the Family Planning Association all disagreed over the extent to which they thought the market should play a role in the distribution of contraceptives, and over whether modern sexual discourse should be public or private. The Family Planning Association, Dawson and the Royal Pharmaceutical Society thought that the market had an important role to play in contraceptive distribution, although could not decide on its extent. Given the limited number of direct responses from end consumers, much will be gained by focusing on the types of consumer that firms targeted. To do this, *The Business of Birth Control* will draw on approaches from the history of the book and material culture studies to assess the hitherto neglected significance of the physicality and semiotics of birth control literature, advertising material, mail-order catalogues, product packaging, and shop and window displays, alongside meanings embedded in their text and what their construction reveals about expected consumer audiences.[45] In adopting this approach, the book offers a salutary reminder that historical experience – however powerfully shaped by language, texts and discourses – is also configured by material contexts that require continued historical interrogation.

The book is structured around five overlapping contested processes of contraceptive commercialisation: production, intellectual property, print culture, birth control clinics and retail. This structure aims to break away from conventional linear readings of birth control history and of the linear relationship between production and consumption, and instead emphasises the flows and connections between contraceptives and their stakeholders as they circulated the economy. As we will see, these processes, with the exception of birth control clinics, formed the basis of debates over the Contraceptives (Regulation) Bill and as such, represented battlegrounds in which firms, birth control advocates, social conservatives, medical practitioners and consumers struggled over authority, legitimacy and respectability in this new modern market for contraceptive goods. However, the shift from a chronological to a thematic structure is not straightforward. Indeed, most historians of birth control, with recent notable exceptions, have usefully structured their work chronologically in order to demonstrate that contraceptive efficacy, availability and the acceptability of public sexual discourse grew throughout the course of the twentieth century. To demonstrate why women of the 1960s embraced the Pill, Hera Cook, for example, usefully identifies three chronological stages in the growth of sexual acceptability: a relatively homogenous sexual culture that shared negative attitudes to birth control before the First World War; an emergence and then acceptance of new sexual ideas and technologies in the interwar period; and increased sexual knowledge during and after the Second World War. The Pill then was the result of a longer, almost unstoppable, trend in the increasing acceptability of discourse about sexual practice.[46]

Broad chronological overviews that highlight change are, of course, valuable but their division of time into distinct, neat periods can, again, present a teleology of continual progress and also overly simplify the relationship between change and continuity. In the interwar period in particular, new sexual ideas and technologies did not just passively emerge, but were fiercely contested centred on commercialisation, economic changes and the growth of affluence. Indeed, as David Edgerton has argued, contraceptives provide a good example of the long existence of many alternative means, the significance of declining and disappearing technologies and re-emerging old technologies.[47] The tensions surrounding commercialisation within the interwar period, the period in which contraceptive authority was fiercely contested, therefore must be addressed in more detail than has hitherto been attempted in order to uncover the trade's role in how they were accepted.

Of course, this structure is, like all book structures, an artificial arrangement. Indeed, this particular focus on the interwar decades is in some ways as arbitrary as a broad chronology. Certainly, the sites in which tensions over authority and legitimacy occurred were intimately intertwined, resulting in a great deal of overlap in their discussion in individual chapters. Moreover, change over time still forms an important anchor here; the events occurring in and the social context of 1918 were indeed very different to those in 1939. Nonetheless, a special case should be made for this in-depth focus on the interwar period precisely because of its inherent contradictions and ambiguities. A thematic structure is most useful for uncovering how what could be explicitly bought and sold was being tried and tested in law, medicine, media and commerce, just as what could and should be said about sex and sexual relations was tried and tested in modernist writings, in the cinema, in the politics of welfare and in conversation. It was commerce that brought together the aspects of birth control that historians have typically focused on separately: newspapers, birth control clinics and the law and medicine. Moreover, the focus on the interwar period will allow us to flesh out commercialisation's pre- and post-history. Indeed, as Christopher Lawrence and Anna Mayer have argued, any study of cultural life in Britain in the years between the wars must take into account the transformation in the economic, political and cultural life of the country at the turn of the century.[48] The book will establish how and why the development of commercialisation processes in the late nineteenth century did not lead to such tensions, while identifying how such processes established the future path of contraceptives into the late twentieth century.

It should also be noted that although 'Britain' is used throughout the book, this almost always refers to England and Wales and not to Scotland or Northern Ireland; Scotland and Northern Ireland would require a separate study due to the extent of their religious, demographic, moral and legislative differences, and are therefore excluded here. Moreover, I refer to 'contraceptives' as the material technologies – both rubber appliances and chemical substances – promoted to prevent pregnancy and, in the case of the sheath and condom, to also prevent the spread of venereal disease. However, contraceptives for the purpose of birth control will be the main focus simply because that is how the majority of companies fashioned their goods. Shaping goods into those for birth control does not mean of course that consumers used them for this purpose and thus the book will address the potential for consumers to use contraceptives as prophylactics for venereal disease where appropriate. Similarly, this book does not give much attention to abortion; this is not because abortion was a less important practice for limiting fertility than contraceptives but because contraceptive manufacturers did not enter into abortion (although surgical stores sold 'female pills') and birth controllers advocated contraceptives as a remedy to abortion.

Focusing on production as the first stage of the commercial process, Chapter 1 demonstrates the tensions between old and new manufacturing methods among British manufacturers, the medical profession, social conservatives and consumers. From artificial sponges to intrauterine devices, production methods have been integral to modern contraception. Most contraceptive appliances made from the late nineteenth century to the 1960s were made from rubber, but it was the introduction of latex in the early 1930s and contraceptive testing by the National Birth Control Association in 1935 that not only resulted in increased output and factory employment but also drew increasing public attention to the trade's reputation. Social conservatives protested against the increasing feminisation of the latex contraceptive workforce that made contraceptives visible to adolescent girls for the first time, while the Association sought to ensure that the trade conformed to its medical standards. However, what is clear is that such changes were not wholesale during this period. Not all firms adopted latex production, and while it was in a firm's interest to supply the Association, firms largely ignored protests about workforce feminisation. In short then, this chapter demonstrates that the introduction of latex in the interwar period did not result in a technological revolution as some historians have suggested, but that old uncomfortably sat alongside new.

Following on from production, Chapter 2 turns to the next battle ground in the commodification process in this transitional period: packaging, branding and trademarking. While it was only from the late 1930s at the earliest that LRC's famous brand 'Durex' (registered in 1929) became synonymous with the condom, this chapter draws attention to the importance of packaging, branding and trademarks before 'Durex'. It does so by drawing on two prominent examples of branded contraceptives and outlining the numerous infringement battles over these brands in the interwar period: W. J. Rendell's 'Wife's Friend' soluble quinine pessary, registered in 1894 and aimed at the chemists' market, and Lambert's 'Pro-Race' rubber cervical cap, registered in 1922 and made to supply Stopes's birth control clinics under the Society for Constructive Birth Control and Racial Progress. Tensions between manufacturers and surgical store retailers in particular (as the former commonly accused the latter of infringement) not only indicated the perceived commercial value of brands and trademarks but were also indicative of firms' attempts to establish themselves as the legitimate authorities on birth control in a more open market for such goods. Branding and trademarks, both a mixture of traditional and modern designs, were a way to convince consumers of the quality and reliability of products, and evidence from the Rendell company archive suggests a degree of success. Rendell's customers, in particular, viewed these contraceptives as reliable through the identification of their branding and trademarks.

Establishing consumer trust with brands and trademarks was intimately linked to print promotion. Chapter 3 uncovers how firms attempted to demonstrate their authority in birth control through the promotion of their brands in a range of print media. Increasingly prominent and explicit advertising featured in a variety of respectable and non-respectable newspapers and magazines and in mail-order catalogues, and formed part of a plethora of medical and non-medical printed material on sex and birth control throughout the interwar period.[49] It was this increasing visibility in print that resulted in a backlash against this new and modern public discourse on sexual topics. Of particular concern to medical authorities, birth control advocates and social conservatives were firms' own advertising publications shaped into medical tracts, some of which were delivered unsolicited to the homes of consumers. Such tracts confused unknowing consumers who were unable to discern legitimate medical contraceptive knowledge and commercial knowledge. Such was the blurring of medical, sexual and commercial publications that even authorities like Stopes could not distinguish between them.

While Chapter 3's discussion of print culture begins to uncover contraceptive distribution via manufacturers and various types of wholesaler, chapters 4 and 5 focus on the two other trade intermediaries: birth control clinics and retailers. Chapter 4 revisits the impact of the growing public acceptability of the birth control movement, and of the Society for Constructive Birth Control and Racial

Progress and the Family Planning Association in particular, on the interwar contraceptive production introduced in Chapter 1. While increasing numbers of case studies reveal how birth control clinics were established and managed across the country, we know little about the relationship between clinic management and commercial companies.[50] This chapter highlights the tensions surrounding the increasing competitive nature of clinic supply following the Association's introduction of standardised contraceptive testing in 1935. A growing number of firms attempted to align themselves with clinics as new medical authorities on contraception, who sought to re-define 'reliable' contraceptives with their tests. Yet, as we will see, the Association's attempt to narrowly define what constituted birth control largely failed until the 1950s. Before the war, agreed standards of contraceptives were still in flux and the Association considered the products of certain firms reliable even when they failed the tests. Much of this related to the acceptance of lower standards of product quality during wartime, but it also impinged on the fact that clinics continued to rely on firms who had earned their trust. Price and quality only began to override firm goodwill and loyalty in the 1950s.

The focus of Chapter 5 shifts to retail distribution, a commercial process largely neglected in current historical scholarship on birth control, but one in which the tensions and ambiguities of the interwar years and birth control in this period were the most obvious. The chapter examines how Dawson, birth control authorities, social conservatives and consumers responded to the growing visible and unmediated promotion and sale of contraceptives from retailers such as chemists' shops and surgical stores. Retail outlets became increasingly important to contraceptive distribution as they adopted 'scientific salesmanship' and brightly coloured and branded window displays, as did mechanised contraceptive slot machines placed outside the shops of chemists, barbers and new sites of leisure. It brings us back to Alison Neilans and the heated debate on the 'conscience-less' commercialisation of contraceptives during the 1930s, and outlines how the failure to find consensus on how to accept the rights of married adults to access birth control appliances via retailers and slot machines while simultaneously preventing access to adolescents meant that legislation was largely abandoned by 1950. Ultimately, free trade, and with it, overt commercialisation, triumphed and contraceptives were freely available from, if not freely advertised by, chemists' shops as the contraceptive Pill was introduced. The Epilogue reveals how industry structures of this period provided the foundations for the mass-contraceptive industry of the late twentieth and twenty-first centuries. Companies in this trade that we now consider to be largely reliable, authoritative and trustworthy played no small part in establishing their own reputations during the period under study, although as the Epilogue will demonstrate, many of the commercial practices the contraceptive firms of today follow are no less questionable than those of the interwar period.

Structuring this book around the tensions surrounding each commercial process in the interwar period then reveals how the late twentieth-century availability of contraceptives was not inevitable but rather was the outcome of an interwar struggle between various different interest groups, including long-neglected commercial firms. Commercialisation can thus be seen as one viable discourse, co-existing among and influencing many others on sex and contraception in this period in flux. It urges us to reconsider the importance of viewing contraceptives as commodities in the marketplace – not just as medical technologies for preventing pregnancy and as objects of social morality and sexual liberation – and in doing so, thus work beyond the constraints imposed by the various sub-disciplinary frameworks within the discipline of history. Indeed, there is much unexplored territory in the historical hinterland where the study of the market, medicine and morality overlap. By taking seriously such overlaps, the book becomes not solely about contraceptives, as detached from medical, social and cultural life, but also shows how the debates around the acceptability of commercial knowledge regarding birth control were part of a more general response to modernity itself, a response that forces us to reconsider the importance of commercial concerns before the so-called sexual revolution of the 1960s.

Notes

1 For more on the Association between the wars, see J. A. Laite, 'The Association for Moral and Social Hygiene: abolitionism and prostitution law in Britain (1915–1959)', *Women's History Review*, 17:2 (2008), 207–23.
2 Contraceptives Bill, Parliament: House of Lords, no. 110 (London: The Stationery Office, 1934); Contraceptives (Regulation) Bill, Parliament: House of Commons, no. 115 (London: The Stationery Office, 1938).

3 For more on the legal regulation of contraceptives, see M. Latham, *Regulating Reproduction: A Century of Conflict in Britain and France* (Manchester: Manchester University Press, 2002).
4 On 'moral panics' more broadly, see S. Cohen, *Folk Devils and Moral Panics* (London: MacGibbon and Kee, 1972).
5 H. Perkin, *The Rise of Professional Society in England since 1880* (London: Routledge, 1989), p. 218. For a positive interpretation of the interwar period, see M. Pugh, *We Danced All Night: A Social History of Britain between the Wars* (London: The Bodley Head, 2009).
6 For some preliminary discussion on the interwar trade, see, for example, J. Borge, '"Wanting it Both Ways": the London Rubber Company, the Condom and the Pill, 1915–1970' (PhD thesis, University of London, 2017); S. Szreter, *Fertility, Class and Gender, 1860–1940* (Cambridge: Cambridge University Press, 1996), p. 559; H. Cook, *The Long Sexual Revolution: English Women, Sex and Contraception, 1800–1975* (Oxford: Oxford University Press, 2004), p. 139; K. Fisher, *Birth Control, Sex, and Marriage in Britain, 1918–1960* (Oxford: Oxford University Press, 2006), p. 7; R. Jütte, *Contraception: A History* (London: Polity Press, 2008); R. Porter and L. Hall (eds), *The Facts of Life: The Creation of Sexual Knowledge in Britain, 1650–1950* (New Haven and London: Yale University Press, 1995). For more on the post-1960s, see Cook, *The Long Sexual Revolution*, pp. 263–337; L. Marks, *Sexual Chemistry: A History of the Contraceptive Pill* (New Haven and London: Yale University Press, 2001); B. Mechen, '"Closer together": Durex condoms and contraceptive consumerism in 1970s Britain', in J. Evans and C. Meehan (eds), *Perceptions of Pregnancy from the Seventeenth to the Twentieth Century* (Cham: Palgrave Macmillan, 2016), pp. 213–36; P. Jobling, 'Playing safe: the politics of pleasure and gender in the promotion of condoms in Britain, 1972–1982', *Design History*, 10:1 (1997), 53–70.
7 P. S. Brown, 'Female pills and the reputation of iron as an abortifacient', *Medical History*, 21 (1977), 291–304; J. Peel, 'The manufacture and retailing of contraceptives in England', *Population Studies*, 17 (1963), 113–25; P. Knight, 'Women and abortion in Victorian and Edwardian England', *History Workshop Journal*, 4 (1977), 57–68; A. McLaren, *Birth Control in Nineteenth-Century England* (London: Croom Helm, 1978).
8 Borge, '"Wanting it Both Ways"', pp. 332, 390; Peel, 'The manufacture and retailing of contraceptives'. See also C. L. Jones, 'Under the covers? Contraceptives, commerce and the household in Britain, 1880–1960', *Social History of Medicine*, 29:4 (2016), 734–56.
9 D. G. Sloan, 'The extent of contraceptive use and the social paradigm of modern demography', *Sociology*, 17:3 (1983), 380–7. For an in-depth

discussion of the fertility decline, see Szreter, *Fertility, Class and Gender*, pp. 9–66.

10 S. Szreter and K. Fisher, *Sex Before the Sexual Revolution: Intimate Life in England, 1918–1963* (Cambridge: Cambridge University Press, 2010), pp. 229–67; Szreter, *Fertility, Class and Gender*, pp. 559–65; Fisher, *Birth Control, Sex, and Marriage*; K. Fisher and S. Szreter, '"They prefer withdrawal": the choice of birth control in Britain, 1918–50', *Journal of Interdisciplinary History*, 34 (2003), 265–91.

11 L. S. Florence, *Birth Control on Trial* (London: Allen and Unwin, 1930); E. Lewis-Faning, 'Report on an enquiry into family limitation and its influence on human fertility during the past fifty years', Papers of the Royal Commission on Population, 1 (London: HMSO, 1949). Szreter cites the Lewis-Faning report as 'the most technically rigorous source of systematic information available on contraceptive practices throughout the first half of the twentieth century', in *Fertility, Class and Gender*, pp. 402, 405–6. However, it should be noted that Lewis-Faning only interviewed women.

12 Cook, *The Long Sexual Revolution*; J. Banks, *Victorian Values: Secularism and the Size of Families* (Aldershot: Gregg Revivals, 1994); J. Banks and O. Banks, *Feminism and Family Planning in Victorian England* (New York: Shocken Books, 1977); P. Branca, *Silent Sisterhood: Middle Class Women in the Victorian Home* (London: Croom Helm, 1975); D. Gittins, *Fair Sex: Family Size and Structure, 1900–1939* (London: Hutchinson, 1982); Fisher, *Birth Control, Sex, and Marriage*.

13 G. Aly and M. Sontheimer, *Fromms: How Julius Fromm's Condom Empire Fell to the Nazis* (New York: Other Press, 2011); J. Richdale, 'Ladies' and gentlemen's toilet and rubber requisites: the development of New Zealand's commercial trade in contraceptives and birth control literature 1900s–1940', *Health and History*, 15:2 (2013), 72–92; A. Tone, 'Contraceptive consumers: gender and the political economy of birth control in the 1930s', *Journal of Social History*, 29 (1996), 485–508; *Devices and Desires: A History of Contraceptives in America* (New York: Hill and Wang, 2001); 'Making room for rubbers: gender, technology, and birth control before the Pill', *History and Technology*, 18 (2002), 51–76.

14 Like the literature on birth control, the literature on the history of consumption is vast. The beginnings of the consumer as a form of identity can be traced back to mid-Victorian Britain. F. Trentmann, 'The evolution of the consumer: meanings, identities, and political synapses before the age of affluence', in S. Garon and P. L. Maclachlan (eds), *The Ambivalent Consumer: Questioning Consumption in East Asia and the West* (Ithaca: Cornell University Press, 2006), pp. 37–42; B. Webb, *The Discovery of the Consumer* (London: Benn, 1928); F. Mort, 'Paths

to mass consumption: historical perspectives', in P. Jackson, M. Lowe, D. Miller and F. Mort (eds), *Commercial Cultures: Economies, Practices, Spaces* (Oxford and New York: Berg, 2000), pp. 7–14. See also, J. Benson, *The Rise of Consumer Society, 1880–1980* (London: Longman, 1994); W. Hamish Fraser, *The Coming of the Mass Market, 1850–1914* (London: Archon Books, 1981); M. Hilton, *Consumerism in 20th-Century Britain: The Search for a Historical Movement* (Cambridge: Cambridge University Press, 2003); F. Trentmann, *Empire of Things: How We Became Consumer from the Fifteenth Century to the Twenty-First* (London: Allen Lane, 2016). For a discussion on the history of 'Americanisation', see C. Waters, 'Introduction: beyond "Americanization": rethinking Anglo-American cultural exchange between the wars', *Cultural and Social History*, 4:4 (2007), 451–9.

15 T. MacNamara, *Birth Control and American Modernity: A History of Popular Ideas* (Cambridge: Cambridge University Press, 2018), p. 31. There is no simple definition of 'modernity', but it has generally been seen as a description of major changes both social and material, particularly the emergence of the modern state, industrial capitalism and new forms of science and technology, and of the growing consciousness of the novelty of these changes. As historians and other scholars have argued since the 1990s, there are and have been multiple temporal and geographic 'modernities'. See, for example, B. Short, D. Gilbert and D. Matless, 'Historical geographies of British modernity', in D. Gilbert, D. Matless and B. Short (eds), *Geographies of British Modernity: Space and Society in the Twentieth Century* (Oxford: Blackwell, 2003), pp. 1–28; D. Sachsenmaier, S. N. Eisenstadt and J. Riedel (eds), *Reflections on Multiple Modernities: European, Chinese and Other Interpretations* (Leiden: Brill, 2002); M. Nava and A. O'Shea (eds), *Modern Times: Reflections on a Century of English Modernity* (London: Routledge, 1996).

16 A. Appadurai (ed.), *The Social Life of Things: Commodities in Cultural Perspective* (Cambridge: Cambridge University Press, 1986).

17 L. Z. Sigel, *Making Modern Love: Sexual Narratives and Identities in Interwar Britain* (Philadelphia: Temple University Press, 2012), p. 11.

18 J. Berger and M. Ward, 'Subtle signals of inconspicuous consumption', *Journal of Consumer Research*, 37 (2010), 555–69; C. Campbell, *The Romantic Ethic and the Spirit of Modern Consumerism* (Oxford: Basil Blackwell, 1987); M. L. Smith, 'Inconspicuous consumption: non-display goods and identity formation', *Journal of Archaeological Method and Theory*, 14 (2007), 412–38.

19 Hilton, *Consumerism in 20th-Century Britain*, p. 19.

20 For example, J. Baudrillard, *System of Objects* (London: Verso, 2006).

21 J. Weeks, *Sex, Politics and Society: The Regulation of Sexuality since 1800* (Harlow: Longman, 1989), p. 1.

22 M. Borell, 'Biologists and the promotion of birth control research, 1918–1938', *Journal of the History of Biology*, 20:1 (1987), 51–87; I. Löwy, '"Sexual chemistry" before the Pill: science, industry and chemical contraceptives, 1920–1960', *British Journal for the History of Science*, 44:2 (2011), 245–74; R. Soloway, 'The "perfect" contraceptive: eugenics and birth control research in Britain and American in the interwar years', *Journal of Contemporary History*, 30 (1995), 637–64; N. Szuhan, 'Sex in the laboratory: the Family Planning Association and contraceptive science in Britain, 1929–1959', *British Journal for the History of Science*, 51:3 (2018), 487–510. For chemists, see S. Anderson and V. Berridge, 'The role of the community pharmacist in health and welfare, 1911–1986', in J. Bornat, R. Perks, P. Thompson and J. Walmsley (eds), *Oral History, Health and Welfare* (London: Routledge, 2000), pp. 48–74.

23 The literature on Marie Stopes is vast. See, for example, R. Hall, *Marie Stopes: A Biography* (London: Virago, 1978); J. Rose, *Marie Stopes and the Sexual Revolution* (London: Faber and Faber, 1992); R. Soloway, *Birth Control and the Population Question in England, 1870–1930* (Chapel Hill: University of North Carolina Press, 1982); R. A. Peel (ed.), *Marie Stopes, Eugenics and the English Birth Control Movement* (London: Galton Institute, 1996).

24 Medicalisation, as a concept, developed in the post-war era of scepticism over the ability of modern medicine to cure society's ills and has been applied to various periods and spaces to depict a nebulous but dynamic process resulting in medical control over ideas, practices or knowledge. For example, I. Illich, *Medical Nemesis: The Expropriation of Health* (London: Marion Boyars, 1974); C. Jones and R. Porter (eds), *Reassessing Foucault: Power, Medicine and the Body* (London: Routledge, 1994).

25 L. M. Beier, *For Their Own Good: The Transformation of English Working-Class Health Culture, 1880–1970* (Columbus: Ohio State University Press, 2008).

26 Cook, *The Long Sexual Revolution*, p. 50.

27 Porter and Hall, *The Facts of Life*; Sigel, *Making Modern Love*; J. Rose, *The Intellectual Life of the British Working Classes* (New Haven: Yale University Press, 2001).

28 H. Cook, 'Sex and the doctors: the medicalization of sexuality as a two-way process in early to mid-twentieth-century Britain', in W. de Blécourt and C. Usborne (eds), *Cultural Approaches to the History of Medicine: Mediating Medicine in Early Modern and Modern Europe* (Basingstoke: Palgrave Macmillan, 2004), pp. 192–211. For later medicalisation of contraceptive health, see A. Tone, 'Medicalizing reproduction: the Pill and home pregnancy tests', *Journal of Sex Research*, 49:4 (2012), 319–27.

29 M. Ertman and J. Williams, *Rethinking Commodification: Case Readings in Law and Culture* (New York: New York University Press, 2005) in R. Holz, *The Birth Control Clinic in a Marketplace World* (Rochester, NY: University of Rochester Press, 2012), p. 4. See also, P. Jackson, M. Lowe, D. Miller and F. Mort, 'Introduction: transcending dualisms' in P. Jackson *et al.* (eds), *Commercial Cultures*, pp. 1–4.
30 N. E. Himes, *Medical History of Contraception* (Baltimore: The Williams and Wilkins Company, 1936), p. 326.
31 Trentmann, 'The evolution of the consumer', p. 40.
32 For the development of a late twentieth-century consumer identity, see L. Black, '*Which?* craft in post-war Britain: the Consumers' Association and the politics of affluence', *Albion*, 36:1 (2004), 52–82; Hilton, *Consumerism in 20th-Century Britain*; Trentmann, 'The evolution of the consumer'. For the late twentieth-century emergence of the consumer-patient, see A. Mold, *Making the Patient-consumer: Patient Organisations and Health Consumerism in Britain* (Manchester: Manchester University Press, 2016).
33 F. Trentmann, 'Knowing consumers – histories, identities, practices: an introduction', in F. Trentmann (ed.), *The Making of the Consumer: Knowledge, Power and Identity in the Modern World* (New York and Oxford: Berg, 2006), p. 5.
34 Szreter and Fisher, *Sex Before the Sexual Revolution*; Cook, *The Long Sexual Revolution*.
35 Fisher, *Birth Control, Sex, and Marriage*, p. 26.
36 Porter and Hall, *The Facts of Life*, p. 248.
37 Szreter, *Fertility, Class and Gender*, p. 396.
38 H. Cook, 'The Long Sexual Revolution: British Women, Sex and Contraception in the Twentieth Century' (D.Phil thesis, University of Sussex, 1999), p. 182.
39 Trentmann, 'Knowing consumers'.
40 Gittins, *Fair Sex*; A. McLaren, *A History of Contraception: From Antiquity to the Present Day* (Blackwell, 1990); J. Benson and L. Ugolini, 'Introduction', in J. Benson and L. Ugolini (eds), *Cultures of Selling: Perspectives on Consumption and Society since 1700* (Abingdon: Ashgate, 2006), pp. 1–28; E. Rappaport, *Shopping for Pleasure: Women in the Making of London's West End* (Princeton: Princeton University Press, 2000).
41 Fisher, *Birth Control, Sex, and Marriage*, pp. 76–108.
42 M. Schofield, *The Sexual Behaviour of Young People* (London: Longman, 1965).
43 The Association's immediate predecessor was the National Birth Control Council. In 1930, five societies amalgamated as the National Birth Control Council: the Society for the Provision of Birth Control

Clinics (established in 1924), the Birth Control International Information Centre (1929), the Worker's Birth Control Group, which joined the National Birth Control Association in 1930, and the Birth Control Investigation Committee.

44 For the methodological problems of Mass-Observation, see P. Gurney, '"Intersex" and "dirty girls": Mass-Observation and working-class sexuality in England in the 1930s', *Journal of the History of Sexuality*, 8:2 (1997), 256–90.

45 For example, R. Darnton, 'First steps towards a history of reading', *The Kiss of Lamourette: Reflections in Cultural History* (New York and London: W. W. Norton and Co., 1990); L. Howsam, 'What is the historiography of books? Recent studies in authorship, publishing, and reading in modern Britain and North America', *Historical Journal*, 51:4 (2008), 1089–101.

46 Cook, 'The Long Sexual Revolution', pp. 174–5.

47 D. Edgerton, *The Shock of the Old: Technology and Global History since 1900* (New York: Oxford University Press, 2007), p. 22.

48 C. Lawrence and A. K. Mayer (eds), *Regenerating England: Science, Medicine and Culture in Inter-War Britain* (Amsterdam: Roldophi, 2000), p. 2.

49 A. Bingham, *Family Newspapers? Sex, Private Life, and the British Popular Press 1918–1978* (Oxford: Oxford University Press, 2009); Cook, 'Sex and the doctors'; Sigel, *Making Modern Love*.

50 For example, K. Fisher, '"Clearing up misconceptions": the campaign to set up birth control clinics in South Wales between the wars', *Welsh History Review*, 19:1 (1998), 103–29; J. Grier, 'Eugenics and birth control: contraceptive provision in North Wales, 1918-1939', *Social History of Medicine*, 11:3 (1998), 443–8; E. L. Jones, 'The establishment of voluntary family planning clinics in Liverpool and Bradford: a comparative study', *Social History of Medicine*, 24:2 (2011), 352–69.

1

The dynamics of production: contraceptive manufacturing

Alison Neilans's refusal to endorse the Contraceptives (Regulation) Bill led to an exodus of the more religious and social purist members from the Association for Moral and Social Hygiene in 1937. In their letter of resignation quoted in *The Times*, Dr Katharine Bushell, Miss Forsaith and Florence Booth, wife of Bramwell Booth (son of the founders of the Salvation Army), claimed that British contraceptive manufacturers created a 'powerful vested interest' and were 'enriching themselves by encouraging lust' in men, women, boys and girls.[1] And yet, Dawson's detailed enquiries into the trade a few years earlier revealed little to suggest that rubber contraceptive manufacturing was morally corrupt or corrupting. In fact, far from demonstrating a 'powerful vested interest', his research, the most thorough in existence at the time, stated that contraceptive manufacturing was 'as respectably run as any other trade. The factories are well constructed; the workers belong to a high class, are well treated and well-behaved'. Thus, Dawson argued, there was 'no justification for referring to the trade as "vicious"'.[2]

The respectability of manufacturing, both in terms of the items produced and disseminated to consumers and in terms of the workers who produced them, formed a key part of the debates over contraceptive commercialisation in the interwar years, and yet historical work to date has overlooked its significance. Instead, historians have followed Norman Himes and his 1936 publication *Medical History of Contraception* to focus on the impact of technological development on manufacturing, arguing that mechanised latex manufacturing in particular transformed condom production and stimulated demand by allowing consumers to purchase a more reliable, thinner and disposable product at a more affordable price than pre-existing methods of moulded sheet rubber production. Himes, an interwar social and medical scientist and protagonist of birth control, claimed that latex contraceptive manufacture was nothing short of revolutionary, and thereafter historians endorsed latex production as the most significant technological achievement after the nineteenth-century vulcanisation of rubber.[3]

Certainly, the trade's rapid growth in the 1930s was aided by the introduction of latex manufacturing. By Dawson's 1934 estimates, LRC of Chingford, as the first British firm to adopt latex manufacturing in 1932, was producing over 8.5 million latex condoms per year, while E. Lambert and Son of Dalston, LRC's closest rival that relied on sheet rubber production, produced 3.7 million reusable sheaths. By 1939 LRC claimed to dominate half of Britain's condom market.[4] But the impact of latex manufacturing on the trade in the 1930s was far more complex than has hitherto been outlined. Indeed, to focus only on technological change, success, novelty, innovation and radical breaks with the past neglects the wider production dynamics of the trade in this period, its implications for demand and on the workforce, and its effect on the 'moral panic' surrounding contraceptive commercialisation.

It is more accurate to see Himes's attempt to break with the traditional past as part of his own modernist vision, rather than as a reflection of the 1930s trade itself, and to view subsequent emphasis on revolution as part of longer chronological narratives that seek to explain a later technological triumph. Latex manufacturing was certainly not quick to replace older, more traditional manufacturing methods, and as suggested by Dawson's investigations into the trade, new, modern latex manufacturing sat alongside older, smaller-scale methods for producing contraceptive goods made from moulded sheet rubber, including caps, enemas and reusable sheaths. It was only in the 1950s that fully mechanised production methods allowed LRC to dominate the contraceptive trade with latex condoms and diaphragms, and permitted the arrival of the modern condom.[5]

Moreover, home production in the 1930s formed a negligible part of the wider economy and of the contraceptive trade. Britain's contraceptive trade was largely sustained by five times as many imports of cheap contraceptive goods from France, Germany and the United States.[6] German production, for example, reached 100 million units in the 1920s, half of which was exported.[7] Perhaps most significantly, however, neither the former members of the Association of Moral and Social Hygiene, who opposed contraception in its entirety, nor Dawson, as one of the most informed interwar commentators on birth control, made any distinction between old and new methods of manufacturing; this suggests that new production methods meant little to contemporary debates. Dawson, for example, continued to use 'sheath' to refer to both the new latex condom and the older rubber sheath, despite the fact that LRC was making attempts to distinguish its own latex condom from older models of sheaths. Instead, what mattered in the interwar period was manufacturers' respectability and the perception of this respectability among both the contraceptive workforce and consumers.

Structured by Dawson's investigations then, this chapter examines the blend of modern and traditional methods used to produce different types of rubber contraceptives in interwar Britain in the context of the manufactory and wider debates around respectability. In doing so, it reveals that latex production alone did not revolutionise the trade nor was it an immediate catalyst for demand. Indeed, the interwar changes that most affected production – the National Birth Control Association's introduction of standardised contraceptive testing, the feminisation of the workforce and the outbreak of the Second World War – impacted latex and non-latex contraceptive manufacturers alike. As we will see, the contraceptive workforce not only represented firm respectability but was also an important barometer of the extent to which sexual and contraceptive knowledge was disseminated in the workplace.

Rubber manufacturing: the beginnings

By the time LRC introduced its latex condoms, rubber contraceptive manufacturing was well established in Britain. British manufacturing of general rubber goods first began in 1820 in Thomas Hancock's London workshop, but the introduction of the vulcanisation process in the 1840s transformed rubber from a volatile substance into one that was stable and odourless, allowing more firms to more easily and safely produce all manner of rubber goods from flooring and footwear to washers and waterproof garments.[8] Prompted by developments in vulcanisation, several entrepreneurs diversified into contraceptives. Friedrich Adolph Wilde reportedly designed the first rubber device to cover the cervix (a cervical cap or occlusive pessary) in 1838, while in 1842 W. P. J. Mensinga produced the first rubber diaphragm (or Dutch cap), a rubber device with a metal spring-loaded rim that covered the cervix by expanding against the walls of the vagina.[9] The first vulcanised rubber sheath was reportedly produced in 1843 by moulding raw crepe and vulcanising it by burning sulphur, although some historians push the date back into the 1850s, with rubber penis tips being produced from 1858.[10]

While it is likely that a few of the first British contraceptive manufacturers gathered in the industrial districts of Manchester alongside Charles Macintosh's famous waterproof garment factory, no fewer than eight contraceptive firms clustered around Hackney Wick by 1883.[11] Both Manchester and Hackney were key sites of small-scale rubber good production into the twentieth century. Firms in the workshop districts of Hackney Wick and nearby Dalston included those of James George Ingram, a Scottish engineer, who had established his manufactory in 1866, John George Franklin, established in 1864, and Edward Lambert and Son, established in 1877. Conveniently located next to the River Lea, workshops in Hackney Wick and Dalston were able to receive large shipments of rubber and to recruit from the abundance of local skilled and unskilled workers, some of whom were likely to have been Jewish. Increasing immigration had by the 1880s brought perhaps five thousand Jews to Dalston, making up over 20 per cent of Hackney's residents. As we will see throughout this book, anti-Semitism within the British birth control movement (Marie Stopes being the most vocal anti-Semite) and among Christian moralists helped to justify and promote the trade's disreputability.

Of the manufacturers of rubber goods that diversified into contraceptive goods, it was Lambert of Dalston that sold directly to the public and thus became the best known. Established as a contraceptive wholesaler in 1860, Lambert initially sold imported cervical caps, Mensinga diaphragms and sheaths made from rubber and from animal skin to a small number of retailers and consumers via mail order.[12] Lambert's establishment of his own contraceptive manufactory in 1877 in two large mansions and two accompanying workshops on Queen's Lane, Dalston, provided space, materials and machinery for the processes of rubber moulding and vulcanisation, and was prompted not only by a desire to move away from a reliance on imports but also to take advantage of the small but growing late nineteenth-century demand for contraceptives. Before the First World War the majority of people within all classes and age groups in society shared broadly similar negative attitudes to sex, but Lambert was able to draw on his seventeen years of experience in the wholesaling trade, its supply chains and customers in order to tap into and expand existing demand among a key market of middle- and upper-class married couples who were actively seeking to control their fertility. Indeed, Lambert's transformation from wholesaler to manufacturer in 1877 was no coincidence. Manufacturing its own goods allowed the firm to exploit the small level of demand that resulted from the publicity surrounding the infamous trial of Charles Bradlaugh (1833–91) and Annie Besant (1847–1933) that found the pair guilty of publishing and distributing Charles Knowlton's *Fruits of Philosophy*, and from the establishment of the Malthusian League, a largely middle-class neo-Malthusian movement with a small membership of over one thousand, which sought to control population through fertility regulation.[13] However, Lambert's success at tapping into and expanding contraceptive demand could only be assured through his appeal to physicians, surgeons, chemists, nurses and other forms of medical practitioner through the production and sale of all manner of medical rubber goods, including teats for feeding bottles, hot-water bottles, hernia trusses and urinals. The firm produced and promoted these medical goods alongside contraceptives, and thus could legitimately describe themselves as 'surgical appliance makers'.

Lambert's first contraceptives – syringes, seamless enemas, cervical caps and a range of rubber pessaries – appealed to both practitioners for their use in medical treatment and to married couples for birth control. With their ability to clean bodily orifices, syringes and enemas appealed to practitioners. Higginson's syringe, first made and patented in 1874 by Ingram, was the first and best known, but Lambert soon developed and produced his own model called 'Lambert's Improved Vertical and Reverse Current Syringe'. Medical and nursing literature, such as *Hints on Nursing* in 1889, referred to the importance of the cleansing power of Lambert's syringe.[14] But it was the ability of such douching appliances to flood and thus clear out the vagina with water after intercourse that appealed to middle-class married couples and its innocuous use as a hygienic aid meant the syringe could be widely produced, promoted and sold without offending unknowing consumers in the prevailing, relatively homogeneous, negative sexual culture.

Syringing for contraceptive purposes was not new to the late nineteenth century – Charles Knowlton had mentioned it in 1834 – but the seamless nature of the rubber syringe meant it was able to syphon water more effectively and more simply with one instrument compared to earlier forms of the appliance made from brass, caoutchouc tubing and detachable ivory pipes.[15] At around 5s the rubber syringe was also cheaper than the earlier brass model, which cost 15s. The rubber syringe's apparent improved contraceptive function was highlighted in birth control publications throughout the late nineteenth century and into the interwar period. Noted pioneering sensationalist journalist and birth control advocate William T. Stead, for example, wrote in his diary on 20 January 1889: 'I have from the birth of Willie (1875?) practised simple syringing with water. Of late always withdrawal. We never used anything but this'.[16] The disguised nature of the syringe also did not go unnoticed by commentators. As part of her data collection work among working-class householders north of the Humber for the Eugenics Laboratory, Ethel Elderton reported in 1914 that the number of enemas sold in Guisborough 'was far larger than could be accounted for on the ground that they were required for ordinary purposes'. Yet, like all those within Elderton's report, this statement was largely based on the testimony of mainly middle-class local doctors, chemists and philanthropic workers, and thus not necessarily reflective of consumers' intended use.[17]

Similarly, Lambert's check and stem pessaries appealed to practitioners treating female patients for prolapsed uteri, while simultaneously appealing to married couples for their ability to create a barrier in the cervix.[18] The firm explicitly sold and promoted such goods as both pessaries for uterus support and as contraceptives. Its 1897 catalogue text to promote the Mensinga pessaries, for example, stated that the device was used for 'supporting and covering the womb' and 'is also useful as a support in early cases of falling of the womb, and for the application of remedies in cases of ulceration of the womb'; but promotion of the appliance simultaneously featured under the heading 'contraceptives' with text explaining that it could be used by the woman 'without inconvenience or knowledge of the husband'.[19] The distinction between a pessary for contraceptive purposes and one to support a prolapsed uterus or vagina may be obvious to historians of birth control but was unlikely to have been so for unknowing consumers or even medical practitioners. Indeed, by 1910 there were almost one hundred different designs of vaginal and intrauterine pessaries available, while the only identifying characteristic was often its description in printed advertising as a 'preventative'.[20] Even Marie

Stopes in 1920 was unable to distinguish between caps that could be used for uterus support and those for contraception.²¹

The initial success of Lambert's douching appliances and early rubber caps and pessaries then resulted from their dual purpose as both contraceptives and innocuous hygienic and medical aids; their meaning changed dependent on the user and their requirements. While the reliance on access to water, a degree of privacy and, for the cap or pessary, knowledge of the appropriate methods of fitting, meant that such contraceptives had limited appeal beyond women of the upper and middle classes until the mid-twentieth century, their popularity among such couples prompted other firms to take on production of their own versions, as well as a variety of other designs of all shapes and sizes.²² Wholesalers such as the Marvel Whirling Syringe Company began to specialise in syringes alone. Marvel's products were readily available via mail order and from retailers; such products were available well into the 1950s.²³ Lambert's reputation for the production and sale of rubber medical appliances then aided his reputation as a reliable contraceptive goods manufacturer. Indeed, no reputable company was reckless enough to make contraceptives its primary articles of commerce, but Lambert's manufacture of general medical rubber goods meant it could sit alongside other firms in the respectable medical marketplace.

Lambert's success with douching appliances and caps prompted its experimentation with the 'cement' process of rubber manufacture in order to produce an appliance that could only have a sexual association: sheaths or 'French letters', named after the nation the English most associated with rampant sexual vice. First pioneered in Germany, Lambert's sheath production process involved dipping glass moulds into a solution of crepe rubber in petroleum solvent. Once a film had formed and dried, the moulds were dipped again according to the thickness required and finally vulcanised by exposure to sulphur dioxide gas. This process made sheath production cheaper and easier than early vulcanisation processes; it used minimal equipment and allowed the production of standard batches in Lambert's small manufactory. In fact, it was so cheap and easy, sheaths could be produced in one room, and numerous entrepreneurs with makeshift manufactories emerged into the market too.²⁴ Many of these entrepreneurs remain unknown, but we do know that Durrant and Sons, chemists of Bristol, made its own sheaths in the back of its shop between 1900 and 1920, while a Tommy Horton established production in a garage in Merthyr Tydfil in 1915, having consulted with Lambert about the most suitable methods.[25]

To appeal to the Malthusian League and its supporters, Lambert named the first sheath it produced in 1886 the 'Malthusian', and its first washable and reusable seamless sheath the 'Paragon' (1891), alongside variants such as the 'American' that covered only the glans, and a variety of paraphernalia enabling users to care for their sheath. Such paraphernalia included chalk, powder, rolling mounts and protective cases to prevent cracking after washing and enabling users to carefully roll the sheath onto the penis when next in use. Replacing the first vulcanised sheaths – which were reportedly expensive, thick and characterised by a seam that joined the sheets together, making them uncomfortable – the washable and reusable nature of the new cement-process sheaths appealed to Lambert's established customer base of upper- and middle-class consumers. Indeed, the relatively high expense of sheaths, averaging 4s each, plus sheath rollers and cases priced at between 1s 6d and 3s, meant that they may have been out of the reach of working-class consumers.

Identifiable sheath consumers were often only brought to light due to their association with high-profile scandal, although it is difficult to know if the sheaths they purchased were produced by Lambert. For example, in her testimony in her own divorce case in 1886, Virginia Crawford claimed that Sir Charles Dilke, radical Liberal MP, had used 'French letters' during their adulterous affair.[26] But there is some non-scandalous evidence of high-profile middle-class couples using sheaths too. These include several among the 420 middle-class women that socialist Enid Charles interviewed for her 1932 publication *The Practice of Birth Control*, who began using the sheath in 1880.[27] The League and some of its more vocal members began to promote Lambert's 'Malthusian' in their tracts and publications, alongside the firm's syringes and Mensinga pessary, in order to target its membership. For example, Henry Arthur Allbutt, the medical practitioner and neo-Malthusian most famous for his publication of *The Wife's Handbook* in 1885 and his expulsion from the medical profession in 1886, initially promoted all three of Lambert's contraceptive types, while fellow neo-Malthusian Annie Besant referred to Lambert's cap in her *Law of Population*.[28] Lambert's advertisement in *The Malthusian*, the League's journal, from April 1887 and in each edition thereafter similarly referred to its 'New Scientific Malthusian Appliance', and its 'Higginson's Syringe with Improved

Vertical and Reverse Current (just out), recommended by Dr Allbutt and others'.[29]

The lack of extant production or sales figures means that it is difficult to be precise about the extent of demand for Lambert's contraceptives in the firm's first decades of production. The impact of the Bradlaugh–Besant trial, and of the late nineteenth-century birth control movement more generally, on the dissemination of sexual and contraceptive knowledge was almost certainly more limited than early commentators, demographers and historians have suggested. Indeed, Himes's claims that the effect of the trial 'upon the public mind was electric' and 'there can be no doubt that the publicity gave wide advertising to the idea that contraception was possible' exaggerated the impact of the birth control movement on the general population.[30] While family limitation may have been increasingly popular among the middle classes, Lewis-Faning's survey conducted for the Royal Commission on Population of 3,281 women of all ages in 1946 and 1947 suggested that among respondents from two marriage cohorts of 1900–9 and 1910–19 only 2 per cent and 9 per cent, respectively, acknowledged use of any form of 'appliance method'.[31] Nonetheless, Lambert's reported production of between a quarter of and half a million sheaths per year by the 1890s and its subsequent workforce expansion to around twenty employees that included appliance makers, wrappers, packers, shippers and testers suggests a small level of demand that was sustainable alongside the production of other rubber medical appliances.[32] While only a fraction of the twenty-eight thousand workers engaged in British rubber manufacturing by 1912 produced contraceptives, Lambert, Ingram, Franklin and other contraceptive firms were able to sustain a productive and satisfied workforce, many of whom were in the trade for fifty years or longer.[33] Demand certainly came from the neo-Malthusians and their audience, but it also came from middle-class consumers not connected to the Malthusian League and a variety of medical practitioners who used syringes and caps for non-contraceptive purposes.

Lambert was, of course, not able to predict demand, and moral sensibilities meant that the firm had limited ways of shaping it, but its relationship with the neo-Malthusians and medical practitioners before the First World War ensured a reasonable level of demand from birth control advocates of the interwar period. As we will see in subsequent chapters, Lambert was the first, and for some years the only, British manufacturing firm that Marie Stopes and the National

Birth Control Association trusted to produce and supply reliable rubber goods, which stimulated further demand from the wider population seeking medically sanctioned contraceptives. By the outbreak of the Second World War, Lambert supplied the majority of birth control clinics and medical practitioners across the country. With its success and goodwill in the trade established, latex production, when possible from the 1930s, was not an obvious business diversification for Lambert. The firm reluctantly stated in 1934 that it was prepared to supply latex goods but only when specially ordered. It placed much greater emphasis on experimentation in sheet rubber production with different methods of rubber vulcanisation and new machinery.[34]

The introduction of latex production

It is no coincidence that in 1932 Lionel A. Jackson, the founder of LRC, established his latex manufactory on Shore Road in Hackney. Aware of Lambert's success, the Hackney location benefited the firm not only through its close physical association to manufacturers in the area but also from its existing industrial and transport structures and skilled workforce. Like Lambert, Jackson did not begin his foray into the contraceptive business through manufacturing. Born in 1894 to Russian Jewish immigrants, Jackson changed his name from Jacoby and, prompted by the increasing publicity that sheaths (and venereal disease) received during the First World War, established his sheath selling business in East London in 1915 at his father's hairdressing and tobacconist shop, a form of retailer where sheaths had long been available on request.[35] Just like the Jewish immigrants likely employed in Lambert's Dalston manufactory, Jackson seemingly viewed the contraceptive trade, albeit with its precarious status and dubious reputation, as way for enterprising Jewish immigrants to make a profitable, honest living. Indeed, as we will see in subsequent chapters, the proprietors of surgical (or rubber) stores, a form of retailer that were among the first to sell 'every variety of French and American skin', alongside obscene saucy books, photographs and neo-Malthusian publications, were often Jewish, which in turn served to enhance the trade's disreputability in the eyes of the birth control movement and possibly the public. But this disreputability was an opportunity for Jackson. It is likely that Jacoby used the name 'Jackson' in order to associate himself and his business with L. Jackson, another London-based entrepreneur who claimed to have been importing pessaries since 1850. This L. Jackson ran a retail store known as Constantine and Jackson on Wych Street, off the Strand, which was infamous for its shops selling pornography and other indecent books. He may have had connections with at least two other Jacksons based in London who were involved in contraceptive retailing, although there is no evidence of this connection.[36] While Lambert had sought to gain credibility through the production of contraceptives alongside other rubber medical goods, there was no such opportunity for Jackson, who specialised in sheaths. Jackson's change of name from Jacoby and his naming of the firm as the London Rubber Company were reputational moves to distance himself and his company from the disreputable Jewish retailers of the trade. Benefiting from general increased publicity during and after the war, Jackson was able to employ twenty people by 1920 and had established his own wholesale business on Aldersgate Street, a surgical store on Mincing Lane and additional offices at Old Street to accommodate a mail-order business.[37]

LRC's motives for becoming the first British company to enter latex manufacture in 1932 are, however, not immediately obvious. Unlike Lambert, the firm was certainly not encumbered by the machinery, equipment and skilled workforce used to make sheaths, caps and enemas from moulded sheet rubber. Indeed, it would have been difficult and costly for Lambert to convert its pre-existing production methods and materials to latex manufacture, even if the firm's management had wanted to. Instead of moulds or 'mandrels' being dipped into a solution of crepe rubber in petroleum solvent, latex production consisted of dipping into liquid latex (the sap of the rubber tree suspended in water). Cylindrical brushes then rolled a protective bead onto the open end of the condom on the moulds. The condoms were then vulcanised in an overhead hot-air-and-water bath, dried and dusted with talc, then stripped with brushes and taken on continuous conveyor belts where they were removed and straightened out. Manufacturing processes consisted of compounding, drum storage, batch mixing, dipping, finishing, testing, packing and distribution.[38] The prohibitively high cost of machinery for latex conveyor belt production also deterred other firms from entering into the trade, indeed resulting in bankruptcy for some that attempted. International Latex Products Ltd, for example, went bankrupt attempting to cover the costs of its heavy machinery for its newly established latex manufactory in 1936.[39]

Jessica Borge has argued that the slump in the cost of raw rubber meant that the 1930s was the right time for LRC to enter latex manufacture, but this was unlikely to be an impetus in itself and neither does it account for Lambert's continued reliance on sheet rubber processes.[40] It seems more likely that LRC's entry into latex manufacture was prompted by both its failure to make any significant inroads in a small market in which Lambert dominated and its successful retailing of the 'Dreadnought', the first American latex condom produced by Young's Rubber Corporation from 1929. Indeed, during the 1920s and early 1930s, LRC failed in its attempts to build a relationship with Stopes and the National Birth Control Association. The firm's limited commercial success with non-latex condoms is suggested by the fact that advertisements for its first 'Durex' brand only appeared intermittently in 1927.[41] Standing for Durability, Reliability and Excellence, LRC's first 'Durex' condoms were likely to have been rebranded non-latex imports, but the brand name embodied the attributes the firm assumed consumers most wanted from contraceptives. Jackson's registration of the 'Durex' trade mark in 1929, the same year as Young began production, was seemingly a first indication of his move into latex production.[42]

LRC's first promotional catalogue emphasised the benefit of latex condoms. Its 'infallible Durex protectives' were 'of amazingly fine texture, made by an exclusive process from the sap or milk of the rubber tree, without the use of gasolines or chemicals of any kind, and being cured in boiling water untouched by hands at any time during production, are completely sterilised. Half as thick yet five times as strong as ordinary rubber. The strongest, thinnest and silkiest protectives in the world'.[43] Beginning the distinction in terminology between condoms and sheaths, LRC's condom was also elastic, disposable and portable, meaning that consumers were no longer required to care for their sheaths and could more conveniently carry them on their person. But as the firm's failure to supply birth control advocates suggests, demand for latex products had to be created in a market where washable and reusable sheaths made from sheet rubber, as well as paraphernalia such as re-rolling kits, and even animal skin sheaths, had long been sold and promoted and where female contraceptives, such as the cap and syringe, could be successfully produced, bought and sold without the association to venereal disease and prostitution.[44] Indeed, the continued promotion of both rubber sheaths and those made from animal skins into the 1930s and 1940s demonstrates that products made from new materials like latex did not wholesale replace those made from existing materials. For consumers, the benefits of the latex condom cited by LRC (and subsequently by historians) were not immediately obvious. The firm had to continually reiterate these benefits for consumers to accept the latex condom and, as we will see in subsequent chapters, it did so aggressively.

Jackson's motivation aside, the firm's move to latex manufacture allowed for greater economies of scale, product standardisation, reduced manufacturing time and less risk of fire resulting from the combustible chemicals used during the cement process. Indeed, fire was a long-standing hazard of rubber good production and there had been a serious fire caused by these chemicals at a London rubber works in 1891.[45] But it also meant that LRC was able to meet the British Royal Navy's order for condoms in 1933 for the prevention of venereal disease, the year in which fertility in marriage was at its lowest. Borge has argued that neither prophylactic knowledge nor condoms were commonly available to British soldiers during the First World War, but prophylactic treatment had shifted away from chemicals and towards condoms by the 1930s and the Navy became the firm's first large intermediary customer with a reported 300 ships and 161,000 men by 1939.[46] Alongside production for the Navy, LRC began to supply growing numbers of retailers and clinics of the National Birth Control Association, which had a growing interest in latex goods. Birth control researchers Griselda Rowntree and Rachel Pierce found that male approval of birth control rose faster than that of women in the 1930s, but the increasing adoption of latex goods by the National Birth Control Association demonstrates that they were also being recommended to women.[47]

LRC was, however, met with fierce competition by newly established latex manufacturer Prentif. W. T. Harrison, Prentif's director, recognised the benefits of latex manufacture, but his move into latex manufacturing was strategic. It aligned Harrison with the Association and the medical profession; in fact, it was the Association that prompted Harrison to overcome the high manufacturing costs and enter latex manufacturing. But like Jackson and his earlier enterprise, turning to latex also allowed Harrison to distance his new firm from its wholesale and retail origins as the infamous and disrespectable London rubber store W. George.[48] W. George was founded in the same disreputable part of London as Constantine and Jackson in the mid-nineteenth century and similarly associated with pornography and vice. Harrison was a director of both W. George and Prentif and was related to W. R. Harrison, who had run W. George on Holywell Street since the late nineteenth century. Harrison aimed to significantly reduce costs through the simultaneous supply of products of his own manufacture to his retail and wholesale business and to the medical profession. By 1938 Prentif was promoting that its state-of-the-art air-conditioned plant gave 'control over both temperature and humidity – most important features in this type of rubber manufacture – in addition, the air is water-washed and freed from dust and impurities'.[49] Expansion in production also had a significant impact on the growth and demographics of its workforce, much to the dismay of moralists (as we will see in the last section of this chapter).

Along with the general expansion in production, it was the National Birth Control Association's research into finding the most effective contraceptive possible that resulted in a significant change to contraceptive manufacturing. Estimates of contraceptive reliability before the mid-1930s varied so widely that they provided little accurate information. Most indicated a low degree of reliability for existing products. Norman Haire, medical practitioner and birth control advocate, suggested in 1928 that over 86 per cent of cervical caps were faulty, as were 51.4 per cent of condoms. Enid Charles estimated that the failure rate for caps was 28 per cent, 21 per cent for Dutch caps and 18 per cent for condoms.[50] LRC had accepted the imperfectibility of its condoms and admitted in 1934 that it discarded one-third of those it produced on account of their imperfections, but stated: 'we do not mind however because the remainder is perfect'.[51] But in order to supply the Association, manufacturers of both latex and non-latex contraceptives had to pass new Association specifications of product testing, notice of which was sent to clinics and other interested parties via an approved product list. Tests of inflation, ageing, elongation (to 900 per cent its length prior to break), tensile strength, dating (in order to give goods a three-year guarantee) and visual assessment for tears and splits, introduced from 1935 and developed throughout the 1940s and 1950s, not only represented the beginning of standardised contraceptives in Britain, but also signalled the Association's and, with it, the medical profession's, attempt to dominate and medicalise contraceptive supply.[52] Testing was, of course, not altogether new. Manufacturers had long claimed that they subjected their products to rigorous testing. Retailers of the 1910s, such as W. George, stated that every contraceptive was tested by a 'special testing machine', while C. F. Charles and Co. Ltd stated that 'all sheaths are tested – we can guarantee them to be quite fresh and free from fault'.[53] But manufacturer and retailer claims are difficult to prove and their goods appear ineffective in light of estimates of contraceptive reliability. The National Birth Control Association's standards were more rigorous and standardised than any previous testing.

Accordingly, old and new manufacturers, and those using latex and the cement process alike, dedicated an increased amount of factory space to contraceptive testing. Testing procedures were labour intensive – it took skilled workers between twenty and thirty minutes to complete a batch – and thus not only demanded a greater amount of factory space but also increased production costs.[54] The newly established Prentif was able to immediately dedicate the required factory space for testing and conducted what it called the 'Factory test' on every condom it produced. LRC developed testing space too and, like Prentif, developed dedicated workbenches for testing sheaths by air inflation and visual inspection. Male workers at the factories of LRC and Prentif were required to manually test condom elasticity and strength. At the Prentif factory, two operators inflated every condom produced by blowing into them then visually examining them for minute holes, weak spots and creases (fig. 1), while at LRC, workers suspended chairs using condoms (fig. 2). Condoms that passed the tests were wrapped in individual envelopes (or boxes for washable sheaths), date stamped and dispatched; those considered defective fell through tubular runaways incorporated into the benches and into the catcher. Defective stock was then reportedly destroyed, but it is clear that manufacturers sold on such stock to surgical stores. Selling on inferior stock was a common practice by the 1930s, which allowed manufacturers to make a small profit. For Prentif, defective stock was sold through its own retailer, W. George, which graded sheaths into up to five qualities with prices that corresponded. We return to the significance of testing on improved contraceptive efficacy in Chapter 4.

Increasing demand led to increased manufacturing capacity and allowed LRC to claim 50 per cent of the market for sheaths in 1939. Indeed, the firm's move to a larger factory in Chingford, on the outskirts of London, under the name British Latex Products Ltd, allowed for continuous assembly lines common to other interwar industries. A large proportion of LRC's new manufactory

Figure 1 'The factory test'. Condom testing by air inflation and visual inspection at Prentif's latex manufactory, St Mary Cray, Kent, c.1937.

consisted of large vulcanising ovens and space for condensed dripping and drying, providing the capacity for the firm to produce over 2.5 million condoms per day. However, the size of the market meant that the firm produced nowhere near to capacity. Indeed, for the most part, condom production, and contraceptive rubber production more generally, remained small-scale, manual and workshop based until LRC introduced fully automated production in 1951, marking what Hera Cook has described as the arrival of the modern condom.[55]

Latex production at the end of the 1930s certainly did not resemble the factories mass producing all manner of white household goods that were becoming central to the British economy during the interwar period, and neither did it bear much resemblance to latex production in North America by the late 1920s. Tone describes the pioneering condom production plant of Fred Killian in Akron, Ohio, which consisted of a 5,000 ft conveyor belt that automatically, rapidly, continuously and without the intervention of human hands dipped glass moulds into liquid latex at the rate of one per second.[56] In Britain, demand was still not large enough to warrant fully mechanised mass-production techniques. The firms that made the costly

THE DYNAMICS OF PRODUCTION

Figure 2 Condom testing by elongation at LRC's latex manufactory, Shore Road, Hackney, 1938.

investment to enter latex production still relied on manual methods and the skill of their labour force. Employees at LRC had to hand dip multiple mandrels into latex tanks in batches and hand deliver them to ovens through a labour-intensive system of hand-operated pulley-assisted racks, and women workers were required to manually unroll and snap the latex to remove wrinkles that might make the condom stick.[57] Prentif claimed that two male workers undertook the laborious process of monitoring 'electronically operated' tanks of latex with 'absolute precision in speed', in order to ensure an even texture and to avoid even the slightest vibration, which would spoil all of the condoms on a frame.[58]

It was only after the Second World War that supply and demand for latex contraceptives far exceeded supply and demand for contraceptives made from standard rubber. The war both disrupted domestic contraceptive production and provided the opportunity for LRC's further expansion. Lambert and Prentif suffered under the Ministry of Supply's policy to supply materials only to industries deemed of national importance. Supplies of rubber, spring steel for use in rubber cervical caps and quinine for the manufacture of chemical pessaries were significantly reduced and grew worse as the war went on. Supplies of rubber were so low by 1944 that Franklin shifted its production to rubber sealing for fuel tanks on aircraft and boats, informing Lambert that it was no longer able to supply the firm with enema syringes.[59] While the Ministry did grant extra rubber supplies for medical and surgical purposes (such as that for vaginal prolapse and hence caps under this description), much to the disgust of moralists, this still gave Lambert only one-third of the rubber it required to match its pre-war levels of production.[60] Contrastingly, LRC's bulk purchases and on-site storage of latex at its Chingford site meant it was less affected by fluctuations in the rubber market. On-site storage proved vital for the firm's completion of its contract to supply HM Armed Forces. The firm's 'Durex' branded condoms became standard issue following the full mobilisation of British and US forces throughout Europe, the Middle East and the Mediterranean in 1942, and production of condoms ran at thirty-six million per year for the remainder of the war, a production increase of over 300 per cent since Dawson's investigations seven years earlier.[61] This figure also included a tenfold increase in the number of chemists LRC supplied. With eight thousand chemist customers keen to benefit from increased condom publicity from the war, LRC supplied almost half the chemists in the country. Prentif, LRC's closest domestic competitor, supplied five thousand.[62]

The feminisation of the contraceptive manufactory

With increased production from the 1930s came increased employment. It was largely women and girls who filled new roles in the contraceptive manufactory. Women were certainly increasingly employed by firms at the manufactories in Hackney Wick and Dalston that continued to use the sheet process of rubber manufacture. Indeed, Lambert's workrooms consisted of twelve women binding, stripping and finishing 'Lam-butt' sheaths and diaphragms, alongside rubber gloves, and were presided over by a woman overseer (fig. 3).[63] But the adoption of mechanised latex production resulted in the feminisation of contraceptive manufacturing on a greater scale. In his early investigations of LRC in 1933, Dawson revealed that the firm's workforce was made up mostly of girls, aged about sixteen, and claimed that these workers belonged to a high class and were well-behaved; they

Figure 3 'One of the workrooms where "Lam-butt" contraceptive appliances are made', Lamberts Prorace Ltd.

earned between 10s and £10 conducting much of the easy and repetitive dipping work required to make latex sheaths. Like male workers at other contraceptive manufactories, women workers had long careers at LRC. Doris Groom, for example, came to work for LRC on leaving school in 1929 and stayed with the firm until she retired in 1965.[64]

The growth in contraceptive production concerned interwar and post-war moral purists for its effect on consumers, and also for its influence on young impressionable women that worked inside the contraceptive manufactory. In 1934 John Robertson, Medical Officer of Health for Birmingham, reported on his experience of the dissemination of contraceptive knowledge in the factory more generally: 'pamphlets on birth control are now sold inside and outside factories both to men and women. Agents for the sale of contraceptives exist either inside the factory or at the factory door', and male workers regularly used a condom vending machine placed near to a factory in Leicester.[65]

Such concerns feed into wider historical debates about the role of the workplace in disseminating sexual knowledge and shaping values and ideals on birth control in gendered, largely female, social networks, or 'communication communities' in England and Wales in the late nineteenth and early twentieth centuries. Historians have long argued that the workplace was a space in which contraceptive knowledge could be shared, with some drawing particular attention to the influence of the workplace distribution of contraceptive handbills and pamphlets by Richard Carlile (1790–1843), Robert Owen (1801–99) and Charles Knowlton (1800–50), the birth controllers of the early nineteenth century.[66] Certainly, low fertility rates in some localities where working-class women had steady employment after marriage, such as the cotton textile industry in Lancashire, wool textiles in the West Riding of Yorkshire and hosiery in the East Midlands, suggest that there is a positive correlation between sexual knowledge and factory work more generally.[67] Moreover, Elderton's report certainly highlighted that her middle-class respondents believed that working-class women shared birth control information. In Gorton, a Manchester textile manufacturing district, for example, one respondent stated that 'the subject is freely talked about in the workshops where girls and young women work, and also during the dinner hour', while one Lancaster respondent reported 'an afternoon gathering of women, many of whom were "good church-workers" and the subject under discussion was not the legitimacy of restriction, but the most effective means of restriction'.[68]

More recent historical interpretations, however, suggest the impact of workplace propaganda and 'communication communities' on contraceptive uptake and thus fertility was more limited. Kate Fisher has argued that the evidence suggests that among women friends, both before and after marriage, sex and therefore birth control were rarely discussed.[69] In fact, she argues that the oral culture of handing down knowledge may not have solely been an integral part of 'female culture' and that it was much more common to male social networks in workplaces. When sex was discussed by male sections of the workforce, women could deliberately close off their ears and avoid such knowledge. Ignorance was privileged. Reinforcing this view, reports from the 1930s suggest that workplace social networks reinforced morally conservative viewpoints on contraceptive appliances. The Public Health Society's official in the Midlands stated in 1934 that:

> Within the last five days I have had experiences quoted to me by married women, one of whom gave up her job at a big factory, because of the open discussion concerning sex and promiscuity 'made safe by birth prevention articles' ... a short time ago a well-known doctor for women's diseases said that contraceptives must be blamed for much of the trouble. Numerous girls in good positions coming to me for advice on venereal disease blame contraceptives introduced by men to them, as the cause of their downfall, what they mean is, of course, that but for the safety assured them by the men, they would never have risked sex intercourse.[70]

While such reports should be interpreted with care given the fact that report authors often opposed the open sale and advertisement of contraceptives, Dawson's more detailed investigations into the workforce of the contraceptive manufactory itself also confirmed reinforcement of these morally conservative viewpoints. His research suggested that dissemination of sexual knowledge among factory girls at LRC was decidedly low; these girls were not only 'of a good class' but were 'quite unconscious of their work'.[71] How Dawson determined that girls were 'quite unconscious of their work' is difficult to know, and again the ignorance of these girls may have been performative, but it nonetheless suggests that the circulation of birth control knowledge in the factory was more limited than moralists and many subsequent historians have assumed.

The trade's rapid increase in female employment during the war, as part of a more general increase in women in the workforce from nearly 20 per cent in 1938 to 27 per cent in 1945, heightened concerns about the dissemination of sexual knowledge within factories.[72] Conscription meant a shortage of male workers, and the Bishop of St Albans complained that employment of women in contraceptive factories across Britain ran into the thousands. While twenty-four girls made up the majority of the workforce of wrappers and packers of the 'Wife's Friend' quinine and cocoa-butter soluble pessaries (a spermicide placed in the vagina) at W. J. Rendell's manufactory in Hitchin in 1943, the Lambert workforce of forty in 1940 consisted of eleven males and twenty-nine females. Ten of Lambert's workers were over 70 years old and seven were under 14, highlighting the difficulty of retaining male workers of conscription age.[73] With the assistance of Joan Malleson (1900–56) of the Family Planning Association, Lambert had to rely on certificates of exemption to prevent its last vulcaniser and spring-maker being called up for service in August 1943. For recruiting female labour, Lambert was also reliant on the Hackney Labour Exchange, the local branch of the state-run department that allocated workers between the armed forces, civil defence and industry, as suggested by its 'most urgent demand' for more girl workers to work 8 a.m. until 6 p.m. with Saturdays off at 46s per week.[74] The firm complained about how unsuitable these girls were for work in the contraceptive manufactory. Of course, newly recruited girls lacked the experience necessary to make contraceptives to the firm's standards and it took about six months to train them. But others the firm simply viewed as degenerate. The firm described one as 'about fifty years of age, who appeared somewhat strange in her manner. However, we took her on and after three days she informed the Manageress that she had been certified and had been "inside" three times. Naturally, she had to go as the other hands refused to work with her'. This inexperienced and unsuitable workforce had as significant an effect on the quality of products as lack of materials; Stopes complained that the cervical caps the firm sent during the war were badly finished.[75] The bombing of Lambert's factory in October 1944 made the labour shortage worse; it left the firm with only skeleton staff, as many workers who had lost their homes had to leave Hackney.[76] In March 1945 Lambert reported to Stopes that the factory had no roof and that the firm was 'hanging on by the skin of our teeth'.[77]

But it was LRC's employment from 1942 of one hundred local girls aged 14 and 15 to dip the latex and test and pack the condoms in paper wrappers in order to meet its contract with the armed forces that garnered the greater condemnation. The firm employed these girls because they were four or five years below the registration threshold for women at the employment exchange and it was able to entice them straight from school with high wages. School leavers started on £2 5s per week and could earn as much as £2 17s per week at the end of four to six weeks, a wage comparable with other factory work during the war.[78] Concerned about the moral effects of this work, particularly with renewed concerns around venereal disease and promiscuity during the war, the Anglican Church argued that it occupied 'the minds of adolescents at the puberty age with an unpleasant side of sex and also gives the impression to the young that sexual intercourse can be indulged in without the dangers of being found out'; it published its concerns in a ten-page pamphlet, *The Prevention of Venereal Disease*.[79] Dr Josephine Letitia Denny Fairfield, Senior Medical Officer for London County Council and birth control opponent, reiterated this statement: 'It takes little imagination to realise the corrupting effect on the young of this work.'[80] Such concerns about the corruption of youth, particularly the 'lipsticked' and 'silkstockinged' young working girl, fed into wider reconceptualisations of childhood, adolescence and the emergence of the 'teenager' with her or his own disposable income and wider concerns about the growing numbers of young people who were turning away from the Church for moral guidance.[81] However, the Minister of Supply was 'unwilling to withdraw the girls from an occupation in which they are already engaged' and attempts to prevent these girls from going into this work failed 'as parents cannot resist the high wages offered'.[82] Yet, while there is evidence of camaraderie and solidarity among women engaged in factory work during the war, as well as a mix of married and unmarried women and girls, there is little evidence to suggest that they were any more sexually informed or in favour of mechanical contraceptives than they had been in the 1930s (fig. 4).[83] Again, reinforcing morally conservative viewpoints, some married woman who had been appointed to Rendell's and Lambert's factories under the National Service Acts were released from the work of packing contraceptives by machine on religious and moral grounds.[84] In general factories too, the increased sale of contraceptives in the workplace in wartime caused a large proportion of the married female workers to walk out.[85]

Figure 4 Women manually dipping and drying condoms, LRC, Chingford, c.1940.

Figure 5 Girl testing condom by air inflation, LRC, Chingford, c.1950.

Post-war, latex and non-latex production expanded. Ingram's completion of its new factory in Hackney with three workshops dedicated to washing, cutting and moulding sheet rubber in 1947 meant the firm now possessed 'a large modern factory measuring three and a half square acres where mass production methods adequately coped with quantity as well as quality'; it allowed them to produce thousands of rubber contraceptives every day, many of which it supplied to

Lambert.[86] By 1950 Franklin employed five hundred workers.[87] LRC exceeded pre-war production levels in line with increased demand from a broader range of consumers, but its transference to fully automated production (each condom took eight minutes make) meant that women became a larger and permanent part of its workforce.[88] Women continued to undertake the most labour-intensive parts of condom production, including wrapping and testing (fig. 5). While the firm's new Rotoseal machine allowed it to move away from women hand-packing condoms into paper envelopes to automated foil packing, women were still required to mount condoms onto electronic testing probes and line them up on the Rotoseal conveyor.[89]

The firm's automated production allowed it to claim that its share of the condom and diaphragm market was 95 and 75 per cent, respectively, in 1952.[90] By 1961 LRC employed over two thousand people and were the largest manufacturer of dipped latex products in Europe, and the third largest in the world. But it is unclear the extent to which factory working in the post-war period was responsible for the dissemination of sexual knowledge. Some female workers continued to claim they were unconscious of the nature of the work. One female worker stated that her employment at LRC, beginning in the mid-1950s, was an unusual introduction to contraceptives. She stated that 'nothing was mentioned during my interview and no one enlightened me beforehand!'[91] But even during her employment, she claimed not to have discussed sex and contraception with female co-workers, suggesting not only that workers viewed their employment as a job like any other, but that the existence and importance of communication communities for the circulation of birth control knowledge may have been exaggerated. Such views seem to confirm the new concept of citizenship of the post-war period that placed a premium on the sexual behaviour of women and girls with social legislation reinforcing the traditional role of females as wives and mothers.

Conclusion

By the late 1930s, contraceptive production in Britain had shifted from a disparate trade made up of small and often non-identifiable manufacturers to a few large companies who dominated home manufacture until LRC was able to monopolise supply by the 1960s. This chronology can be charted against technological progress and growing sexual knowledge. Contraceptive supply and demand increased in line with the gradual dissemination and acceptance of new sexual ideas in the interwar period. Growing uptake of birth control among married couples and its rising acceptance among the medical profession and birth controllers correlates with expanded contraceptive manufacture. But while technology may have been the means, it did not result in increased product ranges or designs, nor did all manufacturers choose to shift to latex manufacture. As Cook has argued, technology 'was born of human desires and needs, and the pace and shape of its development was bound up in ideology'.[92] Simplistic narratives of quick technological progress do not fit the British pattern of manufacture, and what is clear is that the form of manufacturing depended on the preference of key customers. Toeing the line between respectability and creating demand was difficult, but decisions to enter contraceptive manufacturing in the late nineteenth century and to shift to latex in the 1930s or to remain a sheet rubber good producer were reliant on contemporary, not future, consumer demands. Lambert was able to supply the birth control clinics of Marie Stopes, the Malthusian League and the National Birth Control Association/Family Planning Association because it continued to produce sheet rubber products, along with other firms in Hackney Wick, and had built up the goodwill they had established as pioneers of the cement process fifty years earlier. LRC's embrace of latex, for whatever reason, allowed it to obtain the large contract with the Royal Navy and then HM Armed Forces with its 'Durex' brand condoms, which became popular among the customers of chemists' shops. Prentif attempted to meet the needs of birth control advocates by supplying both latex condoms and rubber caps. This was the shape of Britain's contraceptive manufacturing trade, and amid moral purists' complaints about the immorality of the industry, Dawson found that the factories were no less respectable than those in any other industry. There is certainly no evidence to suggest that workers in the contraceptive manufactory were unhappy; in fact many took pride in their work, but by the 1930s Dawson's claim that women and girls at LRC were 'quite unconscious of their work', or at least not self-conscious about it, suggests that the industry was not as morally corrupting as the social conservatives feared. Moreover, rather than encouraging promiscuity, wartime factory work reinforced morally conservative viewpoints among some.

Such perspectives then complicate our view of technological progress in contraceptive manufacture, the role of supply and demand

and also the role of the factory in disseminating sexual knowledge. Lambert aligned itself with medical rubber manufacture more generally, but did not adopt latex because it was expensive. It had a skilled workforce, relevant expertise and some degree of commercial success with sheet rubber products, all assets that birth control reformers prized. Prizing technological advances appears to be a later distortion of the historical record. Certainly, in the interwar period, the industry is an example of new, modern methods of production sitting alongside older skills-based techniques. The old was preferred by some into the 1950s. Similarly, there is little evidence to confirm that contraceptive manufactories were of the kind of 'communication communities' highlighted by Simon Szreter and others. Uncovering the passing of information orally is of course difficult, but it seems that for many workers it was a job that paid well and, certainly among the rubber makers at Ingram's and the female workers at LRC, was one in which they enjoyed working, allowing them to develop skills and forge long careers. We are left then with an impression of a manufacturing industry shaped by demand that was reasonably respectable, however opaque. As we will see when we examine methods of promotion and distribution more closely, this respectability was not all that it appeared.

Notes

1 'Sale of Contraceptives', *The Times* (5 February 1937), p. 11.
2 Hansard, 'Contraceptives Bill', HL vol. 90, col. 805 (13 February 1934). See also, London Metropolitan Archives (hereafter LMA), A/PMC/067, report on the growth of contraceptives, Contraceptives (Regulation) Bill 1939.
3 Himes, *Medical History of Contraception*, p. 202; Borge, '"Wanting it Both Ways"', pp. 65–9; P. Fryer, *The Birth Controllers* (London: Secker and Warburg, 1965), p. 25; Peel, 'The manufacture and retailing of contraceptives', 122; R. McKibbin, *Classes and Cultures, England 1918–1951* (Oxford: Oxford University Press, 1998), p. 305; H. Cook, 'The English sexual revolution: technology and social change', *History Workshop Journal*, 59:2 (2005), 111–12.
4 Hansard, 'Contraceptives Bill', HL vol. 90, col. 805 (13 February 1934). See also, 'This contraceptive business', *Lancet* (9 April 1938), p. 852. This is higher than Peel's estimate of LRC's production of two million latex condoms, which he obtained following an interview with Angus Reid, LRC's director, in 'The manufacture and retailing

of contraceptives', p. 122. Wellcome Library (hereafter WL), PP/BED/B.2, Personal papers of Bertrand Edward Dawson, 'Population and birth control', letter from Krohne and Sesemann to Dawson, 15 June 1933.
5 Cook, *The Long Sexual Revolution*, p. 139; Szreter and Fisher, *Sex Before the Sexual Revolution*, p. 240.
6 Szreter and Fisher, *Sex Before the Sexual Revolution*, p. 240 n. 35.
7 J. Woycke, *Birth Control in Germany, 1871–1933* (London: Routledge, 1988), pp. 39, 113.
8 W. Woodruff, *The Rise of the British Rubber Industry during the Nineteenth Century* (Liverpool: Liverpool University Press, 1958), p. 71.
9 V. L. Bullough, 'A brief note on rubber technology and contraception: the diaphragm and the condom', *Technology and Culture*, 22:1 (1981), 104–11.
10 Bullough, 'A brief note on rubber technology and contraception', 107; Tone, *Devices and Desires*, p. 56; J. Tully, *The Devil's Milk: A Social History of Rubber* (New York: Monthly Review Press, 2011), p. 44.
11 Trade directories list contraceptive makers under 'surgical instrument makers' or 'wholesale chemists'. *Post Office Directory* (London, 1883). J. G. Ingram, *A Century of Progress, 1847–1947* (London: Ingram, 1947), p. 1.
12 C. Wood and B. Suitters, *The Fight for Acceptance: A History of Contraception* (Aylesbury: Medical and Technical Publishing Co. Ltd, 1970), p. 115.
13 Cook, *The Long Sexual Revolution*, pp. 58–61; F. D'Arcy, 'The Malthusian League and the resistance to birth control propaganda in late Victorian Britain', *Population Studies*, 31:3 (1977), 430.
14 E. Lambert and Son [*Catalogue*] (n.p., 1891), p. 32; M. Drew, *Hints on Nursing* (London: R. Forder, 1889).
15 Cook, *The Long Sexual Revolution*, p. 58. See, for example, H. Wright, *A Catalogue of the Most Approved Surgical Instruments, Trusses, &c.* ([London]: 1834); J. Read, *A Vindication of Read's Patent Syringe* (London: W. Glendinning, 1826).
16 McLaren, *Birth Control*, p. 122.
17 E. Elderton, *Report on the English Birth-Rate: Part I, England North of the Humber* (London: Eugenics Laboratory Memoirs, 1914), p. 149. For a more detailed critique of Elderton, see Szreter, *Fertility, Class and Gender*, p. 400.
18 For nineteenth-century medical accounts of the usefulness of pessaries to support the uterus and vagina, see J. Blundell, *Observations on Some of the More Important Diseases of Women* (Philadelphia: A. Waldie, 1837); E. J. Tilt, *A Handbook of Uterine Therapeutics* (New York: Wood, 1863); Cook, 'The Long Sexual Revolution', p. 174.

19 E. Lambert and Son [*Catalogue*] (n.p., 1897), pp. 28, 38.
20 J. G. Franklin, *Catalogue of Surgical Goods* (n.p., 1910), p. 78; See 'Patent fluid ring pessary (8920)', E. Lambert and Son, *Special List of Domestic & Surgical Specialties* (n.p., 1911), p. 26.
21 British Library (hereafter BL), Add. MS 58638, letter by Marie Stopes to Lambert, 26 September 1920.
22 Cook, 'The Long Sexual Revolution', p. 68. See, for example, Franklin, *Catalogue*, 1910; Ingram, *A Century of Progress*; Evans and Wormull, *Catalogue of Surgical Instruments* (n.p., 1876), p. 268.
23 The Marvel Co., [*Catalogue*] (London: Constantine and Jackson, 1882).
24 T. J. Buckingham, 'The trade in questionable rubber goods', *India Rubber World* (15 March 1892), cited in Tone, *Devices and Desires*, pp. 61–2. For the similar American context, see Tone, *Devices and Desires*, p. 49.
25 Blue glass condom mould for rubber or latex moulding, Durrant and Sons, Bristol, England, 1900–1920, Science Museum, Object number 2014–380, http://collection.sciencemuseum.org.uk/objects/co8421629/blue-glass-condom-mould-for-rubber-or-latex-moulding-condom-mould [accessed 16 July 2019]; T. Horton, *The French Letter King* (Bloomington: Author House, 2014), p. 29.
26 L. A. Hall, *Sex, Gender and Social Change in Britain since 1880* (Basingstoke: Palgrave Macmillan, 2013), p. 40.
27 E. Charles, *The Practice of Birth Control* (London: Williams and Norgate, 1932), p. 23.
28 A. Besant, *The Law of Population: Its Consequences, and Its Bearing upon Human Conduct and Morals* (London: Freethinker, 1889), pp. 32–3. Historians have long highlighted Allbutt's part in the neo-Malthusian movement. For example, Fryer, *The Birth Controllers*, p. 170; McLaren, *Birth Control*, pp. 112, 132–3, 152, 186, 223, 225; Hall, *Sex, Gender and Social Change*, p. 40; Fisher, *Birth Control, Sex, and Marriage*, p. 27; Peel, 'The manufacture and retailing of contraceptives', 117.
29 For example, 'Malthusian Appliances', *The Malthusian* (April 1887), p. 31; (June 1887), p. 47; (August 1887), p. 63; (May 1888), p. 38; 'The new vertical and reverse current syringe' (February 1889), p. 15; (December 1889), p. 95; 'Our special illustrated list' (February 1892), p. 15.
30 Himes, *Medical History of Contraception*, p. 243; Szreter, *Fertility, Class and Gender*, p. 15.
31 Lewis-Faning, 'Report on an enquiry into family limitation'.
32 Monopolies and Mergers Commission, *Contraceptive Sheaths: A Report on the Supply of Contraceptive Sheaths in the United Kingdom* (London: HMSO, 1975), p. 11.
33 P. Dawson and T. R. Schidrowitz (eds), *History of the Rubber Industry* (London: W. Heffer, 1952), p. 338.

34 WL, SA/FPA/A7/66, memo from Lambert to the FPA, 30 November 1934; July 1940.
35 Borge, "'Wanting it Both Ways'", pp. 91–2, 97, 100, 103, 125.
36 Lewis Jackson had a business in Victoria, while Harvey Jackson, his father, ran Paddington's Surgical Store. BL, Add. MS 58639, 203–4.
37 BL, Add. MS 58638, letter by Lamberts to Stopes, 1 October 1921.
38 J. Murphy, *The Condom Industry in the United States* (London: McFarland, 1990), p. 18.
39 WL, SA/FPA/A7/61, letter from Smith and Hudson to National Birth Control Association, 5 October 1937.
40 Borge, "'Wanting it Both Ways'", p. 105.
41 For example, *The New Generation*, 55 (October 1927), p. 4; Borge, "'Wanting it Both Ways'", p. 114.
42 'Durex', *Trade Mark Journal*, 2677 (17 July 1929).
43 Durex [Price list], BL, Add. MS 58640.
44 For continued promotion of reusable animal sheaths and sheath paraphernalia, see, for example, Lamberts Prorace Ltd, *Revised Price List of Up-to-Date Contraceptive Appliances* (n.p., 1933), p. 13; *Latest Price List of Approved Contraceptive Appliances* (n.p., 1941), pp. 10–14. W. George, *Contraceptive Methods and Appliances* (n.p., 1940), pp. 8, 12.
45 Tully, *The Devil's Milk*, p. 53.
46 Borge, "'Wanting it Both Ways'", pp. 100, 243.
47 G. Rowntree and R. M. Pierce, 'Birth control in practice: part one', *Population Studies*, 15:1 (1961), 4, 11, 15.
48 WL, SA/FPA/A7/100, memo of telephone call with Mr Harrison, 1 October 1937.
49 Prentif, *Contraceptive Practice: A Quarterly Bulletin dealing in Family Spacing and Allied Subjects*, 2 (February 1938), 3–5.
50 Cook, *The Long Sexual Revolution*, p. 140.
51 London Rubber Company, *Price List* (n.p., 1934?), p. 1.
52 Szuhan, 'Sex in the laboratory'; WL, SA/FPA/A7/1, Approved list correspondence and papers including minutes of ad hoc committee of National Birth Control Association (NBCA), 1935–1942; SA/FPA/A7/3, Approved List 1952; SA/FPA/A7/5, Copies of printed Approved Lists, 1937–1974. The Pearl Index for contraceptive efficacy was introduced in the United States in 1934. See, Holz, *The Birth Control Clinic*, p. 60.
53 W. George, *Most Modern and Up-to-Date Special List of Domestic and Surgical Appliances* (n.p., 1912), p. 1; Charles and Company, *Price List of Surgical Appliances and Rubber Goods* (n.p., 1910), p. 1.
54 Himes, *Medical History of Contraception*, p. 206.
55 Cook, *The Long Sexual Revolution*, p. 139.
56 Tone, *Devices and Desires*, p. 194.

57 Borge, '"Wanting it Both Ways"', p. 69.
58 Prentif, *Contraceptive Practice*, 2, p. 3.
59 WL, SA/FPA/A7/66, letter by Lambert to J. Malleson, 1 December 1944.
60 The Bishop of St Albans complained that the Ministry of Labour was promoting this work as if it was of national importance. While the government denied the Bishop's claim, it did admit that 'special arrangements' had been made for the manufacture of rubber surgical goods and medical supplies, particularly those supplying the forces. 'State and War Industries', *The Times* (8 April 1943), p. 2; BL, Add. MS 58639, 143, letter by Lambert to Stopes, 1 August 1944.
61 Monopolies and Mergers Commission, *Contraceptive Sheaths* (1975), p. 11; Borge, '"Wanting it Both Ways"', p. 113; BL, Add. MS 58641, 60, letter by LRC to Stopes, 15 December 1944.
62 WL, SA/FPA/A7/71, letter by LRC to FPA, 1 September 1936; SA/FPA/A7/101, letter by Prentif to FPA, 7 August 1940.
63 Lamberts Prorace Ltd, *Revised Price List of Up-to-Date Contraceptive Appliances* (n.p., 1936), p. 3.
64 London Rubber Company, *London Image: The Staff Magazine of the LRC Group* (Spring/summer 1966), p. 22.
65 LMA, A/PMC/067, Report of Sir John Robertson CMG, MP.
66 For example, Gittins, *Fair Sex*; K. Ittmann, 'Family limitation and family economy in Bradford, West Yorkshire 1851–1881', *Journal of Social History*, 25:3 (1992), 554; A. McLaren, 'Women's work and regulation of family size', *History Workshop Journal*, 4:1 (1977), 70–81; R. Roberts, *The Classic Slum: Salford Life in the First Quarter of the Century* (1971; Harmondsworth: Penguin, 1973), pp. 55–6.
67 Szreter used 'communication communities' in *Fertility, Class and Gender*, p. 533. See also, C. Creighton, 'The rise and decline of the "male breadwinner family" in Britain', *Cambridge Journal of Economics*, 23 (1999), 521; Gittins, *Fair Sex*, p. 46; Soloway, *Birth Control*, p. 278. Outside of work, such communities have been called 'circles of consultation' and 'gossip networks'. E. Freidson, *Profession of Medicine: A Study of the Sociology of Applied Knowledge* (Chicago: University of Chicago Press, 1988); S. C. Watkins and A. D. Danzi, 'Women's gossip and social change: childbirth and fertility control among Italian and Jewish women in the United States, 1920–1940', *Gender and Society*, 9:4 (1995), 469–90.
68 Elderton, *Report on the English Birth-Rate*, pp. 61, 34.
69 Fisher, *Birth Control, Sex, and Marriage*, p. 61. See also, M. Tebbut, *Women's Talk? A Social History of Gossip in Working-Class Neighbourhoods, 1860–1960* (Aldershot: Scolar Press, 1995); E. Roberts, 'Working wives and their families', in T. Barker and M. Drake (eds), *Population and Society in Britain, 1850–1980* (London: Batsford, 1982), pp. 140–71.

70 LMA, A/PMC/067, evidence from Public Health Society's official (Midlands).
71 WL, PP/BED/B.2, Reid to Dawson, 9 March 1933.
72 P. Summerfield, *Women Workers in the Second World War* (London: Croom Helm, 1984); I. Gazeley, 'Women's pay in British industry during the Second World War', *Economic History Review*, 61:3 (2008), 653.
73 'State and war industries', *The Times* (8 April 1943), p. 2; WL, SA/FPA/A7/66, particulars re employed, March 1940.
74 BL, Add. MS 58639, 152–9, letter by Lambert to Stopes, 11 September 1945. From March 1941, all women aged 19 to 40 had to register at employment exchanges. S. Bruley, *Women in Britain since 1900* (Basingstoke: Palgrave, 1999), p. 60.
75 BL, Add. MS 58639, Stopes to Lambert, 8 July 1942.
76 BL, Add. MS 58639, 147, Lambert to Stopes, 20 Oct 1944.
77 BL, Add. MS 58639, 149, Lambert to Stopes, 26 March 1945.
78 Lambeth Palace Library (hereafter LPL), Archbishop of Canterbury Archives, W. Temple 14, ff. 384–96, 385, Juvenile employment – contraceptives, 13 September 1943–8, April 1944; Mass-Observation (hereafter M-O), File report 1494–5, War Factory, November 1942, p. 87.
79 LMA, A/PMC/69, venereal disease.
80 LPL, 397, letter by Fairfield to Archbishop of Canterbury, 20 November 1943; Soloway, *Birth Control*, p. 274.
81 S. Alexander, *Becoming a Woman and Other Essays in 19th and 20th Century Feminist History* (London: Virago, 1994), p. 103; D. Fowler, *The First Teenagers: The Lifestyle of Young Wage-Earners in Interwar Britain* (London: The Woburn Press, 1995).
82 LPL, 394, letter by Bishop of London to Fairfield, 6 April 1944.
83 Bruley, *Women in Britain since 1900*, p. 66; M-O, File report 1494–5, War Factory, November 1942.
84 'Conscripted to contraceptives', *Truth* (16 April 1943); 'Population ethics', *Harrow Observer and Gazette* (15 April 1943); 'House of Lords – Contraceptive supplies', *The Times* (8 April 1943).
85 LMA, A/PMC/69, report from Swindon.
86 Ingram, *A Century of Progress*, p. 7.
87 J. G. Franklin, *Catalogue of Surgical Goods* (n.p., 1950), p. 179.
88 Monopolies and Mergers Commission, *Contraceptive Sheaths* (1975), p. 22; Borge, '"Wanting it Both Ways"', p. 142.
89 Borge, '"Wanting it Both Ways"', p. 148.
90 Borge, '"Wanting it Both Ways"', p. 137.
91 Mrs W., pers. comm., 24 January 2017.
92 Cook, 'The Long Sexual Revolution', p. 100.

2

Shaping markets: packaging, brands and trademarks

Contraceptives as things – as rubber appliances or as chemical substances – did not concern interwar moralists. What did concern these opponents to contraceptive commercialisation was the growing visual distinctiveness of such technologies and their potential to take advantage of ignorant consumers by attracting them through new forms of colourful packaging, eye-catching brand names and memorable trademarks. Indeed, as Dawson commented during his reading of the Contraceptives (Regulation) Bill in the House of Lords in 1934, contraceptives themselves 'are extremely dull looking things. They would not attract the attention of anybody more than once'.[1] It was the shaping of these technologies into attractive commodities – of which the aforementioned colourful packaging, eye-catching brand names and memorable trademarks were key indicators – that caused the greatest alarm. While neither the 1934 Bill nor its 1938 amendment addressed packaging, brand names and trademarks directly, two clauses of the Bill that sought to prohibit contraceptives promoted by 'any picture, diagram or written matter' and 'any box, bottle or wrapper' highlighted parliamentary awareness of the importance of such forms of intellectual property to enhancing contraceptive consumption.[2]

As this chapter will demonstrate, it was during the interwar period that packaging, brands and trademarks were first beginning to become of significant commercial value to contraceptive firms. Historians and sociologists of consumption have argued that it was in the nineteenth century that visual merchandising first transformed mundane technologies into commodities that had a 'symbolic virtue', a virtue that signalled to consumers the trustworthiness and authenticity of a manufacturer's products.[3] But as legal-technical artefacts common to the business world, packaging, brands and trademarks only fully represented contraceptive manufacturers' perception of the high commercial value of their products as birth control was becoming increasingly accepted during the interwar period.

Contraceptive manufacturers' use of packaging, brands and trademarks signalled their ambitions to shape their industry into a respectable one amid the mass consumption of general branded and pre-packaged goods. A key indication of the value firms placed on their intellectual property was the increase in the number and frequency of legal disputes. Of course, it is 'Durex', LRC's famous latex condom brand launched in 1932, and its monopolisation of the late twentieth-century contraceptive market that is most commonly cited. The success of 'Durex' condoms during the Second World War attracted imitation from an American firm called Durex Products Inc. in the 1940s.[4] But 'Durex' was certainly not the first contraceptive brand to be fiercely contested. Moreover, Durex's later dominance of the market has seemingly obscured from historical view a variety of other contraceptive brands and trademarks for female contraceptives that were more recognisable and popular before the Second World War than those for condoms. Competition, trade rivalry and legal disputes during the interwar period did not centre on the male contraceptive at all, but most frequently occurred between manufacturers and imitators of the two most common yet historiographically invisible brands for female contraceptives – W. J. Rendell's 'Wife's Friend' quinine and cocoa-butter soluble pessary and Lambert's 'Pro-Race' cervical cap; these goods were frequently imitated and imitators were most commonly the growing number of disreputable 'surgical' or 'rubber' stores that sought to profit from existing demand.

In focusing on the importance of intellectual property before 'Durex', this chapter draws attention to the tensions between the traditional and the modern in this period – Rendell's 'Wife's Friend', first manufactured in 1885, had long been established by the interwar period, while Lambert's 'Pro-Race' cervical cap was newly developed in 1920. End and intermediary consumer responses to such brands, discussed in the final section of this chapter, demonstrate the extent to which brands and trademarks were successful. In some cases, consumers considered the reliability and authenticity communicated by brands as more important than price. Intellectual property then is the second battle ground in the trade covered in this book, one which again complicates our existing knowledge of contraceptive supply and demand before the contraceptive Pill.

New brands, trademarks and packaging: marketing tools of distinction

From its establishment in the late nineteenth century, Lambert, as Britain's largest and most successful British contraceptive manufacturer, registered as trademarks distinctive yet simple titles for its goods. Amid the backdrop of growing consumer markets and the changing legislative framework of the Patent and Trademarks Acts that made it easier and cheaper for firms to register their intellectual property, Lambert's 'Dumas' and 'Vimule' rubber cervical pessaries (registered in 1884 and 1897) and its 'Paragon' and 'Malthusian' sheaths sat alongside the recognisable household brands of Beecham's Pills, Eno's Fruit Salts and Lever's 'Sunlight' soap in the medical marketplace.[5] Yet, while Lambert's trademarks firmly established the firm's contraceptives as consumer products and distinguished them from the products of competitors, the registration of such marks for ambiguous surgical and medical purposes meant they provided little distinction from other surgical and medical rubber goods. Crucially, such trademarks meant that Lambert's contraceptives remained unremarkable technologies and were potentially unrecognisable for their contraceptive function to even knowing consumers.

It was Walter John Rendell's 'Wife's Friend' soluble quinine pessary that became the most recognisable and successful early contraceptive brand well into the interwar period. Rendell, a chemist in Clerkenwell, first began to produce his quinine pessaries with a cocoa-butter base in the back of his shop in 1885. Like Lambert, Rendell refrained from registering a trademark that distinguished his product as a contraceptive. But rather than a simple word trademark, it was his packaging of twelve pessaries together in a bright red box featuring a facsimile copy of his signature that distinguished his products not only from other contraceptives but also from the many branded 'female pills' meant to procure abortion that had long been on the market by the 1880s (fig. 6). With the assistance of Horn and Co., a registration agent, Rendell registered the 'W. J. Rendell' red ink facsimile signature as the firm's first trademark in the UK in 1886 (trademark number 182668), followed by his registration of the brand name 'Wife's Friend' in 1894 (182689) and its extension

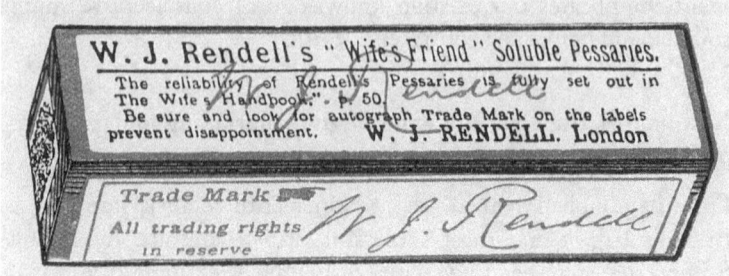

Figure 6 W. J. Rendell's 'Wife's Friend' Soluble Pessaries, with its recognisable red box and featuring Rendell's signature, were widely advertised throughout the late nineteenth and early twentieth century. This image appeared in one of the catalogues of an imitator that sought to profit from the Rendell name.

in Australia, India, South Africa, Argentina, Germany and Canada.[6] As Horn and Co. argued, registering the 'Wife's Friend' trademark and brand secured the good will of 'honest trading, is a guarantee to the public against fraudulent imitators and is the sign manual of patriotic efforts to maintain the prestige of British manufacturers in the home and foreign markets. ... the monopoly once granted is practically perpetual'.[7]

Rendell's distinctive product, on sale for 2s 6d, became immediately popular among neo-Malthusians. In fact, Rendell (a neo-Malthusian himself) claimed that his development of the pessaries was a solution to the burden of large families experienced by many of his local working-class customers. Rendell's pessaries were first mentioned soon after production in the *National Reformer*, co-edited by Annie Besant, and the goods were regularly promoted in J. R. Holmes's neo-Malthusian tract.[8] An anonymous correspondent also wrote to *The Malthusian* in order to draw readers' attention to 'the highly meritorious efforts of a dispensing chemist'. The correspondent went on to say that

> Mr Rendell has, amid great difficulties, and during a protracted period, examined into the different conditions under which human spermatozooids can live; he has, under the advice of a distinguished medical practitioner – whose name I am not at liberty to mention – experimented with various therapeutical agents that would be likely to destroy the fecundating power of the same.[9]

This distinguished medical practitioner was undoubtedly Henry Allbutt. In the following edition of the journal, Allbutt brought to readers' attention that Rendell's 'device' would be 'referred to in my forthcoming little work, *The Wife's Handbook*. I am also of opinion that Mr Rendell has discovered a "check" of very great value'.[10]

Rendell's distinctive brand found natural alignment with Allbutt and his *The Wife's Handbook*. Indeed, Rendell and Allbutt worked together, the similarity in language between the 'Wife's Friend' and Allbutt's publication resulting in a shared promotional opportunity. No copies of Allbutt's first edition of *The Wife's Handbook* of 1885 seemingly exist, but in the third edition of 1886, Rendell's pessaries appeared alongside Lambert's syringe, the Mensinga pessary, a sponge and 'Dr Henry Paterson's French letters' with a disclaimer: 'it is but right to say that these pessaries are at present only on trial. Time will show whether they be relied upon to prevent conception. My opinion is that they will do all their inventor claims for them.'[11] But it was following Rendell's death in 1890, and with it the firm's takeover by partners John Pullen and Frederick John Ward, that *The Wife's Handbook* became little more than a promotional tool for Rendell's 'Wife's Friend' (fig. 7). Initially, their business arrangement meant that Pullen and Ward paid Allbutt £3 10s for a two-page advertisement, while the partners included Allbutt's testimony of the reliability of their pessaries in promotional literature and leaflets accompanying the product; but in 1891 Allbutt assigned the partners exclusive advertising rights to the publication.[12] Since his removal from the medical register in 1886, Allbutt had fully embraced commercial activities. Writing to the editor of the *Leeds Mercury* in 1889, Allbutt stated that despite the General Medical Council's attempts 'to try and crush me ... I am in a better pecuniary position, have a better practice, better fees and more reputation than ever and can afford to snap my fingers at the Council'.[13] Subsequent editions of *The Wife's Handbook*, the last of which was seemingly published in 1926, thus only promoted Rendell's pessaries and Allbutt's own appliances, removing any mention of Lambert and other firms.

The popularity of Allbutt's *The Wife's Handbook*, which sold over 250,000 copies by 1900 with more than a half a million in circulation in the interwar years, undoubtedly raised the profile of Rendell's 'Wife's Friend' beyond the small middle-class membership of the Malthusian League.[14] The popularity of the publication may have

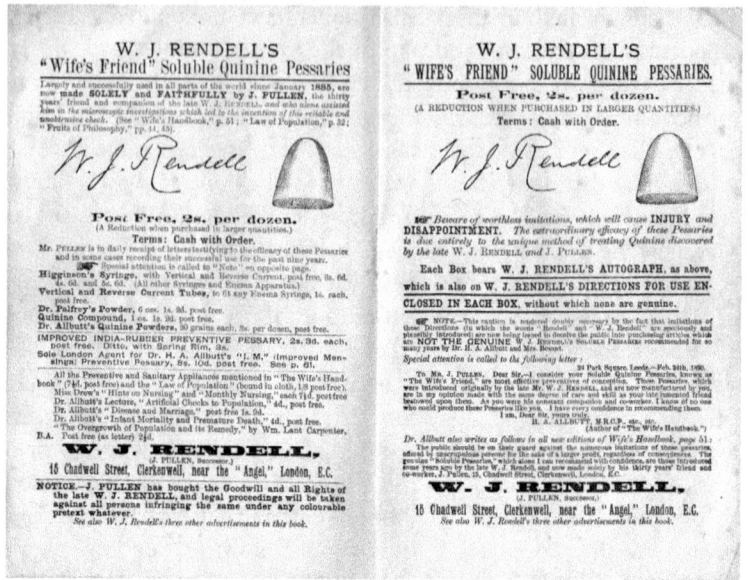

Figure 7 H. A. Allbutt's *The Wife's Handbook*, promoting Rendell's 'Wife's Friend'.

increased consumer requests for the 'Wife's Friend' from chemists, which aimed to be a 'one-stop shop' for all household medicaments and appliances by the late nineteenth century, and from new forms of retailer, such as the American drug store and the department store. The latter was the new retail icon of modernity, with stores ranging from the up-market Selfridges on Oxford Street to the mass-market Woolworths. Growing numbers of these retailers began to stock the product, alongside all manner of rubber female contraceptives promoted as innocuous hygienic and medical aids. Chemists, of which there were over eight thousand in Britain by 1900 and nearly fifteen thousand by 1939, were not solely retailers but were able to provide contraceptive manufacturers with some form of medical legitimacy because they employed or were run by qualified professional pharmacists.[15] Indeed, chemists' growing appeal to married middle-class women for the supply of all forms of medicaments and appliances, as well as medical services such as tooth extraction, extended to contraceptives too. Contrary to common opinion, Charles Killick Millard, Leicester's Medical Officer of Health who had long been in support of birth control, confirmed that it was women also who purchased sheaths from chemists, although chemists did not always stock them.[16]

But it was Rendell's packaging, with its recognisable signature trademark and bright red box that the public regarded as representing authenticity, which aided the development of consumer loyalty and encouraged retailers to always have the goods in stock. The 'Wife's Friend' was among the first products to form part of a new and increasingly standardised retail practice that replaced generic and unpackaged contraceptive goods with those that were pre-packaged and branded. This practice formed part of a wider retail trend for packaged and branded goods, particularly medicines. Known as proprietary medicines, pre-packaged and branded medicinal liquids and pre-pressed tablet form drugs were increasingly sold to consumers as more convenient and hygienic consumptions than loose chemicals mixed and wrapped by a pharmacist.[17] The gradual rise in the brightly coloured pre-packaged and branded good, as the ultimate sales tool and as a distinctive work of art in itself, formed part of a new set of retail practices. These practices were subject to standardisation, heightened planning and new measures of efficiency, and were geared towards the generation of sales of goods in ever larger quantities to expanding numbers of shoppers who were consuming more varied products and experiencing rising disposable income.[18] Indeed, as an economist stated in 1928: 'The fancy package, together with the advertising of it, stimulates the senses, arouses the imagination, and therefore creates a fictitious value.'[19] The growing importance of the packaging of contraceptives throughout the interwar years was highlighted in 1934 by *Shelf Appeal*, the British trade journal dedicated to retail packaging, when it commented on Johnson and Johnson's Ortho-Gynol contraceptive jelly: 'There is no reason why an attractive pack should not help sales for such products.'[20] These new retail practices, specifically the retail display of packaged and branded products, will be examined further in Chapter 5. But by the mid-1920s, retail sales of Rendell's pessaries, along with those sold via mail order, exceeded half a million boxes annually at a time when 50–60 per cent of the average turnover of a chemist came from pre-packaged goods.[21]

Meanwhile, Lambert expanded its trademark registration in line with its product range to include ointments and gels, as well as chemical and rubber pessaries and sheaths. The firm's new trademarks included 'Anti-Geniture', 'Racial', 'Chinobut', 'Contraceptalene',

Figure 8 E. Lambert and Son, 'Pro-Race' cervical cap, England, 1915–25.

'Tophet', 'Contoil', 'Bymeston' and 'Lam-butt'.[22] One of the firm's most significant trademarks of the 1920s, 'Pro-Race', a crested ribbon that featured the product name and that the firm applied to a rubber cervical cap (fig. 8), however, was not solely supplied to the growing numbers of retailers willing to stock contraceptives; the 'Pro-Race' was also the primary contraceptive supplied via the growing number of Marie Stopes's clinics of the Society of Constructive Birth Control and Racial Progress.[23] In fact, Lambert first made its 'Pro-Race' to Stopes's design specifications in 1920 and supplied the first gross free to her in order to ensure continued favour. The 'Pro-Race' was much smaller than most other caps, and in order to be held in place by suction, had to be fitted so that it perfectly covered the cervix.

Between 1921 and 1945 the firm's caps were supplied to 80 per cent of the forty thousand female patients that visited Stopes's six Constructive Birth Control clinics located in London (the first was on Whitfield Street), Leeds, Aberdeen, Cardiff, Belfast and Swansea.[24] It was the growing popularity of the cap beyond the clinic, in part resulting from Stopes's recommendation of the product within her publications, that prompted Lambert to sell the cap to chemists too. *Married Love*, her first book of 1918, sold two thousand copies within two weeks of publication and went through seven editions in the first year; it provided Stopes with a ready readership for her subsequent books, although none sold as well.[25] *Wise Parenthood*, as the more practical sequel to *Married Love*, sold nearly half a million copies by the mid-1930s, while *Contraception: Theory, History and Practice*, her new textbook of 1923, sold forty thousand copies by 1927.[26] But it was Stopes's *A Letter to Working Mothers on How to Have Healthy Children and Avoid Weakening Pregnancies* that was the most explicit on contraception by type. As Stopes's response to the condition of working-class women who visited her first clinic, *A Letter to Working Mothers* recommended the cap as part of a review of different contraceptive methods and appliances and as part of her explanation of conception in simple terms. Stopes gave away many copies of the publication and it was also bought in bulk to give away free by welfare workers. Keen to profit from this publicity, Lambert targeted chemists via advertisements placed in the *Chemist and Druggist*, the chemist trade's main journal, which seemingly had profitable results. The firm's later journal advertisements proclaimed to chemists that 'the demand is already phenomenal. YOU SHOULD BE GETTING ENQUIRIES!' Advertisements regularly placed in the journal shortly after by Rendell, the Winchester Manufacturing Company and LRC suggest that chemists were ordering other brands of rubber and chemical pessaries too.[27]

Despite the fact that Lambert made the pessary under her instruction and received her permission to use the clearly eugenic 'Pro-Race' brand name, Stopes explicitly stated her wish to have no commercial involvement in the product. Such a wish reflected her wider hostility to the contraceptive trade, but in reality Stopes's relationship with Lambert and the promotion of the 'Pro-Race' in her publications demonstrate her intimate involvement in trade activities. While she refused any involvement in the firm's registration of the 'Pro-Race' trademark design in March 1922, Stopes directed Lambert to mark on each cap 'The Pro-Race, Lambert, 3–/'.[28] Stopes refused to take any payment from the relatively small number of the poorest working-class women who attended her clinics, but her clinics sold on 'Pro-Race' caps for between 4s and 6s to women who could afford them, giving them a role in business transactions; nurses at the Whitfield Street clinic also directed women to Lambert to make their contraceptive purchases.[29] Stopes undoubtedly saw her involvement with Lambert as helping the birth control cause and may have naively assumed that her work did not constitute trade activities; but nonetheless, her explicit statements to the contrary did not reflect the reality of her involvement in the contraceptive trade. Outwardly distancing herself from the trade was of vital importance for her and for the wider charitable birth control movement at a time when birth control knowledge and its authorities were in flux. It was also why Lambert supplied its 'Pro-Race' pessaries to her clinics packaged in plain white boxes, while those it supplied to chemists were stamped and packaged with the brand name, trademark and firm name. Indeed, the firm continued its supply of non-branded products to Stopes's clinic in the 1930s with its new cap and soluble pessaries called the 'Racial'.[30] The manufacturer of the 'Racial' was unlisted in all of the advertising of the Society for Constructive Birth Control and Racial Progress.[31] For Stopes, attracting consumer attention was unimportant. What was important instead was reassuring patients that she had secured the most reliable contraceptives to date. Plain packaging and limiting her association with Lambert assured this reliability.

While Lambert altered its 'Pro-Race' packaging according to whether it supplied clinics or chemists, the development of different and distinct brands for clinic and for chemist customers became an established practice in the contraceptive trade by the 1930s, particularly for condoms. Clinics under the control of National Birth Control Association, who like Stopes claimed to want no involvement with the contraceptive trade, were supplied with unbranded Prentif reusable moulded rubber sheaths and disposable latex condoms, allowing only chemists supplied with branded packaging to benefit from consumer recognition and loyalty to the firm's products.[32] LRC claimed to sell its range of 'Elarco' branded rubber and chemical contraceptives only to the Association, while targeting chemists and other reputable retailers with its 'Durex' branded products, the firm's premier brand. Sold in what became its characteristic modernist packaging featuring several geometric shapes at 2s 6d (the same price as Rendell's 'Wife's Friend') and only in packs of three as a way of disassociating the product from frivolous and impulsive sexual intercourse, 'Durex' products aimed to signal high quality to those consumers who believed more expensive contraceptives were more reliable.[33] In one of its first catalogues of the early 1930s, the firm stated that 'VALUE FOR MONEY is the watchword of every really keen and clever buyer … We do not claim to be the cheapest – we have too much regard for our good reputation – but we do certainly offer you unequalled value'.[34] In contrast, LRC and Prentif sold its 'Ona' and 'Diplomat' brands of condom, which the firms both recognised as of inferior quality to their chemist brands, in single brightly coloured branded paper packets for 6d each via slot machines, barbers and the growing number of rubber shops in order to target bachelors about town.[35] Yet, while providing clinic and chemist customers with separate contraceptive brands was well established by the 1930s, Lambert was the first manufacturer to attempt to supply both forms of intermediary with just one brand (the 'Pro-Race'), and as we will see in the next section, only did so with limited success.

The 'sundry infringers': surgical stores, imitation and trade disputes

As Britain's most recognisable branded and pre-packaged contraceptives during the 1920s, Rendell's 'Wife's Friend' and Lambert's 'Pro-Race' cervical cap were regularly imitated. Imitation of Rendell's 'Wife's Friend' was not new following the First World War. The initial success of the product and the distinctiveness of its packaging had quickly attracted several imitators to brand their own pessaries and abortifacients 'Wife's Friend' or derivatives thereof. Concerned about the volume of such products and their influence on the falling national birth rate, the *British Medical Journal* in 1914 commented that there was 'a great army of "Lady's Friends" [and] "Lady's Doctors"'.[36] Rendell was concerned too, and accordingly made several chemists and pharmaceutical firms, including Lambert, sign affidavits prohibiting them for selling their own versions of the 'Wife's Friend'.[37] Attempting to profit from the popularity of both the 'Wife's Friend' and *The Wife's Handbook*, Lambert produced its own advertising publications, *The Wife's Adviser* in 1892 and *The Wife's Guide and Friend* in 1896, and branded its pessaries Lambert's 'Wife's Friend' (fig. 9).[38] An injunction prompted Lambert to remove the name 'Wife's Friend' from all of its promotion, packaging and price lists. Reference to the name was crossed out in black pen in all subsequent promotional literature, although the firm continued to draw on the date of invention for its own pessaries as 1885, the date of Rendell's invention, to demonstrate longevity.

It was Stopes's recommendation of Lambert's 'Wife's Friend' pessaries, alongside its 'Pro-Race', in new editions of her *A Letter to*

"WIFE'S FRIEND" SOLUBLE QUININE PESSARIES.

A most successful method is the use, by the wife, of the Soluble Quinine Pessarie. One is inserted, and, as it dissolves, it sets free the Quinine, which instantly neutralises the activity of the fluid. The Pessarie contains nothing to cause irritation or injury in any way. From the experience of many years during which we have manufactured and sold these Pessaries, we can recommend them with complete confidence.

Soluble Quinine Pessaries ⸻⸻⸻⸻⸻⸻⸻⸻ manufactured by us, and extensively and successfully used to prevent conception. *Beware of imitations* that are being advertised by other firms as "Tablets," "Tabloids," and similar misleading titles. Directions bear our registered trade mark, without which none are genuine.

In boxes of 1 dozen, post free	...	...	...	2	0
,, 3 ,, ,, ,,	...	...	...	5	0
,, 6 ,, ,, ,,	...	...	...	9	6
,, 12 ,, ,, ,,	...	...	...	18	0

Ladies can communicate with Mrs. Lambert.

Figure 9 E. Lambert and Son, *Revised List* (1897).

Working Mothers that prompted Rendell's renewed threat of legal action in 1926.[39] Stopes was no stranger to legal dispute. Indeed, she had brought a libel action against the Roman Catholic doctor Halliday Sutherland in 1923 and continued thereafter to threaten individuals who offended her with litigation.[40] Yet, in the case of the 'Pro-Race', Stopes sought Lambert's assurance that her name would not be dragged through the courts. The firm stated: 'We have been using these words ['Wife's Friend'] for rather over 40 years and we therefore do not think they [Rendell] can claim them.'[41] Rendell dropped the lawsuit on the condition that Lambert persuaded Stopes to omit 'Wife's Friend' in subsequent editions of her publication. Accordingly, Lambert asked Stopes to 'refer to the soluble pessaries only in a general way' and with Stopes's guidance, renamed its soluble pessaries the 'Lam-butt Odourless', incorporating it into its 'Lam-butt' umbrella brand of goods.

Earlier in 1918 Rendell had been threatened with libel not by Lambert but by Annie Besant for including her name in its advertising and on the pessaries box. The firm claimed that the 1891 edition of Besant's *The Law of Population*, a neo-Malthusian tract first published in 1877 that sold 175,000 copies, stated Rendell's 'Wife's Friend' could 'be obtained from the address given on his advertisements and that is the one which from a very wide experience I recommend as at once the most certain and least inconvenient'. Unlike Allbutt, Besant claimed not to have given Rendell permission to associate her name with the product. In fact, she claimed not to have mentioned the pessaries at all, and from 1889 disavowed the neo-Malthusian theory in her own publication. There was then no official 1891 edition of *The Law of Population*, although the Malthusian League seemingly continued to publish it after she left and had turned to theosophy. Rendell agreed to withdraw this quotation and settled out of court.[42]

But together, Rendell and Lambert faced a new and more serious threat in the 1920s from the growing number of rebranded imitations sold directly to consumers by the increasing number of surgical stores, the proprietors of which sought to take advantage of what Lesley Hall has called the increased discussability of birth control following the war.[43] And it is in the 1920s that we see the firms' defence of its trademarks and brand names most fiercely tested. A growing number of proprietors adopted the name 'surgical' or 'hygienic' stores for their retail outlets as a way of shielding the unknowing consumer from their true purpose, while projecting an image of medical authority and legitimacy to the knowing consumer in ways similar to the innocuous hygiene aids themselves. Opening on high streets across Britain and thus providing easier access to consumers seeking contraceptives, surgical stores were established in Brighton, Nottingham and Glasgow, while London stores established branches in Liverpool, Bristol, Birmingham, Wolverhampton, Plymouth, Bradford, Manchester and Hereford, Portsmouth, Chatham, Reading and Ipswich.[44] While not every British town or city had a surgical store – by 1932, for example, there were apparently no 'rubber shops' in Sheffield – they were accessible to most urban consumers.[45] Such stores sold cheap branded contraceptives manufactured at home and abroad, ranging from female contraceptives under the well-known and long-established American brand name 'Dr Henry Paterson' to individually packaged branded sheaths and condoms with all manner of vague brand names unconnected to any firm, including 'Reliable', 'Useful', 'Hygienic', 'Neverrips', 'Seamless', 'Zephyr', 'Transparent' and 'Deluxe'. Stores also sought to profit from the success of contraceptives that were already popular retail goods through the sale of imitations for a few pennies.[46]

It was surgical stores and their imitations that most concerned moralists and later campaigners of the Contraceptives (Regulation) Bill. Imitations of products that experienced a degree of market success were considered inferior to the originals; but packaged as they were in similar wrappings and offered at a range of prices, they preyed on consumer ignorance. While imitation branded contraceptives became common, not all imitations resulted in legal disputes. Le Brasseur Surgical Manufacturing Company, a surgical store established in Birmingham in 1915 and one of the most flagrant imitators of British manufacturers' goods, launched its own version of LRC's 'Durex' condom in the 1930s called the 'Durateste'.[47] While packaged in a similar paper wrapping and sold at the same price as 'Durex', LRC did not consider Le Brasseur's imitation a threat, presumably because LRC had secured the Royal Navy contract and because demand for latex condoms was not yet sufficient to launch an expensive legal case. But demand for Rendell's 'Wife's Friend' and Lambert's 'Pro-Race' in the 1920s was sufficient not only to prompt imitation on a relatively large scale but also to spur the manufacturers into defensive action. Indeed, Constantine and Jackson, and W. George, Britain's oldest rubber contraceptive retailers, both sold generic pessaries under the 'Wife's Friend' brand name at the cheaper price of 2s per box.[48] W. George not only sold an imitation of Rendell's product but traded off Rendell's name by advertising soluble pessaries under the names of 'Rendell's and Co', 'Rendell's Drug Stores' and 'Rendell's Surgical Manufacturing Company'.[49] The Hygienic Stores, another London-based surgical store with connections to Constantine and Jackson, even promoted its 'Illustrated Pro-Race Catalogue' in 1925.[50] Both Rendell and Lambert compiled lists of 'sundry infringers' in 1926. In addition to W. George and Constantine and Jackson, Rendell's and Lambert's lists of 'sundry infringers' included Blake's Surgical Stores in Bristol and Liverpool, Johnnie's Rubber Stores in Villiers Street, Dr Paterson's Hygienic Stores in Glasgow, Ray's Surgical Appliance Store in Soho, F. W. Timberlake of Dulwich and Ward's Surgical Company.[51] Lambert had warned Stopes that 'the sale of cap pessaries is being greatly abused' as early as 1922 and passed her the firm's sundry infringers list.[52]

To subvert interwar imitators, Rendell and Lambert used their promotional literature to warn consumers against copies. Rendell used its ownership of Allbutt's *The Wife's Handbook* to state: 'The public should be on their guard against the numerous imitations of these pessaries offered by unscrupulous persons regardless of consequences. The genuine "Rendell's Pessaries" which alone I can recommend with confidence are those introduced some years ago by W. J. Rendell and now made only at Ickleford Manor, Hitchin, Herts. W. J. Rendell's Registered Autograph and Trade Mark are on each box and directions for use are enclosed'.⁵³ Allbutt's testimonial appeared on all company packaging too, alongside the contested one from Annie Besant. In its catalogues, Lambert stated that it would issue a reward to 'any person bringing to our notice any infringement of our registered names', although there is no evidence to suggest any person brought notice of such infringement or of any reward being given.⁵⁴ Concerned over imitation of Lambert's 'Pro-Race' cap, Stopes warned readers of *A Letter to Working Mothers* that 'though most of the really good shops do stock them; poor women too often trust the nasty kind of "rubber shops", herbalists, etc., and there they often get terribly cheated ... I am very angry to discover that many of these shops misuse my name and foist off their goods by telling the poor women they are "what Dr Stopes recommends".' Stopes drew attention to the fact that some rubber goods stores were taking advantage of ignorant consumers by charging up to 30s for imitation caps and stated that 'you are being cheated if more than 3s is charged'.⁵⁵ Indeed, infringement was so widespread that the Robilton Company was established in London as 'an exclusive agency for the supply of genuine contraceptives'. Claiming 'YOU ARE SAFE', the agency aimed to only supply contraceptives of 'proved worth and reliability', stating that the number of defective contraceptives currently on the market was as a high as 17 per cent, although there is no further mention of this agency beyond one advertisement.⁵⁶

Yet, 'sundry infringers' and imitators used this defensive strategy too, warning consumers about imitation of their own products and thus presenting consumers with confusing messages about authenticity. George, for example, stated that every box of its quinine pessaries 'bears my registered TRADE MARK thus. Without this – even if my name should appear on the box – the pessaries are not of my manufacture, and should be refused. Unscrupulous dealers may attempt to substitute imitations, for the sake of larger profit, but they dare not use my Trade Mark, which is printed upon every box that I send.' The firm went on: 'I hereby caution our customers and the public that all goods of our make have our Trade Mark on the wrapper or the article itself. If it is not there the things are not ours and should be rejected.'⁵⁷ The number of surgical stores claiming to supply the 'genuine article' while warning about imitations confused consumers, but it also demonstrates that the word 'trademark' itself formed a regular part of the promotional rhetoric of manufacturers and distributors alike.

When their warnings failed to prevent imitations, Rendell and Lambert launched legal proceedings against surgical stores. Changes to the law, under the Trade Marks Act of 1905, which provided a statutory definition of a trademark for the first time, meant that prosecutions were more likely to be successful than they had been previously because courts were more able to establish an owner's right to a trademark through its connection with the goods by certification, rather than solely by the act of trading.[58] But evidence for a prosecution was not always strong enough. In Lambert's 1927 case against Le Brasseur, the judge claimed there was not enough evidence of deliberate infringement and ruled in Le Brasseur's favour. The judge argued that 'Pro-Race' was 'common to the trade to indicate a rubber occlusive pessary of known shape and character'.[59] Moreover, he argued that Lambert had not established any goodwill associated with the trademark because as a manufacturer rather than a retailer 'the public never know them in the transaction', demonstrating that its packaging was not sufficient to portray ownership. Le Brasseur was permitted to continue using the word 'Pro-Race' in its catalogues and advertisements, in the same manner as hitherto. Out of court, however, Le Brasseur indicated to Lambert that it would undertake to sell the genuine Lambert 'Pro-Race', although there is little evidence to suggest this occurred. In fact, the firm continued to promote its own version of the 'Pro-Race' in its catalogues throughout the 1930s, including the line 'as recommended by Dr Marie Stopes in her book "Wise Parenthood"'. It stated:

> A WORD ABOUT OUR PRO-RACE GOODS. The manufacture of Pro-Race goods is regarded as a very serious part of our huge business, for we realize that there is probably no article bought where so much depends upon reliability. THE FINEST EQUIPMENT IN THE WORLD IS USED FOR MANUFACTURING PRO-RACE GOODS AND PREVENTIVES, and being in the unique position of personally guaranteeing their manufacture right through to the finished stage it at once enables us to offer only those goods of the highest possible quality, flawless in manufacture, thoroughly dependable in use, absolutely fresh and at a price which defies competition.[60]

The firm included an image of Lambert's 'Pro-Race' packaging, complete with Lambert's registered design and number; the blurring of the registration number in print in order to make it illegible highlights Le Brasseur's intention to pass an imitation.[61]

Even if successful prosecutions took place, they commonly failed to stop imitators. After Rendell's victory in its 1926 case against Constantine and Jackson, for example, the defendants continued to use Rendell's packaging. Cecil Jamblin, the managing director of Constantine and Jackson, claimed that Rendell's trademark was invalid because 'Wife's Friend' was understood by both the trade and public as having reference to pessaries in general, in just the way Le Brasseur had argued for the 'Pro-Race'. Rendell was supported by over twenty of its chemist customers from across the country, who testified that Rendell's was the original article. Jamblin, Rendell claimed, was buying Rendell's pessaries from a third party and then selling them on to consumers under the brand name 'Dr Henry Paterson's Wife's Friend Soluble Pessaries'. The pessaries were also displayed in the store's shop window via a large notice board to attract passers-by.[62] Yet, despite ruling in Rendell's favour and for Constantine and Jackson's removal of the name 'Wife's Friend' from its product packaging, the surgical store continued to sell soluble quinine pessaries in similar red boxes with the 'registered signature' of 'Dr Henry Paterson'. Constantine and Jackson had thus only loosely interpreted the court's ruling to no detriment. Indeed, the sensitive nature of the subject matter meant that judges were reluctant to even preside over cases. The judge in the Lambert versus Le Brasseur case questioned why he should have to preside over a case in this 'filthy trade'.[63] Before the Second World War, such potential for disregard certainly disincentivised other firms from taking legal action, but also demonstrated the undefined nature of legal responsibility for contraceptive branding and trademarks in the interwar period.

From the manufacturers' point of view, surgical stores appeared villainous. But as their earlier imitation practices suggest, Lambert and Rendell were far from virtuous. Moreover, Lambert's dealings with Marie Stopes and the 'Pro-Race' cap during this period of imitation demonstrate that manufacturers' dubious business practices continued. It was by preying on Stopes's fear of association with the disreputable surgical stores she so despised that Lambert was able to gain her permission to register the 'Pro-Race' brand name. Stopes stated that 'I have spoken to my publisher about the registered name of the recognised cap. Neither of us like it but under the circumstances of which you tell us, it is probably the best course to pursue'.[64] Lambert also persuaded Stopes to include its company name, along with the 'Pro-Race' name, within the text of *Wise Parenthood* itself, rather than within an inserted page, after pointing out that surgical stores were physically cutting out reference to the company in order to sell their own caps, although as we have seen with the court case against Le Brasseur, registration of the 'Pro-Race' or inserting its name within the text of *Wise Parenthood* was not enough to prevent imitation. Much of Lambert's strategy of aligning with Stopes also played on her anti-Semitism and xenophobia. Lambert highlighted the fact that the proprietors on its list of sundry infringers were of Jewish or 'foreign extraction', including Manistead, the managing director of Constantine and Jackson; Waretski of Wards Surgical Co and Son; and Sevacbe of Ray and Co.

Stopes's increasing reliance on Lambert to defend what she saw as her intellectual property from rubber stores manifested itself in requests for Lambert to do her bidding.[65] In 1923, for example, she asked the firm to prevent a surgical store on Euston Road from advertising her books in the *Daily Herald* and from sending abortifacient literature when readers of *Wise Parenthood* wrote to the firm for details of the 'Pro-Race' cap, more on which will be examined in Chapter 3.[66] It was also by highlighting Lionel Jackson's Jewish heritage that Lambert dissuaded Stopes from purchasing rubber caps from LRC in 1921. Lambert claimed that the sample cap LRC had sent to her was in fact one of its own make that the firm had ordered from them. Although no names were mentioned, Lambert also implied that Jackson had broken into its factory and stolen moulds and patterns for rubber pessaries with the aim of passing off Lambert's products as those of LRC.[67] Such information meant that Stopes did not deal with LRC again until at least the mid-1930s when her clinics began to stock a small volume of its latex condoms.

In her correspondence, Stopes appears naive in her dealings with Lambert, but on several occasions she became aware of some of the firm's unscrupulous business practices. She was horrified to discover that the firm's directors were not only applying the 'Pro-Race' brand name to other contraceptive goods of which she did not approve but had also registered the 'Pro-Race' trademark under a series of subsidiary companies, including Madame Dumas Ltd and Prorace Ltd.[68] The firm itself went through a series of name changes and restructures during the 1920s, not least because H. W. Lambert and A. Lambert, the two sons of Edward Lambert, the firm's founder, fell out and the company split into two. H. W. Lambert with his son E. W. went into partnership with P. M. C. Watkins, a sales manager at the firm, to form the largest part of the original company called Lamberts, Son and Watkins, and then Lamberts (Dalston) Ltd, while A. Lambert established his own premises a short distance away on 16 Dalston Lane. Lamberts (Dalston) retained ownership of the 'Pro-Race' name, while A. Lambert retained 'Vimule' and *The Wife's Guide and Friend*. But by registering the 'Pro-Race' name under different companies that did not manufacture or sell the goods, Lamberts (Dalston) could act as its own agents and could earn 6d per cap, as well as earning profits from the cap's sale. It also allowed the subsidiary company to sell on inferior caps that were not good enough for Stopes's clinic to surgical stores without any association with the Lambert name.

Stopes was equally horrified to discover that Lamberts (Dalston) (hereafter Lamberts) had been distributing leaflets for its 'Dumas Anti-Geniture' rubber cap to its 'Pro-Race' mail-order customers; Lamberts had done so as a way of boosting the disappointing sales figures of the expensive 'Anti-Geniture' cap (sales averaged only 1,500 annually by 1922).[69] But Stopes argued that such distribution incorrectly suggested that she supported this product. Her anger increased when she discovered that a customer had become pregnant after using the 'Anti-Geniture', thinking that Stopes had recommended it. Arguing that the customer had probably 'heard of Anti-Geniture in a round about [*sic*] way', Lamberts nonetheless promised to end this practice and included the following statement in its 1936 catalogue: 'We never "circularise" customers or "follow up" after having received an order. This is a point worth considering as some firms have this objectionable habit.'[70] Stopes also threatened the firm with legal action in 1930 when she discovered it was distributing *A Letter to Working Mothers* to the very surgical and rubber stores it denounced (more on which will be discussed in Chapter 3). There were also tensions surrounding the firm's new brand of chemical pessaries, the formula to which Lamberts refused to give Stopes, to which she responded: 'you are merely developing my ideas and that in making the Racial Solubles for us you are acting as our manufacturer and should be following my instructions.' In 1934 Stopes requested that the firm omit any mention of her name from its catalogues, although she discovered that it continued to mention the fact that *Wise Parenthood* recommended its occlusive cap, alongside testimonials from the Mother's Welfare Clinic, as late as 1949.[71]

Yet, in spite of her frequent complaints, Stopes did not break her relationship with Lamberts. While tensions remained, Stopes's continued fear of surgical stores and Lamberts' manipulation of this fear meant that Stopes remained largely in Lamberts' debt. Until her death in 1958, Stopes was reliant on Lamberts (among other firms), not just for the supply of rubber cervical caps and for its defence of the 'Pro-Race', her name and publications from all forms of imitation, but also for wider industry knowledge. In fact, despite her protests against any form of trade association, she defended her connection to the 'Pro-Race' until the end. Complaining in 1950 to Lord Horder, president of the Family Planning Association, about the Association's inclusion of Lamberts' Dutch, Dumas and Cervical caps on its lists, Stopes stated: 'I do not know if you are aware that the design of the "Pro-Race" and its name were both invented by myself and then commercially registered many years ago without payment to me by Messrs Lamberts'.[72] A final agreement between Stopes and Lamberts in 1951 bound the firm to apply the trademarks only to goods approved by Stopes and also to provide a royalty to the Mothers' Clinic, thus reinforcing the commercial connection she had always claimed to reject.[73]

Consumer responses to brands and trademarks

The frequent imitation of Lamberts' and Rendell's brands, trademarks and packaging demonstrate the competitive nature of the interwar contraceptive trade, and the firms' defence of these suggests their value for signalling quality and establishing consumer loyalty. But uncovering the impact of brands and trademarks on consumers is of course less straightforward, particularly when price, efficacy, ease of use and other variants also played a part in consumer choice amid widespread ignorance and misinformation. Certainly, many women, unsure of how to distinguish between brands and reliant on recommendations from those they perceived as authorities, were given little choice. Women who visited Stopes's clinics and wrote her letters seeking guidance, for example, were recommended or fitted with Lamberts' 'Pro-Race' cap and occasionally Rendell's pessaries, even if they struggled to afford to pay for them, while the National Birth Control/Family Planning Association only recommended brands from its approved product list to its correspondents.[74] Correspondents seeking professional advice occasionally rejected it, instead preferring to adhere to market signs. One female correspondent from Worcester challenged the Association's recommendation of Prentif's branded condom in 1942, stating that at 2s 6d for three (like 'Durex' and 'Wife's Friend') it was 'rather expensive' and that she wanted to opt instead for a surgical store brand, 'La Victorie', which was packaged in blue paper featuring an illustration of a female Greek goddess and cost 3½d.[75] But in the main, correspondents of and visitors to clinics heeded professional advice and purchased recommended brands.

Some retail and mail-order consumers, however, did develop their own brand preference, thus suggesting that intellectual property had a greater impact on purchasing choices than has hitherto been established. Shopping for contraceptives could be an overwhelming and confusing experience, but intellectual property played a crucial role in encouraging consumption, particularly as consumers were becoming ever more brand conscious and consuming packaged goods more generally. In fact, loyalty to a particular brand formed an important part of consumer beliefs in efficacy, ease of use and price satisfaction. Among the most explicit evidence of brand appreciation is for Rendell's 'Wife's Friend', a product that was not available from clinics and could be fitted without professional intervention (unlike rubber caps). Such evidence is contained within letters received by the firm between 1926 and 1931, which now reside at Rendell's premises in Hitchin, Hertfordshire.[76] Both male and female customers based all over the country and beyond wrote to Rendell. The fact that 20 per cent of letters were written by men correlates with Kate Fisher's finding that husbands could purchase pessaries for their wives, highlighting some male control over the use of spermicides.[77] But the remaining 80 per cent written either by women or both spouses together suggests that women still maintained a great deal of control over this method, even if this control was shared. While co-written letters stating 'my wife and I' or 'my husband and I' suggest the shared nature of contraceptive responsibility, they are not explicit enough to reveal the ways in which this control might have been gendered. Nonetheless, this correspondence demonstrates that the firm's 'Wife's Friend' was not only a popular mail-order product, but that those in countries where its trademarks were valid (Britain, Canada and Egypt) viewed the brand name as an indication of the trustworthiness and reliability of both the product and the firm. All forty-three correspondents emphasised their ongoing satisfaction with the product, some claiming that they had used it with success for twenty or more years, while others admitted to combining its use with a condom or a rubber pessary as a double precaution. Such claims directly contradicted those of birth control researchers in the 1930s, who after subjecting the firm's pessaries to laboratory tests, decried the quinine in Rendell's pessaries as an ineffective spermicide and the cocoa-butter base as a major cause of rubber deterioration to caps or sheaths used in conjunction.[78] But medical practitioners of the time, such as Gladys Cox, acknowledged that the successful practical experience of many women who had used suppositories like Rendell's suggested that they were 'moderately good contraceptives' because the cocoa butter acted as a 'mechanical barrier of oily film, analogous to the rubber occlusive pessary'.[79]

The price of Rendell's 'Wife's Friend', 2s 6d for twelve, would not have been out of the reach of interwar working- and middle-class consumers, coital frequency permitting. Indeed, most contraceptives cost between 1s and 4s by the interwar period: Lamberts' 'Pro-Race' pessary was priced at between 3s and 5s and 'Durex' condoms priced at 2s 6d for three. More expensive syringes and enemas and other more expensive brands of rubber pessaries costing up to 15s, however, would have been less affordable. Average incomes were at around 50s per week for unskilled and semi-skilled men (who comprised half the adult working male population in 1931), while the middle class earned £250 per year or above and in terms of income comprised between 13 and 15 per cent of the population.[80] Yet, while the social class of correspondents is difficult to discern, given their varied locations and the limited information contained within letters, it is likely that Rendell's correspondents were affluent. Correspondents were certainly sexually knowledgeable and several had the pre-existing knowledge and confidence to ask for specific contraceptive advice. A female correspondent from Bideford, Devon, for example, asked the firm the best way of caring for a 'Paragon' sheath to ensure that it was reusable, despite the fact that the firm did not sell them.[81] Female correspondents based in Britain's dominions and colonies may have been spouses of those in the diplomatic service or armed forces. But there is no reason to assume that price was more important to purchasing decisions than brands. Indeed, the similarity in price between these contraceptive brands suggests that other factors were more important. The fact that only 5 per cent of women interviewed by Lewis-Faning in 1949 said that cost was a reason for their continued use of withdrawal, while Mass-Observation reported that 'the financial cost of contraceptives may help to bias poorer people against them, but this aspect of the financial factor is very seldom mentioned' suggests that cost was not the most significant factor in consumption, at least in the 1940s.[82] Cost certainly seemed to be of no object to Rendell's correspondents. Moreover, married couples with higher incomes were more likely to discuss contraceptive methods between themselves, hence accounting for the 20 per cent of couples who co-wrote their letters to Rendell.[83]

Rendell's correspondents took the firm's warnings about imitation seriously and were careful to request 'Rendell's "Wife's Friend" Quinine Soluble Pessaries' by name. Indeed, at a time when no contraceptive, branded or unbranded, was totally reliable and firms admitted as much, consumers relied on firm rhetoric about reliability and imitation as much as their own experience of the product. Demonstrating that foreign firms also imitated Rendell's products, one female correspondent from Alexandria, Egypt, in 1926 was concerned that when buying the firm's pessaries from a local druggist, 'I noticed that the label, the part opposite your signature, instead of having "registered trade mark, number 182688" had "trade mark all trading rights in reserve" and I naturally concluded that he was trying to palm off an imitation of your pessaries'. She then called into four other druggists before she could find a box 'bearing the label with the registration number'. She then 'decided to write and find out whether you have changed the label or if some local commission agent is trying to put in the market some imitation of your good pessaries. I need hardly say that a reply will be heartily appreciated'.[84] Another female correspondent from Vancouver, Canada, requested that the firm send her five boxes because she was not able to get the 'genuine ones for some years here ... There are too many different kinds under the same name here in Canada'.[85] A female correspondent from Swansea requested that Rendell verify some printed leaflets, one of which was included in a box of Rendell's pessaries that did not include the registration number: 'I want you to please advise me if they are genuine or not. I prefer to be cautious as we are not in a position to afford a large family and we have found your pessaries very satisfactory for which we are extremely grateful. We have recommended them to several of our friends who use them with success'.[86] Another female correspondent of Earlsfield, London, stated that she had acquired and used the box-numbered Rendell's pessaries for twenty-three years until the last twelve months when the chemists provided her with a box with 'no 182688 anywhere about it ... the pessaries I have used have always had that number on the box and also inside on the directions'. She then also went to visit four chemists and 'not one had any with the number on the box'.[87] One male correspondent of Forest Hill, London, reported to Rendell in 1931 that the use of a pessary imitating Rendell's had been a distressing experience for him and his wife and 'our faith has been somewhat shaken'. The correspondent described the imitation as having 'a Stork as a trade mark'.[88] This was the non-registered trademark of Abraham Nathan Hancock, the Fleet Street chemist and director of Hancock's of Fleet Street that had entered into the contraceptive retail trade in the 1920s and claimed to do a large trade in 'Soluble Compound Quinine Pessaries or Ladies' Safety Cones', also known as the 'Wife's Friend' and the 'Wife's Protectors'.[89]

Loyalty to the Rendell's brand was so strong among these correspondents that they defended the firm amid wider consumer fears that firms placed one 'harmless' or 'dud' pessary in every box of twelve. One correspondent from Palestine wished to inform Rendell in 1926 of the rumour that this 'dud' was placed in the box 'at the order of the British Government, who otherwise would prohibit their manufacture'.[90] Another from London also wished to inform the firm that the rumour was circulating among a 'considerable body of people' and stated that 'I have had difficulty on occasions to prove otherwise to them'.[91] Stopes's correspondents were aware of these rumours and they persisted into the Second World War when Mass-Observation respondents reported that manufacturers 'were required by law to put some that don't work in each packet. I know Rendells do.'[92] Rendell responded to such fears by stating that it would donate £1,000 to charity if anyone could prove that the firm's packets of pessaries contained one dud, although it is unclear whether anyone offered such proof.[93]

Such a fear was not restricted to Rendell's pessaries. A. Lambert addressed this issue in its catalogue of 1932: 'There is a popular fallacy that manufactures of soluble quinine tablets are bound by law to put one "blank" tablet in every box. This, of course, is quite erroneous and by a special process of compounding, which our long experience in making these tablets has taught us, we are able to guarantee that every "Vimule" tablet contains the full and correct quantity of quinine.'[94] In its 1941 catalogue, Lamberts repeated this claim, stating:

'we guarantee that every "Lam-butt" Soluble Pessary contains the correct quantity of Quinine'.[95] Hancock too claimed that the rumour of one ineffective pessary was 'utterly absurd'.[96] The Kingsland Hygienic Company, a surgical store of East London, attempted to profit from this rumour by stating that it was the mass-production process of manufacturing by other firms that ultimately resulted in 'dud' quinine pessaries. The firm stated that the moulding process made the quinine sink to the bottom of the vessel used for the pouring. Consequently, the first batch of pessaries contained little or no quinine, while the others that were poured later contained too much. The firm stated that it was therefore possible to 'purchase a box of pessaries with not one, but the whole twelve ineffective owing to the lack of quinine'. The firm assured its catalogue readers that the best way to avoid the serious problem of 'duds' was to purchase the firm's own non-mass-produced 'Pessettes' and 'Koneids' soluble quinine pessaries.[97]

Neither was the rumour restricted to chemical pessaries. A BBC journalist noted that 'one rumour in the early days of condom manufacture was that the law required every tenth condom to be faulty, and another said that Catholic workers in condom factories would stick holes in condoms with pins'.[98] As we saw in Chapter 1, it is difficult to determine whether female workers were even aware of the products they were producing, never mind being actively motivated to sabotage them. Crucially, neither were such rumours restricted to end consumers; several doctors seemed convinced that the rumour of a defective pessary or condom in every packet was true.[99] Thus, in a period during which fear of defective contraceptives permeated contraceptive consumer cultures, the letters written to Rendell are notable for their strong defence of the company and its product.

Of course, the letters from Rendell's satisfied customers depict only positive consumer experiences and thus represent only a fraction of the countless other responses to Rendell's pessaries and to contraceptive brands in general. Certainly, evidence beyond this body of correspondence suggests that not all experiences were positive. Rendell's product failed in some cases. One correspondent wrote to Stopes in 1926, for example, to inform her how she did not trust Rendell's 'Wife's Friend' as she became pregnant after using them, while soluble pessaries failed for more than half of the patients sampled by Lella Secor Florence in 1937 at the Cambridge birth control clinic.[100] Middle-class interviewees told Enid Charles that quinine pessaries caused irritation, were greasy, odorous and soiled the bed linen, and were also expensive, while an unknowing consumer purchased them thinking they were throat lozenges.[101] It also must be remembered that pessaries and caps were only used by a fraction of the population as a whole. Claire Davey's close analysis of 1,659 of the 10,000 or so letters written to Marie Stopes between 1919 and 1927 suggests that 11 per cent of working-class correspondents most frequently cited the generic cap with or without generic pessaries as their preferred method, while 33 per cent of middle-class correspondents most frequently cited this method; these figures were likely to be an overestimate of the use of caps and pessaries.[102]

Sales of Rendell's pessaries also declined by over 90 per cent after the Second World War, with only thirty-three thousand boxes being produced and distributed annually. Sustained rumours of 'duds' may have played a part in the declining popularity of Rendell's pessaries, but decreasing sales of the 'Wife's Friend' brand, along with the unpopularity of its new post-war brands ('Santron', 'Silatex', 'Mensinole' and 'Protoco') also formed part of a wider trend in the trade where sales shifted from older female contraceptives (chemical and rubber pessaries) to new modern female goods (diaphragms, spermicidal gels and ointments) and to the condom. The results of post-war tests, both in the laboratory and by women themselves, that confirmed the inefficacy of Rendell's pessaries were taken more seriously, while sales of 'Durex', LRC's chemist brand condom, grew.

The 'Durex' brand name became synonymous with the condom among many men during the war and in the post-war period, both those in the armed forces and those who worked in and purchased from chemists' shops, as we saw at the beginning of this chapter. When interviewed about their experiences of contraceptive sales, Brian Hebert, an apprentice in a chemist's shop in Portsmouth in 1939, and Peter Homan, who worked as a pharmacy manager for Boots in the early 1960s, referred to condoms that their stores did or did not stock as 'Durex'. Similarly, Bill Sides, a youth from an East Durham mining village, requested 'Durex' by name from a local chemist in the 1930s.[103] While no respondent to the Mass-Observation survey on venereal disease in 1942 mentioned 'Durex' (a few women mentioned 'preventives'), chemist customers preferred to spend more on the 'Durex' brand than those offered cheaply and singularly from rubber stores because the brand and the price demonstrated reliability and authenticity.[104] Such consumer confidence helps explain the firm's claim that it dominated over 95 per cent of the condom market by 1952 and seemingly confirms the claim made by Reid, LRC's managing director, that 'there are large numbers of people who will have DUREX and DUREX only'.[105] It was from the 1950s that LRC was able to monopolise the rubber contraceptive market, and by the mid-1970s 'Durex' and LRC's other major Durex brands – 'Gossamar', 'Fetherlite' and 'Nu-Form' – had nearly 96 per cent of market sales. The firm's continued monopoly over the contraceptive market, however, resulted in its investigation by the Monopolies and Mergers Commission in 1975.[106] The Commission found that the firm's policy of high prices had taken advantage of consumers who had long associated quality with price.[107] Yet, despite 'Durex's' dominance as a contraceptive brand in the late twentieth century, it was Rendell's 'Wife's Friend', and with it, Lambert's 'Pro-Race', that had first laid the foundations for brand loyalty in the British contraceptive industry.

Conclusion

Navigating the interwar history of packaging, branding and trademarks in the contraceptive trade is far from straightforward, but uncovering the importance of such forms of intellectual property through examining the lengths to which Lambert/s and Rendell were prepared to go in order to defend them demonstrates their significance, as well as the trade's growing competitiveness. Indeed, while imitation of branded contraceptives was not new in the interwar period, it was the rise of surgical stores, widely despised among birth control advocates and social moralists alike, and their desire to stake a claim in existing successful markets that resulted in the most fiercely contested trade disputes. The ongoing sale and promotion of imitations, alongside genuine articles, were significant in Stopes's continued reliance on Lamberts long after she discovered some of the manufacturer's own dubious business practices. To birth control advocates, a perceptible hierarchy of respectability within the trade thus was being projected, of manufacturers like Lamberts and Rendell (and then LRC) at the apex and surgical stores at the base. But as their actions outlined here (and in the next chapter) demonstrate, manufacturers could be just as unscrupulous as the rubber store distributors that they claimed to deplore; Lamberts profited from selling on inferior products and

LRC relied on high profit margins to the detriment of customers. Respectability and authenticity were thus highly contingent and depended on what companies revealed and concealed. This hierarchy was not clear to consumers either.

The distrust of imitations was key to the development of brand loyalty. The available evidence from a sample of Rendell's correspondents suggests that the firm's trademark and packaging assured both men and women that they were using effective products. Purchasers were of course unaware that laboratory tests found them to be ineffective as spermicides. The significance of packaging, trademarks and branding of contraceptives then contributes to our understanding of the buoyancy of the trade and consumer trust and confidence in contraceptives as consumer goods. Indeed, these features were arguably more important in the interwar contraceptive trade than in any other because no contraceptive could be fully relied on, and retail and mail-order consumers were thus forced to rely on visual signals from firms, as well as their own experiences. Consumer preference for Rendell's brand amalgamated with beliefs in its reliability, ease of use and price. As implied here, and as we will see in the following chapter, brands and trademarks were a central feature of firm's printed advertising output. In a competitive market, manufacturers and surgical stores alike needed to advertise their brands and did so continually.

Notes

1 Hansard, 'Contraceptives Bill', HL vol. 90, col. 954 (27 February 1934).
2 Contraceptives Bill, no. 110; Contraceptives (Regulation) Bill, no. 115.
3 K. W. Parker, 'Sign consumption in the 19th-century department store: an examination of visual merchandising in the grand emporiums (1846–1900)', *Journal of Sociology*, 39:4 (2003), 360; Baudrillard, *System of Objects*, p. 164. For an earlier example of imitation as it related to food adulteration, see E. Rappaport, 'Packaging China: foreign articles and dangerous tastes in the mid-Victorian tea party', in F. Trentmann (ed.), *The Making of the Consumer: Knowledge, Power and Identity in the Modern World* (New York and Oxford: Berg, 2006), pp. 125–46.
4 LRC lost a trademark appeal against Durex Products Inc. in 1946 at the Supreme Court in India because the judge ruled that a trademark

monopoly would restrict much-needed access to contraceptives in a country with a population excess and that Durex Products Inc. applied its name to different products: female contraceptives, rather than condoms. Thanks to Jessica Borge for highlighting this case. See also J. Borge, *Protective Practices: A History of the London Rubber Company and the Condom Business, 1915–1965* (Montreal: McGill-Queen's University Press, forthcoming).
5 'Vimule', *Trade Mark Journal* (26 May 1897), 1000; BL, Add. MS 58639, 179, Wilkinson, Howlett and Moorhouse to Stopes, 27 February 1951. Lambert, [*Catalogue*] (1897), p. 28. Eno's Salt, used since 1872, application 1876 3322 and 3324; Beecham's Patent Pills, used since 1860, application 1876 1416. Patents, in contrast, were relatively rare beyond rubber pessaries; their medical status as support for uterus prolapses made them less controversial. See Tone, *Devices and Desires*, p. 31.
6 W. J. Rendell, Hitchin (uncatalogued papers), Office for British and Foreign trademarks to Pullen, 30 October 1896; [trademark – Canada, 1902]; [Trademarks – English Empire 1902, German 1905, Cape 1909, Victoria 1902, New South Wales and India – perpetual]; [History of the firm].
7 Rendell (uncatalogued papers), pamphlet titled 'The value of trademarks', Horn, Son and Co.
8 J. R. Holmes, *True Morality or The Theory and Practice of Neo-Malthusianism* (Wantage, Berks: 1891), p. 83; *True Morality* (1914), p. 19;
9 Amicus, 'A recommendation', *The Malthusian* (March 1886), p. 21
10 H. A. Allbutt, 'A recommendation', *The Malthusian* (April 1886), p. 30.
11 H. A. Allbutt, *The Wife's Handbook: How a Woman Should Order Herself During Pregnancy, in the Lying-In Room, and After Delivery* (London: W. J. Ramsey, 1886), p. 39.
12 Rendell (uncatalogued papers), letter by Allbutt to Pullen, 2 October 1890. For example, see Allbutt, *The Wife's Handbook* (London: Standring, 1901): 'The Soluble Vaginal Pessaries invented by the late W. J. Rendell in 1885 and now manufactured solely by Mr J. Pullen, Chadwell Street, London are the most reliable pessaries yet introduced. They are simple, convenient, effective and harmless. They are indeed, as Mr Rendell termed them The 'Wife's Friend'. ... To obviate the difficulty and to render the pessaries absolutely reliable, Dr H. A. Allbutt has invented an INTRODUCER, which is most simple in construction'.
13 'H. A. Allbutt', *Leeds Mercury* (25 January 1889), pp. 3–4.
14 Soloway, *Birth Control*, p. 57.

15 A. M. Brownfield-Pope, 'From Chemist Shop to Community Pharmacy: An Industry Wide Study of Retailing Chemists and Druggists, *c*. 1880–1960' (PhD thesis, University of East Anglia, 2003), p. 13.
16 *Medical Aspects of Contraception/being the report of the Medical Committee appointed by the National Council of Public Morals in connection with the investigations of the National Birth-Rate Commission* (London: M. Hopkinson, 1927), p. 115.
17 J. Jankowski, *Shelf Life: Modern Package Design 1920–1945* (San Francisco: Chronicle Books, 1992), p. 11.
18 R. Bowlby, *Carried Away: The Invention of Modern Shopping* (New York: Columbia University Press, 2001), ch. 5, 'The Package'.
19 Bowlby, *Carried Away*, p. 83.
20 Bowlby, *Carried Away*, p. 105.
21 Rendell (uncatalogued papers), pamphlet on the history of the firm; 'Manchester essays', *Chemist and Druggist* (3 February 1923), p. 164; 'Profit squeezing', *Chemist and Druggist* (4 October 1924), p. 514.
22 'Lam-butt 289288', *Trade Mark Journal* (20 March 1907), 501; Lambert, *Special List* (1911).
23 BL, Add. MS 58638, letter by Lambert to Stopes, 24 March 1922.
24 P. Neushul, 'Marie C. Stopes and the popularization of birth control technology', *Technology and Culture*, 39:2 (1998), 247. Stopes also prescribed the 'Clinocap' diaphragm in cases where cervical damage precluded use of the cap, see Neushul, 'Marie C. Stopes', 262.
25 Porter and Hall, *The Facts of Life*, p. 249; Rose, *The Intellectual Life of the British Working Classes*, p. 218.
26 M. C. Stopes, *A Letter to Working Mothers: On How to Have Healthy Children and Avoid Weakening Pregnancies*, 5th edn (London: The Mother's Clinic for Constructive Birth Control, 1926), p. 10. Soloway, *Birth Control*, pp. 213–15, 347 n. 13.
27 For example, 'Surgical appliances of all kinds', *Chemist and Druggist* (22 April 1922), p. xxviii; 'The Pro-Race cap pessary', *Chemist and Druggist* (5 April 1924), p. 40; 'Buy direct – Elarco Rubber Goods', *Chemist and Druggist* (2 December 1922), p. xviii; '"Wimaco" – Specialities, British and best', *Chemist and Druggist* (4 December 1926), p. 36; 'Rendell's quinine soluble pessaries', *Chemist and Druggist* (1 March 1930), p. xxv.
28 BL, Add. MS 58638, Stopes to Lambert, 21 March 1922.
29 Szreter, *Fertility, Class and Gender*, p. 427; BL, Add. MS 58638, Stopes to Lambert, 18 March 1921.
30 BL, Add. MS 58639, Lambert to Stopes, 24 February 1931.
31 For example, WL, SA/FPA/A14/91, 'Racial price list', *c*. 1950.
32 WL, SA/FPA/A7/101, letter by Prentif to FPA, 7 August 1940.

33 WL, SA/FPA/A7/71, letter by LRC to FPA, 4 July 1938; Borge, "'Wanting it Both Ways'", pp. 113–15.
34 Bold type in original. London Rubber Company, *Price List*, p. 1.
35 WL, SA/FPA/A7/101, letter by Prentif to FPA, 10 February 1943; Borge, "'Wanting it Both Ways'", p. 114.
36 'The restriction of births', *British Medical Journal* (17 October 1914), p. 671.
37 Rendell (uncatalogued papers), Affidavit, Marshall Ltd, 19 January 1898; The British Medicinal Capsules Co. Ltd, 28 November 1898; F. Schultze and Co., 24 May 1899; Barclay and Son Ltd, 21 January 1897; Lambert, 15 March 1897, 2 April 1897, no 457.
38 Lambert, [*Catalogue*] (1897), p. 29; Lambert's *The Wife's Adviser* was mentioned in James Joyce's banned work *Ulysses*, along with *Aristotle's Masterpiece*. M. Power, 'The wife's adviser(s): a literary note', *James Joyce Quarterly*, 32 (1995), 706–9. See also, Dorsan and Co., *The Wife's Handbook and Family Medical Guide: A Clear and Practical Treatise of Great Value to Wives and Mothers on the Management of Their Own Health – Including Suggestions for the Effectual Treatment of Most Women's and Children's Ailments* (London: Dorsan and Co., c. 1929).
39 Rendell (uncatalogued papers), legal papers: W. J. Rendell versus Lamberts (Dalston) Ltd. Strellet, Mercer and Co. to Rubstein, Nash and Co., 9 February 1926; 11 February 1926; Rubstein, Nash and Co. to Strellet, Mercer and Co., 19 February 1926.
40 L. Hall, '"The subject is obscene: no lady would dream of alluding to it": Marie Stopes and her courtroom dramas', *Women's History Review*, 22:2 (2013), 253–66.
41 BL, Add. MS 58638, letter by Lambert to Stopes, 12 February 1926.
42 Rendell (uncatalogued papers), Besant versus Watts, 3 September 1918; Mrs Besant, 10 September 1918; Note of suppression and intention, 1918. See also, Fryer, *The Birth Controllers*, p. 12.
43 Hall, *Sex, Gender and Social Change*, pp. 91–2.
44 For example, Walton Rubber Goods Company (Portsmouth, Chatham and Reading) and S. Seymour (Leicester Square, London) were established in 1923; Curtis's Surgical Store in Birmingham; Blake's Medical Stores, with branches in Bristol, Belfast, Birmingham, Leicester, Liverpool, London, Northampton, Plymouth, Sheffield and Southampton; Anglo-Scottish Hygienic Stores had several branches in Glasgow.
45 T. McIntosh, '"An abortionist city": maternal mortality, abortion, and birth control in Sheffield, 1920–1940', *Medical History*, 44 (2000), 75–96.
46 See, for example, W. George, *Contraceptive Methods and Appliances* (1940), p. 8; Le Brasseur Surgical Manufacturing Co., *Revised List of*

Surgical Rubber Specialities and Pro-Race Goods (n.p., 1936), pp. 4–5, 8–9. 'Dr Paterson's pills' were commonly sold in the nineteenth century. E. J. Bristow, *Vice and Vigilance: Purity Movements in Britain since 1700* (London: Gill and Macmillan, 1977), p. 204.
47 Le Brasseur, *Revised List of Surgical Rubber Specialities* (1936), p. 9. Date of establishment based on 'Surgical rubber goods', *Illustrated Police News* (11 November 1915), p. 10.
48 W. George, *Special List of Domestic and Surgical Appliances* (n.p., 1912), p. 8; (n.p., 1915), p. 10; L. Jackson, *Price List of Rubber Goods* (n.p., 1907), p. 6.
49 'Rendell and Company', *Sporting Times* (21 March 1925), p. 11; 'Rendell's surgical and rubber goods, *Illustrated Police News* (11 November 1920), p. 7; 'Rendell's drug stores', *Illustrated Police News* (12 November 1925), p. 7; *Sporting Times* (21 February 1925), p. 7.
50 'Illustrated Pro-Race catalogue', *Illustrated Police News* (12 November 1925), p. 2.
51 Rendell (uncatalogued papers), Sundry infringers, *c.* 1925; BL, Add. MS 58639, 203 and 204.
52 BL, Add. MS 58638, letter by Lambert to Stopes, 20 February 1922.
53 H. A. Allbutt, *The Wife's Handbook*, 56th edn (London: Bentley, 1922), p. 69.
54 Lamberts Prorace Ltd, *Revised Price List of Approved Contraceptive Appliances* (1933), frontispiece.
55 Stopes, *A Letter to Working Mothers*, p. 10.
56 WL, SA/FPA/A14/32, advertisement for 'The Robilton Company: an exclusive agency for the supply of genuine contraceptives', http://de.muvs.org/bibliothek/artikel/1428?media_id=7502 [accessed 24 July 2019].
57 George, *Special List* (1915), p. 11.
58 P. Duguid, T. da Silva Lopes and J. Mercer, 'Reading registrations: an overview of 100 years of trademark registrations in France, the United Kingdom and the United States', in T. da Silva Lopes and P. Duguid (eds), *Trademarks, Brands and Competitiveness* (New York and London: Routledge, 2010), p. 17.
59 'Prorace Ld v. Le Brasseur Surgical Manufacturing Co. Ld', *Reports of Patent, Design and Trademark Cases*, 44:3 (1927), p. 75.
60 Le Brasseur, *Revised List of Surgical Rubber Specialities* (1936), p. 11.
61 Le Brasseur, *Revised List of Surgical Rubber Specialities* (1936), p. 13.
62 Rendell (uncatalogued papers), Call Dudley John Hedderley Ward to prove, W. J. Rendell Ltd versus Constantine and Jackson Ltd, 1927.

63 Rendell (uncatalogued papers), Statement of claim – W. J. Rendell Ltd versus Constantine and Jackson Ltd, 1927; Affidavit of Mr Frederick John Ward; Court transcript, 15 March 1928; Affidavit of Mr J. M. Dawson, 5 December 1927; Affidavit of Mr C. R. Jamblin, 5 December 1927.
64 BL, Add. MS 58638, letter by Stopes to Lambert, 17 March 1922.
65 BL, Add. MS 58639, 203 and 204, list of sundry infringers.
66 BL, Add. MS 58638, letter by Stopes to Lambert, 17 November 1923.
67 BL, Add. MS 58638, letter by Lambert to Stopes, 27 October 1922.
68 BL, Add. MS 58638, Lamberts Prorace Ltd, 7 February 1929; Add. MS 58639, 179, letter by Wilkinson, Howlett and Moorhouse to Stopes, 27 February 1951; 180, letter by Stopes to Wilkinson, Howlett and Moorhouse, 5 March 1951.
69 BL, Add. MS58638, letter by Stopes to Lambert, 30 April 1922; letter by Lambert to Stopes, 3 November 1922.
70 BL, Add. MS58638, letter by Lambert to Stopes, 19 October 1922; Lamberts Prorace Ltd, *Revised Price List* (1936), pp. 3, 12.
71 Lamberts (Dalston) Ltd, *Revised Price List* (1941), p. 15; BL, Add. MS58639, 166, Stopes to Lambert, 2 December 1949.
72 WL, SA/FPA/A13/46.1, letter by Stopes to Horder, 10 February 1950.
73 BL, Add. MS58639, 195, letter by Stopes to Wilkinson, Howlett and Moorhouse, 2 July 1951.
74 See, for example, R. Hall (ed.), *Dear Dr Stopes: Sex in the 1920s* (London: Penguin, 1978), p. 24; WL, PP/MCS/A.31, letter by Stopes to Mrs B., 20 June 1922.
75 WL, SA/FPA/A7/101, letter by Mrs Y to FPA, 5 February 1942; letter by Prentif to FPA, 10 February 1943; letter by FPA to Prentif, 12 February 1943; letter by FPA to Mrs Y, 12 February 1943; letter by Prentif to FPA, 15 February 1943.
76 Rendell (uncatalogued papers), testimonials 1926–31, numbered 1 to 46.
77 K. Fisher, 'An Oral History of Birth Control Practice c. 1925–50: A Study of Oxford and Wales' (D.Phil. thesis, University of Oxford, 1997), pp. 154, 258, 286.
78 J. R. Baker, *The Chemical Control of Conception* (London: Chapman and Hill, 1935); C. I. Voge, *The Chemistry and Physics of Contraceptives* (London: Cape, 1933).
79 G. M. Cox, *Clinical Contraception* (London: Heinemann, 1933), p. 44.
80 Cook, 'The Long Sexual Revolution', p. 70. McKibbin, in *Classes and Cultures*, pp. 44–5, points out that the definition of 'middle class' solely by income is too restrictive as there were those who earned

much less but considered themselves or others considered them to be middle class, such as petty clerks and salesmen, so constituted approximately 22 per cent of the population.

81 Rendell (uncatalogued papers), testimonial, no. 2, Mrs T., Bideford, North Devon, 9 February 1927.
82 Cook, 'The Long Sexual Revolution', pp. 69, 192; M-O, Topic Collection 12 3/E, Chapter 4, 'Birth Control'.
83 McKibbin, *Classes and Cultures*, p. 299.
84 Rendell (uncatalogued papers), testimonials, no. 2, Anon., Alexandria, 21 September 1926.
85 Rendell (uncatalogued papers), testimonials, no. 5, Anon., n.d.
86 Rendell (uncatalogued papers), testimonials, no. 15. Anon., 9 June 1926.
87 Rendell (uncatalogued papers), testimonials, no. 21. Anon., 7 March 1927.
88 Rendell (uncatalogued papers), testimonials, no. 41. Mr F., 3 November 1931.
89 Hancock and Co. Ltd, *The Shadow of the Stork* (n.p., 1934), p. 15.
90 Rendell (uncatalogued papers), testimonials, no. 14, Anon., 5 August 1926.
91 Rendell (uncatalogued papers), testimonials, no. 1. Mrs F., 27 June 1928.
92 M-O DR 3453 (catalogued also as 1022), reply to April 1944 Directive. Cited in Fisher, *Birth Control, Sex, and Marriage*, p. 181.
93 'Rendell', *The New Generation*, vol. ix, no. 6, p. 68, June 1930.
94 A. Lambert, *Modern Contraceptive Methods and Appliances* (n.p., 1932), p. 11.
95 Lamberts (Dalston) Ltd, *Revised List of Up-to-Date Contraceptive Appliances* (1941), p. 21.
96 Hancock, *Shadow of the Stork* (1933), p. 15.
97 A. Phelps, *Birth Control and What it Means*, 52nd edn (London: The Kingsland Hygienic Co. Ltd, 1940), pp. 18–20.
98 Tully, *The Devil's Milk*, pp. 44–5.
99 WL, PP/MCS/A.278, letter by Stopes to anon.; PP/MCS/A.64, letter by anon. to Stopes; Porter and Hall, *The Facts of Life*, p. 237.
100 WL, PP/MCS/A.45, letter by anon. to Stopes, 27 March 1926; Florence, *Birth Control on Trial*, p. 93.
101 Fisher, *Birth Control, Sex, and Marriage*, pp. 44, 166; M. Sutton, *We Didn't Know Aught: A Study of Women's Sexuality, Superstition and Death in Women's Lives in Lincolnshire during the 1930s, '40s and '50s* (Stamford: Paul Watkins, 1992), p. 90; Szreter and Fisher, *Sex Before the Sexual Revolution*, pp. 243, 256; N. Haire, *Birth Control Methods* (London: G. Allen and Unwin, 1936), p. 73; T. van de Velde, *Fertility*

and *Sterility in Marriage: Their Voluntary Promotion and Limitation* (London: Heinemann, 1931), p. 343.
102 C. Davey, 'Birth control in Britain during the interwar years', *Journal of Family History*, 13:3 (1988), 336.
103 Anderson and Berridge, 'The role of the community pharmacist', p. 66; S. Humphries, *Secret World of Sex: Forbidden Fruit, the British Experience, 1900–1950* (London: Sidgwick and Jackson, 1988), p. 112.
104 M-O, 12 1/B, First Venereal Disease Survey, November–December 1942.
105 WL, SA/FPA/A7/78, letter by A. Reid to Clifford Smith, 16 July 1958.
106 Monopolies and Mergers Commission, *Contraceptive Sheaths* (1975), p. 21.
107 Monopolies and Mergers Commission, *Contraceptive Sheaths* (1975), pp. 65, 74, 76.

3

The print culture of contraceptives: advertising and the circulation of birth control knowledge

Contraceptive firms relied on promotion in print to sell their brands. As in other industries, contraceptive trade advertisements placed in popular newspapers, circulars and catalogues aided the establishment of intellectual property, provided defence from imitation and communicated the reliability of products and the authenticity of their vendor or producer to consumers.[1] Advertising served as a legitimising force within the contraceptive trade and this force was most significant amid the interwar increase of printed material on birth control more generally where medical professionals and birth control advocates sought to stake out their authority. Yet, advertising in the interwar years held a peculiar position; it was circulated in greater quantities than ever before, and certainly in more forms than historians have commonly recognised. Birth control advocates and moralists, concerned about the rise in contraceptive advertising, sought to limit its circulation, not least to the innocent young and unmarried who formed the focus of the Contraceptives (Regulation) Bill. Such measures reflected wider ideas about what constituted legitimate and non-legitimate birth control and sexual knowledge in the public sphere in this period of flux, and who had a right to determine and access this knowledge. At the same time, company attempts to balance attracting consumers and avoiding offending sensibilities meant that interwar advertising still remained invisible to some. As we will see in this chapter, firms attempted to avoid offence and censorship through greater alignment with the medical profession and medical publishing, and through the emulation of birth control pamphlets that were rarely the target of censorship laws.[2]

Through this chapter's focus on contraceptive advertising, we will see how interwar attempts by Marie Stopes and the State to narrowly define sexual and contraceptive knowledge also sought to delegitimise commercial knowledge. However, as we will see from an analysis of advertising outputs, the boundary between commercial and non-commercial information on birth control was not always clear. The combination of old and new ways of viewing birth control information – the increasing visibility of birth control publications but with content that was highly guarded and euphemistic – resulted in a complex and broad range of print material, which confused intermediaries and end consumers alike.

Threaded throughout is an attempt to consider potential readers of such material. While factors such as class, sex, age and geography undoubtedly determined access to literature and the degree of literacy readers brought to reading material, understanding the extent to which such advertisements were 'read', how much knowledge readers took away from them and whether their reading practices were transformed into ordering products is no easy matter.[3] In its surveys of the late 1940s, Mass-Observation reported that while 3 per cent of the general population said they never read anything of any sort, only 8 per cent of respondents to a questionnaire stated that they had found out about sex through reading, although this is probably an underestimate among the population.[4] Most of the population picked up sexual information in a haphazard way – from friends, colleagues, spouses and through print – without necessarily being aware they were doing so. Nonetheless, the lack of information on readerships and the almost serendipitous circulation of sexual knowledge, both in the 1940s and before, is important because it is suggestive of a reading culture that was uncontrollable and unmonitored. And it was of this uncontrollable culture that contraceptive companies could take advantage.

The print trade and mail-order contraceptives

Late nineteenth-century print that addressed sex and contraception was subject to censorship under obscenity and indecency legislation. Forming the background to such legislation was a wider movement for moral reform of sexual behaviour, specifically targeting homosexuality, prostitution and venereal disease. Yet, despite being the only aspect of the contraceptive trade for which there could be any potential for legal recrimination, contraceptive manufacturers, retailers and mail-order entrepreneurs were prolific advertisers prior to the First World War. Their advertising merely required a degree of discretion and for consumers to know where and how to look. Beyond Rendell and the firm's use of Allbutt's *The Wife's Handbook* to promote the 'Wife's Friend' soluble pessary, small, discreet advertisements announcing the availability of euphemistically described 'surgical appliances' featured in both the specialist neo-Malthusian press and the provincial and penny weekly press. Indeed, less restricted by legal, social and moral dogma, and more reliant on the income from advertising rates than the growing number of daily newspapers, provincial titles from the *Brighton Gazette* to the *Cornish Telegraph* regularly included discreet contraceptive advertisements alongside those promoting Beecham's Pills, jewellery, clothing and other consumer goods.[5] Elderton, and historians thereafter, have suggested that proletarian birth regulation was most established in the north of England, and accordingly, more explicit advertisements addressing 'the population question' appeared in the *Derbyshire Courier*, the *Wharfedale and Airedale Observer*, the *Preston Herald* and other northern newspapers. More explicit still were advertisements within cheap penny weeklies for 'special rubber goods' for 'all married people who wish to be happy and limit their families'; they contained cautionary slogans such as 'Look before you leap!' and 'Don't Run the Risk'.[6]

Also advertised in the press were firms' ambiguously titled catalogues and price lists; names such as *Catalogue of Rubber Specialities* and *Special List of Domestic and Surgical Specialities* were common (fig. 10).[7] Within these catalogues and price lists, contraceptives were typically discreetly promoted across a few pages by short product descriptions and an occasional black-and-white line drawing amid more general rubber goods, including bandages, hot-water bottles, urinals and teats (fig. 11); updated every few years, such publications were sent to interested consumers in plain brown envelopes to avoid detection. The catalogues of rubber good stores also tended to include female pills and pills to enhance male virility.[8]

Press advertisements, catalogues and price lists assisted the trade's expansion into mail order. Its advertising success led to Lambert's claim from 1900 that 'a large part of our business is conducted through the post'.[9] Facilitated by the Royal Mail's introduction of postal orders in 1881 and a parcel post service in 1883, mail order was convenient for consumers, both in Britain and abroad; it enabled them to order contraceptives as frequently as required from the comfort

Figure 10 E. Lambert and Son, *Special List of Domestic and Surgical Specialties* (1900), front cover.

and safety of their own home. But Lambert's success as a mail-order business was not only sustained by contraceptive goods, or even its medical rubber goods; it was also aided by its distribution of all manner of books and pamphlets on contraception and sex. Perhaps as many as two million tracts concerning sex and contraception were sold in Britain between 1876 and 1891, providing an existing market that firms such as Lambert could tap into.[10] As the decline in fertility rates began to pick up speed, Lambert developed an extensive library of texts on 'the population question' that it sold and lent to mail applicants. Along with enthusiastic neo-Malthusians, including C. J. Welton of Nottingham and J. R. Holmes of Berkshire, Lambert described and promoted himself as a medical bookseller, and his mail-order business for both texts and contraceptives flourished.[11]

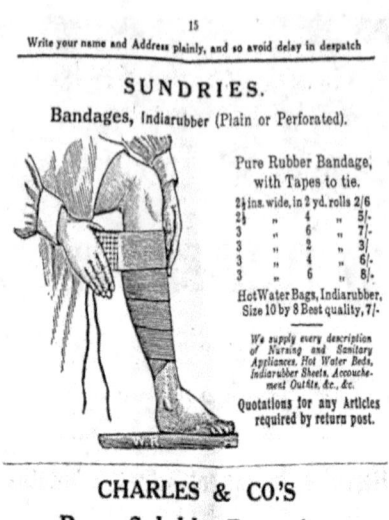

Figure 11 Chemical pessaries are promoted next to rubber bandages.

For its lending library, Lambert charged readers a deposit of between 6d and 2s 6d, depending on the value of the book.[12] Among its lists of almost two hundred books addressing medical topics ranging from consumption to midwifery, books on 'the population question' included Allbutt's *The Wife's Handbook*, the firm's own *The Wife's Guide and Friend*, Foote's *Plain Home Talk* and those by Charles Knowlton and George Drysdale.

The relationship between contraceptives and the book trade was most apparent among the retailers in and around London's Wych Street and Holywell Street. Book dealers on Holywell Street, also known as Booksellers' Row, had developed a reputation for the supply of works on sexual health and popular information on contraception since the 1820s, but they also supplied contraceptives.[13] By the late nineteenth century the explicit advertisements for the 'special rubber goods' of W. George and Constantine and Jackson, suppliers located in this area, featured in the penny weekly press next to manuals on spermatorrhoea, *Aristotle's Masterpiece*, *The Confessions of a Lady's Maid*, *My Uncle Barbasson* and *Memoirs of Fanny Hill*, and ambiguously titled 'chic books' and 'rich, rare and racy books'. The *Illustrated Police News* and the *Sporting Times: Otherwise Known as the 'Pink 'Un'* (on account of its pink pages, a measure taken to reduce publication costs) were among the most prolific advertisers of sexual books and contraceptives (fig. 12); they appealed to largely lower-middle-class and working-class readerships titillated by sensational stories of crime and society scandal. Coverage of the Jack the Ripper case, in particular, made the *Illustrated Police News* one of the most sensational newspapers of the mid- and late-Victorian era.[14]

It was through postal distribution, rather than production, that advertisers could be prosecuted under obscenity laws. Accordingly, penny weekly advertisers used multiple false names, pseudonyms and addresses not only to profit from the success of existing brands (as we saw in Chapter 2 with W. George's use of the name Rendell and Company) but also to avoid prosecution. But such a tactic was not always successful. Charles Froment Haynes, for example, ran mail-order firms under the names of Charles and Co., J. Reid, Madame Froment, Haynes, and Haines from addresses in Tottenham and Bishopsgate Without, and was convicted for obscenity and mailing indecent matter in 1890 and 1901. Haynes was also implicated in the prosecution of Edward de Marney, a pornographic magazine publisher, in 1906.[15] De Marney knowingly supplied a correspondent with advertisements for Reid's 'indiarubber goods', alongside objectionable books, photographs and the 'Magic Revealer', a catchpenny device for revealing an image of a nude woman.[16] Following the sensational coverage of Allbutt's expulsion from the medical register in the press, Lambert too was prosecuted for distributing *The Wife's Handbook*.[17] Prosecutions did not, however, prevent Haynes or Lambert from subsequently selling their 'obscene' books or contraceptives. Lambert avoided further prosecution largely because his other books on the population question were able to blend into his catalogue of medical books.

Figure 12 Contraceptives advertised in the *Illustrated Police News* (30 October 1897).

The underground nature of the pre-First World War mail-order trade for contraceptive goods and its connections to the trade in Malthusian, medical and obscene material means that establishing readerships for these forms of advertising is difficult. While it is clear that provincial newspapers were widely read among all social classes, certainly more widely read than national daily newspapers until at least the 1920s, it is difficult to establish the extent to which euphemistic contraceptive advertisements were even seen, never mind acted upon.[18] Their continual inclusion in the press suggests some level of reader receptivity, a finding that correlates with Elderton's suggestion that advertisements had some influence on respondents in parts of northern England on purchasing habits, but we have little way of establishing the extent of this receptivity. Readers of sensational penny weeklies – circulation figures were between fifty thousand and three hundred thousand for the *Illustrated Police News* and the *Sporting Times* – seemingly possessed some degree of contraceptive knowledge and sought out contraceptives, possibly for non- or extra-marital sex.[19] Indeed, one supplier claimed to have done enormous business and to have contacted hundreds of customers in the 1890s through illustrated magazines like *Photo-Bits* and *Pick-Me-Up*, with the bachelor about town forming the majority of the readership.[20] But again, how reading affected contraceptive demand is difficult to gauge. The obscene market was niche and remained so into the interwar period. Similarly, firms' catalogue readerships and distribution figures are almost unknown, although it is likely that a small level of demand for this form of print came from an existing customer base of middle-class consumers, some of whom had neo-Malthusian sympathies.

'Birth control is here to stay'? Contraceptive print in the interwar period

During the opening up of general print culture to articles on birth control and sex in the interwar years, contraceptive advertising began to be produced and circulated in greater volume, also becoming less opaque in content. The increasing discussability of birth control, following Margaret Sanger's coining of the term in 1914 and Stopes's publications from 1918, resulted in a growth in contraceptive advertising. The provincial press, which maintained a large readership, featured more contraceptive advertisements, and for the first time, contraceptive advertisements appeared in daily newspapers and growing numbers of women's magazines alongside editorials, reports, lectures and correspondence that addressed birth control as a practice. Newspapers before the war had often discussed 'the population question', but there had been little to signal to the unknowing reader that individuals were actively controlling their fertility.

As Adrian Bingham has argued, it was during the interwar period that newspapers began to make public sexual topics that had once been private.[21] As the habit of daily newspaper reading was established across society through the success of papers such as the *Daily Express*, *Daily Mail* and *Daily Mirror*, it was in the *Daily Herald*, a labour movement and socialist newspaper with a daily circulation of 150,000 at its peak in the mid-1920s, that contraceptive advertisements became noticeable. A daily newspaper known for its strong stance on women's rights, the *Daily Herald*'s contraceptive advertisements consisted of nearly half a column.[22] Such advertisements less frequently referred to 'surgical appliances' and instead increasingly promoted 'birth control appliances'. This more explicit rebranding, which reflected broader shifts in language use, was most obvious in the provincial press. Among the first aspects of birth control discussed in the provincial press were Charles Killick Millard's lecture on population and birth control at the Royal Institute in January 1918, Dawson's 1921 address to the Church Congress in Birmingham in which he stated 'birth control is here to stay' and, of course, Marie Stopes's work on birth control, including her publications and the opening of her first clinic.[23] More than fifty different magazines, journals and largely provincial newspapers included advertisements for Stopes's publications and clinics and around a dozen London and provincial newspapers reported on the opening of the Malthusian League's Walworth clinic.[24] Yet, while advertisements for 'birth control appliances' became more visible (certainly more so than in retail, as we will see in Chapter 5), some contraceptive advertising remained opaque, meaning that not all readers could access such information. Indeed, in their quest to maintain an image of respectability and to shape their publications into 'family newspapers', many successful publications, such as the *News of the World*, refused to mention birth control at all, never mind accept advertisements for products explicitly for the purpose of birth control. Other newspapers addressed the topic of birth control, as well as other sexual topics including abortion, venereal disease and homosexuality, but their stance was often neutral and discussions remained largely euphemistic.[25]

Similarly, the increasing incorporation of both sex instruction and contraceptive advertisements within magazines that specifically targeted a female readership with themes of glamour, health and romance also tended to emphasise 'self-protection' in vague language rather than provide new information.[26] Much to the annoyance of other contraceptive firms, it was only advertisements for Rendell's 'Wife's Friend' that began to appear regularly in a range of papers from the 1930s, including *Woman and Home*, *Woman's Magazine*, *Woman's World*, the *Sunday Times*, the *Telegraph*, *Illustrated London News*, *Sketch*, *Tatler* and *London Life*, publications in which some of the firm's correspondents claimed to have seen its advertisements.[27] Rendell's advertisements promoting 'feminine hygiene' featured a character called Nurse Drew in order to convey medical authority, or groups of well-dressed and fashionable ladies conversing in a beauty and hair salon or over lunch in a restaurant, and included simple statements such as 'approved by doctors, Rendells, obtainable from leading chemists everywhere'.[28] Publications accepted such advertisements because, as the Amalgamated Press stated following complaints from Prentif in 1937, they were 'simply reminder advertising and the wording is entirely inoffensive and to the uninitiated, mysterious. Those who know what it all means understand and it serves to remind them.'[29] The continued reticence surrounding birth control and associated advertising meant that it remained unlikely that unknowing consumers received enlightenment. Knowing consumers, however, had a greater number of advertisements to interpret amid growing amounts of sexual information.

Press coverage of birth control was often ambiguous, but it was the form and format of firms' catalogues, as well as the frequency with which they were published and their method of distribution, that experienced significant change. Amid the flooding of the book market with all manner of manuals of sexual instruction, guides to marriage and medical works of sexology suited to all forms of readership, manufacturers and surgical stores increased their catalogue output, updating their editions annually or biannually. Numbers of catalogue editions are difficult to estimate, but catalogue production increased by at least 50 per cent during the interwar period and sat alongside no fewer than fifteen million books, pamphlets and brochures on birth control, as well as an untold growth in mass-market pornography and cheap erotic fiction where sexual activity itself was not mentioned but was hinted at.[30] Ranging in price from 2d to 15s, such books were available from selected booksellers, news agents, increasing numbers of lending and circulating libraries and book clubs and via mail order.[31]

Like advertisements within the press, catalogues increasingly emphasised 'birth control'. Titles such as *Catalogue of Contraceptive Appliances* or *Catalogue of Birth Control Appliances* began to become more common, and catalogues no longer promoted contraceptives across a few pages within larger general rubber appliance catalogues; they instead expanded to up to a hundred pages of all manner of branded contraceptives, becoming catalogues in their own right and further aiding the expansion of mail order. Neither were all catalogues shaped solely as promotional material. Like the growing numbers of manuals of sexual instruction, contraceptive catalogues began to furnish practical contraceptive advice that provided more information on sexual conduct and behaviour but simultaneously maintained ignorance or at least allowed the performance of ignorance. Indeed, firms were aware that the success of Stopes's publications resulted from her skill at knowing exactly how to convey 'the maximum amount of sex education possible' and when to have recourse to 'reticence and inexplicitness'.[32] In particular, while earlier tracts and catalogues integrated information on contraceptives into content on menstruation, pregnancy and marriage, catalogue text of the interwar period aligned the promotion of caps and pessaries to married middle-class women with contemporary ideas about sanitation and hygiene. *A Hint in Confidence: Woman's Guide to Intimate Hygiene*, a Solidol Chemical Ltd catalogue of 1930 consisting of forty-eight pages, for example, promoted douching and 'Lysolats' vaginal disinfecting tablets (forty for 1s 3d) as part of a general routine of intimate cleaning and washing for the modern woman.[33] Alongside pages that continued to promote individual branded syringes, rubber and chemical pessaries, firms dedicated an increasing amount of catalogue space to the sheath and condom, not only indicating company attempts to push the many different types of condom and sheath but also their growing popularity among consumers. Condoms and sheaths were also promoted at the beginning of the catalogue, suggesting that these were the most sought-after items. Firms offered the daunted reader a range of different 'special trial packs' containing six or seven different types of condom, and presented the middle- and upper-class well-to-do bachelor about town or the soldier with condoms disguised as buttonholes, sweet wrappers and cigarette packets; described as 'camouflaged preventives', they were adorned with images of attractive young women in bathing suits. Firms provided aluminium or enamelled carry cases (priced at 1s 9d each or 8s for six cases).[34]

Books (and catalogues), the most serious and legitimate forms in which sexual information could be contained, were more authoritative and respectable if they appeared to be 'medical' and 'scientific' and drew on the rhetoric of the birth control movement. Half of the forty or so sex manuals published between 1918 and 1945 and identified by Hera Cook were seemingly written by medical doctors, while a fifth had substantial involvement in the birth control movement and a fifth were written by women. Whether medical or not, many of these publications adopted the tropes of medical publications by giving married readers candid information about the physical sexual body of men and women, sexual practice and contraceptive recommendations generally said to be based on clinical or personal experience.[35] In *Contraception* (1923), a book aimed at filling the gaps in medical knowledge, Stopes mimicked the tropes she saw in other medical works.[36] Catalogues of the 1930s copied these tropes. Catalogues of Lamberts, of course, drew on Stopes's recommendation of its pessaries in *Wise Parenthood* and other publications, but they also increasingly included details of the firm's successful testing of both rubber and chemical contraceptives. While the 'Lam-butt' cap was 'scientifically correct', halftone images of Lamberts' 'Bymeston' spermicide within four test tubes, for example, promoted the product's foam density in order to demonstrate its ability to kill spermatozoa:

> the purpose of any contraceptive method is to prevent the male sperms connecting with the female cells in the womb and the 'Bymeston' foaming jelly offers the simplest and safest way ... Leading authorities on the subject have said that the main requirement is a highly spermicidal preparation which will not only form a barrier, but will also kill the sperm immediately they leave the male organ.[37]

Walton Rubber Goods Company, established to supply sailors with condoms in the port towns of Portsmouth, Chatham and Ipswich, stated in its 1937 catalogue that 'it is admitted on all sides that the Malthus Sheath is a perfect contraceptive, but opinion is still divided as to whether it is ideal'. Walton's statement was virtually meaningless, but being open about the fact that opinion was divided projected an image of scientific authority in an arena in which consensus had not yet been reached. The firm also included reference to 'Constructive Birth Control' and an extract from Isobel Hutton's 1923 book *The Hygiene of Marriage* to highlight that its own sheaths were 'the simplest and most reliable method which exists'.[38] The 1934 catalogue of Kait's Pharmacies included several pages on conception, complete with illustrations of the uterus, and stated that 'to understand birth control, one must know how pregnancy takes place'.[39] Like authoritative and respectable books, catalogues also needed to be purchased. Charging between 6d and 2s for a catalogue presented to consumers the impression that the information contained therein was valuable.

As sources of instructive content, such 'medical' publications also meant that their publishers and authors might avoid prosecution under obscenity and indecency legislation.[40] Indeed, censorship was still very much in the minds of publishers, and random prosecutions for the publication and distribution of obscene and indecent material still occurred, despite the existence of a more candid discourse on birth control. Libertarian communists Guy Aldred and Rose Witcop were prosecuted for publishing and selling Margaret Sanger's *Family Limitation* in 1923, and the popular fictions of D. H. Lawrence and Radclyffe Hall were subject to censorship.[41] But in reference to medical works, the *British Medical Journal* argued in 1934 that 'what was intended to be a plain statement, giving information, was not capable of being held to be indecent or obscene, but it must be something intended to affect the mind salaciously'.[42] Contraceptive catalogues for the most part then began to draw on the same rhetoric of practical education and directness that appeared in sex and contraceptive advice manuals.

Catalogue expansion and textual shifts towards instruction not only signalled the increasing legitimacy of manufacturers as contraceptive specialists among both general consumers and medical practitioners but also resulted in manufacturers' abandonment of their long-standing role in the book trade as contraceptive booksellers. Indeed, the growing alignment of manufacturers with the medical profession was signalled by the promotion of goods in medical journals and the targeting of medical practitioners with catalogues. Advertisements for Lambert's 'Pro-Race' cap (and Stopes's *Married Love*), for example, appeared in the *Lancet* and the *Chemist and*

Druggist, and the firm's advertisements disappeared from the general press.[43] Prentif even published a medical journal, *Contraceptive Practice*, that it circulated to thirty thousand medical practitioners in 1936, in order, it said, to more fully detail the anatomical underpinnings of reproduction in line within its products. It obtained permission from John Baker, the University of Oxford eugenicist and cytologist working with the National Birth Control Association, Birth Control Investigation Committee and British Drug Houses to develop an effective spermicidal contraceptive, to use his name when writing to medical officers at clinics.[44] Indeed, Lamberts and Prentif were likely to have been among the firms Himes referred to as 'the better manufacturers in England' where 'there is growing up a certain spirit de corps designed to protect the legitimate interests of the business and the public'. Such firms, Himes argued, were 'anxious to cooperate with the medical profession in standardising products and in maintaining high ethical business standards'.[45]

But while manufacturers like Lamberts and Prentif began to distance themselves from general press advertising, bookselling and the seedy reputation of the pornography trade, surgical stores began to fill the gap left behind. Surgical stores expanded their press advertising and bookselling business in the comfort that they were unlikely to be prosecuted for distributing instructive birth control manuals. Company pseudonyms became publishing companies. Le Brasseur, for example, established and ran the Medical Publishing Company, the Medical and Surgical Supply Co. and the London Medical Manufacturing Co. The book circulation lists and press advertisements of surgical stores mimicked those of bona fide medical publishers with titles such as 'Sexual Science Series' or 'Medical Works', and claimed to be 'for the medical profession only'. Such features aimed to appeal to scientific and medical authority and assure readers that they only supplied works on birth control, marriage and sexology by 'medical' experts.[46] S. Seymour of Leicester Square's three-page list of 'Sane Sex Books' published at the back of his 1930 catalogue included, for example, Dr G. Courtenay Beale's *Wise Wedlock (Birth Control)* (which sold one hundred thousand copies by 1939), Walter Gallichan's *Youth and Maidenhood* and Mona Baird's *Matrimony*.[47] Le Brasseur's 'Sex Educational Series' in 1931 included works by Stopes, Sanger and Havelock Ellis in its list of nearly ninety 'Medical Works on Birth Control'. The firm's advertisements for 'birth control' in the *Sporting Times* in 1925 listed Stopes's *A Letter* to *Working Mothers* and *Wise Parenthood* for 3d, and *Married Love* for 6d, alongside Sanger's *Family Limitation* for 7d, while its other advertisements promised to distribute these publications free of charge with contraceptive orders.[48] Advertisements for 'birth control' by Le Brasseur and the Hygienic Stores appeared in the *Daily Herald*, *Daily Telegraph*, publications by Illustrated News (including *Illustrated London News*, *Sketch* and *Tatler*) and the Amalgamated Press (*My Home*) until Prentif informed the publishers that these firms were unethical in 1937.[49]

Again, it is difficult to establish the effect of such publications on readers, particularly given that print runs are underestimates of readership numbers and that readers may have been selective with the material they read. But increases in production and distribution mean that it is likely that the glut of new publications promoting birth control significantly widened the readership for books on sexual topics to women and working-class readers. It is also, of course, possible to gauge Stopes's reaction to them. Indeed, it was surgical stores' mimicking of medical publishers that was most concerning to Stopes as she sought to establish her own authority in contraceptive matters.

The visibility of print and its problems: Stopes and 'spurious pamphlets'

Stopes despised the intrusion of surgical stores into the medical publishing world as much as she hated their imitation of her 'Pro-Race' pessary. Stopes's aim to have total control over the advertising, text and layout of her publications signalled her awareness of the importance of her books as commodities, and her desire for control over her publications also extended to distribution.[50] Her frustration with surgical stores was directed towards their distribution of her own publications alongside works by authors she considered unworthy and accused of plagiarism, such as Courtenay Beale and even Dawson himself, but also included their distribution of unknown numbers of their own published works on birth control.[51] Indeed, building on the trade's older publishing tradition, surgical stores established their own publishing companies not only to distribute new instructive manuals of birth control, but also as a way of distributing their own advertising indistinguishable from these manuals. Moreover, many of the basic facts around sex and reproduction included in both forms of publication were identical and both tended to recommend a particular firm's

THE PRINT CULTURE OF CONTRACEPTIVES   113

products. When writing to Stopes, Lambert described these surgical store publications as 'spurious pamphlets', but for surgical stores these publications projected an image of the firm as authoritative and its contraceptive products as reliable.[52]

Among the most prominent surgical stores that conducted this publishing practice throughout the interwar period, and the one that infuriated Stopes the most, was Le Brasseur. In its various newspaper advertisements and book circulation lists, Le Brasseur listed Dr St Clair Maurice's *Advice to Married Women* (fig. 13), Dr B. Goodman's *Birth Control* and Douglas Neale's *Manual of Wisdom for the Married* alongside publications by Stopes, Sanger and others.[53] Published under the guise of Le Brasseur's own publishers, these books were little more than catalogues for the firm's products, imitating the very birth control advice literature they distributed. Reflective of the language of birth control manuals, St Clair Maurice claimed that 'nothing in these pages will be of interest to the sensational monger, but those who seriously and sensibly wish for knowledge on this all important question will find much to help them in their social and domestic problems'.[54] But St Clair Maurice, Goodman and Neale were company pseudonyms. Indeed, Dr B. Goodman was a wry dig at the conservative establishment and its views on birth control, while portraying a medical status to unknowing consumers. It is also possible that 'Goodman' was a director of the London Medical Manufacturing Company, a subsidiary of Le Brasseur.[55] Each 'author' recommended the firm's other publications, as well as Le Brasseur's products. St Clair Maurice

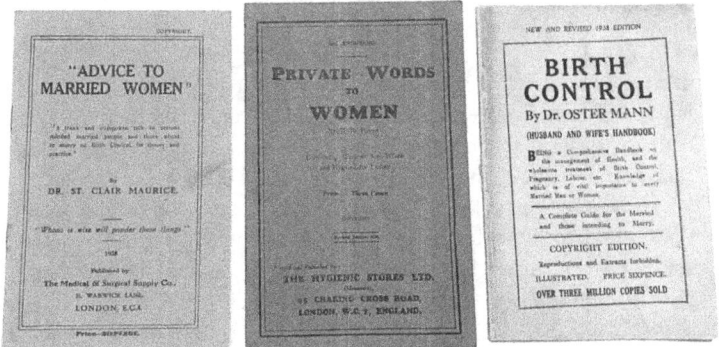

Figure 13 Company catalogues disguised as birth control manuals.

stated 'the most important thing to bear in mind is to purchase these only from a reliable firm; I can personally recommend Le Brasseur Surgical Manufacturing Co. Ltd'.[56]

Other mail-order firms and surgical stores published, promoted and distributed these imitations of birth control manuals. A. Lambert, the firm that had broken away from Lamberts (Dalston) Ltd in the 1920s, updated and adapted the firm's 1896 *The Wife's Guide and Friend* into an imitation of a birth control manual. As early as 1904 the publication became Stewart Warren's *The Wife's Guide and Friend*, but there is no indication that Warren was anything more than a fictional character invented by the firm. Advertising only increased under Warren's supposed authorship. Consisting of one hundred pages, the publication's first section aimed to provide young women with advice about menstruation, pregnancy and labour, while the second section recommended A. Lambert's 'Vimule Soluble Pessaries' for 2/- per dozen, its 'Vimule Seamless Pessary' for between 3s and 5s and its 'Vimule Sheaths' for between 5d each and 24s for six dozen. Advertised in the *New Generation* and a variety of periodicals, A. Lambert claimed to have sold two hundred thousand copies of the publication by 1927.[57] Similarly, Jackson's Hygienic Stores authored and published D. R. Payne's *Private Words to Women: Containing Wisdom for Wives and Hygiene for Ladies* and Dr Oster Mann's *Birth Control (Husband and Wife's Handbook)* in 1926 (see fig. 13), which again discussed reproduction, menstruation, pregnancy and labour, as well as impotence in order to sell vitality pills.[58] 'Oster' in Oster Mann may have referred to the city in Ukraine from which the owner of the Hygienic Stores originated, while 'D. R. Payne' was another sly reference to the medical profession. 'Oster Mann' stated:

> some may be shocked at the publication of such a book as this, perhaps because it provides material for impure minds, yet they will not realise the fact that the same material is shown in many other ways, such as the cinema, some perverted papers, and many theatrical shows which may be seen alike by young and old. The mission of this book, then is this; to show these particular facts to some in a totally wholesome and fresh manner, and to be a help for those who, not knowing, are considering the responsibilities of marriage.[59]

Sexual advice included: 'Matrimonial relation implies reproduction. Reproduction is effected through the union of the ovum with the

Spermatozoon', but there was no information on what these were or practical help on how reproduction occurred.⁶⁰ The Hygienic Stores even developed its own family periodical, *The Popular Herbal Family Medical Guide and Husband's and Wife's Handbook*, which contained practical health information as well as pages of advertisements for the firm's rubber goods and female pills.⁶¹ Other surgical stores adopted possible fictional female authors for their pamphlets to emulate female authorities like Stopes and provide reassurance to female readers. The Kingsland Hygienic Company's Annie Phelps, for example, wrote *Birth Control and What it Means*. For research purposes, Himes had responded to advertisements within the *Daily Herald* in 1927 and had received Stopes's *A Letter to Working Mothers*, alongside six pamphlets on birth control by pseudonymous authors published by surgical stores. One of these pamphlets, Margaret V. Graham's *A Common-Sense Treatise on Birth Control*, promoted Le Brasseur's bookselling services.⁶²

Stopes's solution to this 'spurious pamphlets' problem was to transfer sole agency for the sale and distribution of her most commonly imitated publication, *A Letter to Working Mothers*, to the Medical Trading Company, a medical publisher.⁶³ While Stopes came to rely on Lambert to defend the 'Pro-Race' from surgical store imitation, she also came to rely on the Medical Trading Company to defend *A Letter to Working Mothers* from surgical store distribution, sale and advertisement. By 1925 the Medical Trading Company claimed to have monopolised distribution, sending thirty-three thousand copies of the publication to consumers via mail order and Stopes's Constructive Birth Control clinics. By 1930 approximately twenty Jewish, provincial and workers' newspapers in locations including Liverpool, Hull, Manchester, Glasgow, Bristol, Bradford and Blackburn accepted the company's advertisement for the publication.⁶⁴ Much of the national press refused the advertisement, but an unlikely advertiser was the conservative, patriotic and anti-Catholic weekly *John Bull*, a publication with a circulation of 750,000 by 1914 and the first magazine to sell more than one million copies by 1925. Demonstrating the contradictory stance of the interwar press on birth control, *John Bull's* editor had launched a two-page broadside attacking Stopes in 1922 entitled 'The Bunkum of Birth Control', which associated her publications with 'pornographic French novels and other accessories of vice', but only three years later offered Stopes her own correspondence page, which was widely read among working-class readers and prompted a flood of letters.[65] Accepting that birth control was a legitimate and popular issue among its readership and that Stopes was a birth control authority, the publication was also willing to accept the Medical Trading Company's advertisements.

Stopes also relied on the Medical Trading Company to investigate the authors of surgical stores' 'spurious pamphlets'. Stopes asked the firm to investigate the identity of Dr Grayling Stewart, the author of a pamphlet titled *Wedlock and Birth Control: A Straightforward Talk on a Momentous and Delicate Subject* published by Le Brasseur's the Medical Publishing Company. The firm revealed that there was no Grayling Stewart within the Medical Directory and, having received a copy of his book, asserted that 'if the writer of this pamphlet is a "doctor", his professional studies would appear to have been at the sacrifice of his English grammar'. Stopes agreed that the publication did not read as though he were a medical man. The firm also confirmed that the London offices of the Medical Publishing Company on Ivy Lane had 'merely provided accommodation for the receipt of letters, which are called for daily, but otherwise there is no occupation'.[66] Stopes's request for such an investigation not only demonstrated her own inability to distinguish between birth control manuals and their commercial imitations but also signalled the ability of these imitations to circulate relatively unnoticed. As a non-medically qualified self-styled contraceptive expert, Stopes felt threatened by the medical qualification of other authors of birth control manuals, but at the same time she found the printed output of such authors immensely preferable to that of surgical stores, who took advantage of the ignorant consumer.

Stopes's inability to distinguish between medical manuals and surgical store imitations continued in 1928 with the publication of Michael Fielding's *Parenthood: Design or Accident?* Popular and press attention had been drawn to the publication because H. G. Wells, knowledgeable and in favour of contraceptive methods, provided its preface.[67] But following her experiences with Le Brasseur and other firms, Stopes had come to the conclusion that the publication was little more than a promotional catalogue because it recommended contraceptive products specifically by company and brand name, including Lamberts' 'Lam-butt' pessaries, its 'Dumas' caps, occlusive pessaries, whirling spray, 'Contraceptalene' and its sheaths, alongside quinine pessaries by Rendell and Dockers.[68] But far from being involved in the trade, 'Fielding' was a pseudonym used by Maurice Newfield (1893–1949), a doctor, birth control advocate, eugenicist and editor of the *Eugenics Review*. Fearful of censorship and of repercussions from what the General Medical Council might view as advertising, but anxious that readers had access to what he considered reliable information and effective, bona fide products, 'Fielding' had included the names of firms he trusted and had approached Lamberts asking for permission to mention its products. Lamberts were 'only too pleased to agree', particularly after the book had started to sell well (it sold 150,000 copies by 1940) and, in return, included the fact that 'Fielding' recommended its products in its catalogues. Lamberts recommended *Parenthood* as 'the finest book ever written on the subject of birth control' to various consumer correspondents and in its catalogues.[69] Several authors of other birth control manuals, including Norman Haire, recommended *Parenthood* too. Stopes was clearly unhappy with the firm's endorsement of Fielding's work, not least because she interpreted Fielding's comment in the introduction as a personal attack. He stated that 'there are a number of widely circulated books on birth control in which some of the information is reliable but a great deal is not. Those not written by doctors, with personal experience of contraceptive technique, suffer particularly from this defect'.[70] Complaining to Lamberts that 'Fielding' had plagiarised her work, Stopes demanded, unsuccessfully, that the firm not only 'drop my name altogether out of your catalogues' but also that Lambert reveal the true identity of 'Fielding'.[71] Lamberts informed Stopes that it was 'quite in the dark as to his real identity', although it claimed that the publishers had assured them that the author was a qualified medical man.[72]

While Stopes continued to complain that Fielding's book 'is an absolute crib of me', Newfield's membership of the National Birth Control Association from the early 1930s prompted his attempt to reshape *Parenthood* into a medical publication and to distance himself from the pamphlets of rubber stores.[73] In the 1935 edition, 'Fielding' was clear to state that *Parenthood* was 'not a propaganda leaflet' and removed all mention of the products of Lamberts, Rendell and Dockers. Instead, 'Fielding' recommended that readers write directly to the Association and purchase soluble pessaries and sheaths at a cheaper price than any chemist could offer.[74] Lamberts, however, continued to promote and supply *Parenthood*; an advertisement for the book, including testimonials from the *Lancet* and Haire, filled the back page of the firm's 1936 and 1941 catalogues.

The Medical Trading Company's ongoing inability to distinguish between 'spurious' and genuine birth control pamphlets and between 'rubber stores, herbalists and the like, with reputations good, bad and indifferent' resulted in a tense relationship with Stopes, especially after its monopoly had become formalised in 1930. High demand from all manner of retailers meant that the Medical Trading Company found it impossible to know who to supply with *A Letter to Working Mothers* and who to refuse.[75] Indeed, surgical stores had already subverted the Medical Trading Company's monopoly by convincing other distributors of the publication that they were reputable. Mr Key, manager of Blake's Medical Stores in Bristol, circumvented the Medical Trading Company by purchasing one thousand copies of *A Letter to Working Mothers* from the Holloway branch of Stopes's Constructive Birth Control clinic by emphasising his respectability and legitimacy as a bona fide bookseller. Gwendolen Roberts, the clinic nurse, reported to Stopes that 'he appeared to be an exceptionally nice man, thoroughly respectable and I cannot think why the Medical Trading Company should make themselves such a nuisance over the whole business'.[76] Seymour, another surgical store proprietor, asked H. Lambert, with whom he knew Stopes had a working relationship, to seek assurance from Stopes that the Medical Trading Company would continue its supply of *A Letter to Working Mothers*. Lambert assured Stopes 'that this man is quite straight, and he condemns in strong language the certain firms who advertise that which they cannot deliver – meaning – your *Letter to Working Mothers* ... I would like to put in a good word for Mr Seymour.'[77] Moreover, Stopes was unhappy to discover that the Medical Trading Company also supplied rubber pessaries it obtained from LRC to mail-order customers requesting the publication. To Stopes then, the Medical Trading Company had proved itself to be little better than surgical stores. Her own difficulty in distinguishing between genuine publications and their authors and imitations, as well as the Medical Trading Company's difficulty in knowing which stores were reputable, demonstrates the extent of fluidity of birth control authority in print during the 1920s.

Publication and promotion of surgical stores' 'spurious pamphlets' increased in the 1930s and 1940s. Under the guise of the Medical Publishing Company and the London Medical Manufacturing

Co. Ltd, Le Brasseur republished Douglas Neale's *Guide for Husbands and Wives*, Goodman's *My Views on Birth Control* and Stewart's *Wedlock and Birth Control*, distributing them free of charge to readers who ordered the works of Stopes, Sanger and other authors of birth control manuals. Grayling Stewart's publication even became a long-standing part of a lending library run by the Direct Book Supply Co., alongside works of sexology by Havelock Ellis, sexual advice manuals by Stopes, Haire, Eustace Chesser (1902–73) and Theodore van de Velde (1873–1937), as well as banned novels such as D. H. Lawrence's *Lady Chatterley's Lover* and works 'of absorbing interest to students of torture and flagellation'.[78] Following receipt of the book from the library in 1949, a female correspondent from an affluent part of West London requested more information about Grayling Stewart from the London Medical Manufacturing Company, the pamphlet's stated publisher founded by Le Brasseur's directors, after failing to find his name on the medical register. The firm provided a plausible but unlikely answer stating 'we believe that Dr Grayling Stewart has an American qualification, but are unable to give you details as the original manuscript of which we purchased the Copyright many years ago was unfortunately destroyed when our premises in Warwick Lane were blitzed during the War'.[79] New publications emerged too. The Hygienic Stores Ltd authored, published and promoted Thomas H. Reynolds's *Birth Control: Its Use and Abuse* and republished Payne's *Private Words to Women* promoting them in the penny weekly press by announcing 'GIVEN AWAY, post free'.[80] *An Open Book on the Mysteries of Sex Life* by Kait's Pharmacies Ltd of Camden Town featured a flapper and a male in a top hat and tails on the front cover as symbols of the modern era.

Surgical stores' publications also increasingly directly imitated birth control manuals. Indeed, C. F. Charles promoted its own version of Sanger's *Family Limitation* in its catalogues, products and other books. Le Brasseur's circulars and book lists included the works of George Ryley Scott (1886–1954), the author of a number of books on sex, contemporary morals and erotica, and those of Dr Helena Wright, a birth control pioneer whose work was integral to the establishment of the National Birth Control Association. Yet, the firm's spelling of Ryley as 'Riley' and Helena as 'Helina' suggests that the publications were imitations and of poor quality.[81] Surgical stores then certainly sought to profit from the promotional opportunities offered by publishing activities, but to unknowing consumers much of the information they offered did not appear that different in form and format to that presented by authorities like Stopes.

The visibility of print and its problems: unsolicited distribution

While Stopes felt threatened by the publishing activities of surgical stores and was concerned about their influence over ignorant women, moral purists and MPs were more concerned about how the uncontrolled and unsolicited distribution of contraceptive advertising in general was providing unmarried, immature adolescents greater exposure to unregulated birth control information. Moralists were concerned about the distribution to adolescents of all forms of print that could be classed as obscene; the supposed innocence of these adolescents was thought to be no match for the corrupting influence of modern commerce. Some ministers, such as Richard Acland, expressed concern that there was little way for ignorant newspaper readers to discern an advertisement for the publications of 'gutter manufacturers' from those of the respectable birth control movement like Stopes. But Parliament continued its policy of non-interference in the availability of birth control information to consenting adults, regardless of the source.[82] Indeed, Edward Shortt, Home Secretary of the post-war Liberal government, made it clear in 1922 during discussions of the potential for legislation to make the dissemination of birth control information and contraceptives illegal that a court would not hold a book to be obscene merely because it included reference to contraceptives.[83] The Contraceptives (Regulation) Bills of 1934 and 1938 focused instead on making it unlawful 'to send or deliver or cause to be sent or delivered for the purpose of any trade or business to any married person who has not attained the age of eighteen years, any circular or advertisements relating to any contraceptive'.[84]

Concerns over the moral corruption of young innocents was not new to the interwar period; it had been a main feature of the public morality movement and its drive for regulation since at least the nineteenth century. The most obvious key victory of the movement was raising the age of consent from 13 to 16 under the Criminal Amendment Act 1885.[85] The practice of sending contraceptive advertising unsolicited through the post was not new either. As we saw in Chapter 2, Stopes had chastised Lamberts for sending its 'Pro-Race' consumers advertisements for its 'Anti-Geniture' pessary, but the practice predated the 1920s and had been enabled by the common practice of announcing births and marriages in newspapers. As early as 1891, Henry Young, a barrister and neo-Malthusian on trial for sending a birth control pamphlet and contraceptive through the post, stated that he only sent circulars to men at addresses given in newspapers when births had been announced.[86] Elderton also reported on this practice in Stockport and Huddersfield, stating that new parents who announced a birth in the newspapers received 'illustrated circulars giving very free and unveiled advice and suggestions about the limitation of the family, with full particulars of a long series of "remedies" assured to be "perfectly harmless"'.[87] Birmingham's chief constable complained in 1908 that 'when a woman has a baby, she is flooded with such stuff' and 'I have had numerous letters concerning this from husbands of all classes in life, both from noblemen and labouring men complaining of this sort of literature being sent to their wives'.[88]

But it was the interwar growth in, and hostility to, the postal distribution of birth control literature that led to renewed emphasis on the dangers of unsolicited mail to innocent adolescents.[89] Firms made it explicit in their catalogues that 'we do not retain customer letters or names and address', 'we do not send out circulars or follow up letters, so shall be glad if you will kindly keep this list by you as you will not hear from us again unless we are favoured with your business' and 'a record of all home orders received is kept for eight days, by which time it is presumed the goods have been received by the customer, letters are then destroyed', but the practice of sending unsolicited advertising clearly continued.[90] 'A Father' complained in *The Times* in 1937 that one of the first communications he received after announcing the birth of his child in the newspaper was a pamphlet about contraceptives. He stated that 'it is unthinkable that the great and wonderful facts of sex and birth, and information concerning them, should thus be tampered with, distorted, and exploited by a pushful commercialism, in which birth control is a fine catchword'.[91]

The extent to which this practice extended beyond this prominent example in *The Times* is difficult to establish, although it is possible that lists of customers kept by surgical stores were similar in number to those kept by an interwar pornographic supplier with a list of seven thousand addresses.[92] But it is clear that the practice continued amid increased postal distribution of greater numbers of advertising and birth control publications. The Post Office began to make concerted efforts to intercept commercial, as well as obscene, material sent through the post. Postal interceptions of indecent material increased from 400 papers in 1928 to 1,700 in 1937 and 2,300 in 1938.[93] The prosecution of Amalgamated Publicity Services Ltd in 1934 for sending out 250,000 circulars for Norman Haire's *Encyclopaedia of Sex Practice* to names selected from directories was a prominent example of this curtailing of commercial advertising of birth control publications.[94] The police continued its surveillance of the publisher after the Second World War.

Parliamentary supporters of the Contraceptives (Regulation) Bill unsurprisingly emphasised the widespread nature of the unsolicited distribution of contraceptive advertising. Amid discussion of the Bill in the House of Lords in 1934, Henry Stafford, the Earl of Iddesleigh, complained that four agents of a London contraceptive firm were hand-delivering leaflets to houses in Ashford, Tonbridge, Rochester and Maidstone in Kent: 'They carried out a house to house visitation, leaving at each place, one of these booklets, regardless of the age of the person to whom the booklet was given'. Stafford also suggested that unmarried and largely sexually ignorant university students were a prime target of this printed advertising, and that reading such material 'would come as a great shock' to them.[95] In similar debates in the House of Commons in 1938, Oliver Simmonds (1897–1985), Conservative MP for Duddeston in Birmingham and introducer of the Bill to the Commons, highlighted the potential moral corruption of adolescents, who responded to newspaper advertisements for contraceptive literature with little knowledge of what they were applying for.[96]

Yet, Dawson's own research for the Bill could only confirm that two surgical stores conducted the practice of unsolicited catalogue distribution, either one of whom may have targeted 'A Father'. One was Hancock of Fleet Street, a chemist, birth control specialist and imitator of Rendell's 'Wife's Friend' soluble quinine pessaries. The firm's circular letter, addressed 'Dear Sir or Madam' and sent with its catalogue, asked 'are you interested in birth control?' before announcing its ability to supply books and contraceptives, cash on delivery. One of Stopes's correspondents had sent her one of Hancock's circulars, to which she replied 'I wish one could do something about it'.

She stated that she had considered her own legal action against Hancock's continual solicitation but had decided against it because 'they would simply love that because it would it give their address to the world, which is what they want'.[97] W. George similarly addressed another circular and catalogue to 'Sir or Madam': 'as you could not fail to see the notice printed on the envelope, I start with the advantage of not having to convince you of the desirability of using contraceptives when necessary. My only task is to convince you that it is impossible to obtain, anywhere, contraceptive goods more thoroughly reliable than those I supply'.[98] Both firms suggested that the receiver of these circulars and catalogues pass on the information to married friends 'to whom the knowledge of a reliable source of birth control methods might be a great favour'. Moreover, in response to Dawson's enquiries, Hugh Linstead, president of the Royal Pharmaceutical Society, the professional body of chemists and pharmacists, defended firms by claiming that they did not deliberately target young people, but the circularisation of printed material may nonetheless mean that it accidentally fell into 'the hands of boys or girls'.[99] Other surgical stores prominently labelled their catalogues 'for adults only'. For example, Le Brasseur's 1925 catalogue stated that 'under no circumstances will goods be supplied to minors'.[100] Such claims are of course difficult to verify and firms' monitoring of the age of its consumers would have been practically impossible. As Dawson discovered, firms were not always honest in print. He complained that Lamberts had included an 'inaccurate reproduction of a letter written by me in 1886' in its catalogues into the 1930s without his consent.[101]

But more importantly, there was no way that legislation could stop unsolicited distribution to the young. Indeed, earlier censorship legislation had already failed to stop the postal trade in birth control books and publicity. Dawson too recognised that there would be great difficulty in proving the age of those receiving advertisements by post. Increasing the age restriction from 18 to 21, as a suggested Bill amendment proposed, would only drive the trade further underground and could result in a rise in illegitimacy rates. With the young marrying and maturing earlier than in previous years, this would mean that married 18-year-olds, as legitimate customers, would not be able to access commercial information and products. Neither did restricting the distribution of advertising help readers discern between legitimate and non-legitimate birth control information. Where, for example, would an ordinary newspaper or magazine that happened to contain a birth control advertisement sit within this Bill? Parliamentary debates over a similar bill, the Medical and Surgical Appliances (Advertisements) Bill in 1936, which aimed to prevent 'some of the worse forms of commercial exploitation practised by fraudulent and unscrupulous persons for their own profit' in the advertising of proprietary medicines, surgical appliances and curative treatment, and proposals to amend the Indecent Advertisements Act in 1908 and 1920 were similarly unresolvable. Indeed, amendments to incorporate contraceptive appliances into the Acts were abandoned. The Contraceptives (Regulation) Bill's abandonment on the eve of the Second World War left this issue unresolved, but, as we will see in Chapter 5, concerns around the corruption of innocent adolescents returned after the war centred not on print, but on slot machines vending condoms.

Unregulated by law, surgical stores continued to distribute in the post-war years their unsolicited catalogues and 'spurious pamphlets'. Some of these publications may have been sent to or fallen into the hands of 'innocent adolescents', although there is no evidence of or complaints regarding this. But the continued veiled and euphemistic discussion of birth control and contraceptives in print and manufacturers' sustained use of their own publishing firms to distribute birth control pamphlets and imitations suggests that wider moral sensitivities were sufficient to regulate the trade. Following the Ministry of Health endorsement of the Family Planning Association and wider discussion of birth control by national media outlets from the mid-1950s (including the BBC), LRC, as Britain's most successful contraceptive manufacturer by the 1950s, was able to promote its *Planned Families* pamphlet (titled 'Secret of a Happy Marriage') under its own publishing company called Planned Families Publications in a wide range of newspapers, journals and magazines, as well as in cinemas and through pharmacies and barbers. Writing to the Association in 1956, Reid stated: 'we find it rather intriguing that, for the first time in the history of this country, advertising regarding contraception is being accepted in publications of a national character', and claimed that the advertising campaign led to thousands of requests for the publication.[102] But Reid presented himself as unaware of the fact that his firm was building on the much older printing and publishing traditions of the contraceptive trade.

Conclusion

Interwar contraceptive advertising – within newspapers, catalogues and imitations of birth control pamphlets – created a confusing and contradictory picture to general consumers and birth control advocates alike. With firms taking advantage of more liberal attitudes towards birth control, the overall increase in contraceptive advertising in newspapers and journals, the growth in distribution of catalogues and 'spurious pamphlets', the shift in language from 'surgical' to 'birth control' appliances and the adoption of a more instructive style of prose in line with increasing numbers of birth control manuals meant that contraceptives were more visible in print than ever before. The growing visibility led to a divide in the contraceptive trade whereby manufacturers attempting to be respectable aligned to a medical profession increasingly regarded as authoritative on birth control, while surgical stores expanded their publishing activities to take greater advantage of general consumers. It was surgical store expansion into publishing and its increasing adoption of the tropes of birth control discourse that most concerned Marie Stopes. Uncontrolled distribution of her works, alongside the works of other self-appointed birth control authorities, and surgical stores' imitations of these works challenged Stopes's authority but also sought to take advantage of consumers unable to distinguish between commercial and non-commercial publications. This increase in visibility and its potential to corrupt the innocent and unmarried adolescent was also a key concern of the architects of the Contraceptives (Regulation) Bill, although evidence of this corruption, particularly through the unsolicited distribution of advertising, was limited. Moreover, Parliament could not find a way for the Bill to break the interwar stalemate between allowing married couples to access printed birth control information while preventing access to the innocent and unmarried adolescent.

Yet, at the same time, much of the content of this new outpouring of contraceptive advertising remained implicit, evasive and euphemistic, limiting its appeal among unknowing consumers. Indeed, such ambiguities partly explained how Stopes incorrectly identified 'Fielding' as an imitator and his publication as a 'spurious' commercial pamphlet. The use of vague and euphemistic language continued into the 1950s, even with the Family Planning Association's wider legitimisation. At a time when birth control knowledge was not yet established and access to it in print form remained uncontrolled, both authors of birth control books and commercial firms could be seen as legitimate authorities.

Notes

1. W. Leiss, S. Kline and S. Jhally, *Social Communication in Advertising: Persons, Products, and Images of Well-Being* (New York: Methuen Publications, 1986), p. 42.
2. The most relevant censorship laws included the Vagrancy Act (1824), the Obscene Publications Act (1857) and, with it, the 1868 Hicklin standard, which established a definition for obscenity based on an object's ability to 'deprave and corrupt those whose minds are open to such immoral influences'; the Post Office (Protection) Act (1884), which made it illegal to send obscene and indecent articles through the mail; and the Indecent Advertisements Act (1889). On the effect of this legislation on print on sexual matters, see, for example, S. Bull, 'Managing the "Obscene M.D.": medical publishing, the medical profession, and the changing definition of obscenity in mid-Victorian England', *Bulletin of the History of Medicine*, 91:4 (2017), 713–43; H. G. Cocks, 'Saucy stories: pornography, sexology and the marketing of sexual knowledge in Britain, c.1918–70', *Social History*, 29:4 (2004), 465–84; F. Mort, *Dangerous Sexualities: Medico-Moral Politics in England since 1830* (London: Routledge and Kegan Paul, 1987); Sigel, *Making Modern Love*, p. 21.
3. For a wider discussion on reading and historians' use of reader-response analysis, see Rose, *The Intellectual Life of the British Working Classes*; McKibbin, *Classes and Cultures*, p. 477; R. Hoggart, *Uses of Literacy: Aspects of Working-Class Life with Special and Entertainments* (Harmondsworth: Penguin, 1957).
4. Porter and Hall, *The Facts of Life*, pp. 255–6; Sigel, *Making Modern Love*, p. 35. M-O, A9 Sex Survey 1947–9, 3/C 'report on sex: chapter 2: Discovering Sex'; Mass-Observation, *The Press and Its Readers* (London: Art and Technology, 1949).
5. Elderton's reference to the 'usual' newspaper advertisements in Bingley, St Anne's-on-Sea, Padiham, Tottingham, Clitheroe and Wilmslow and their influence on readers to order such goods suggests her own familiarity with these advertisements, if not those of her respondents, *Report on the English Birth-Rate*, pp. 32, 38, 40, 43, 76, 104. Newspapers including contraceptive advertisements included *Barking, East Ham and Ilford Advertiser*; *Cambrian News*; *Cambridge Daily News*;

Brighton Gazette, Lincoln Gazette, Aberdeen Press and Journal, and the *Cornish Telegraph*.

6 For example, 'GIVEN AWAY. WORDS OF WISDOM FOR OUR WIVES. Being a new treatise of advice and information for the married. It is fully illustrated and contains the population question and other information worth HUNDREDS OF POUNDS. Send at once and you will never regret doing so. Post free. 32 pages. Illustrated lists of rubber appliances, preventives, etc. P. George, 10 Holywell St, Strand, London', *Preston Herald* (23 August 1899); *Derbyshire Courier* (19 March 1898); *Wharfedale and Airedale Observer* (7 January 1898). The *Preston Herald* was a successful bi-weekly paper of Anglican, and often anti-Catholic, persuasion sold across town, including in the poorest areas. See A. Hobbs, *A Fleet Street in Every Town: The Provincial Press in England, 1855–1900* (Cambridge: Open Book Publishers, 2018).

7 For example, Constantine and Jackson announced: 'Just published, Constantine and Jackson's New Illustrated and Descriptive Price List of Malthusian and other rubber domestic and surgical appliance', *Illustrated Police News* (21 November 1896). While no copy seemingly exists, Lamberts advertisement for its first catalogue appeared in the October 1888 edition of *The Malthusian*, p. 79: 'EVERY MARRIED COUPLE should send for our *Illustrated List*, post free, in receipt of stamped envelope'.

8 For example, the Hygienic Stores Ltd, *Revised Catalogue of High-Class Rubber, Medical, Surgical Goods and Domestic Appliances* (London: 1928).

9 The firm made this claim in every catalogue it published from 1900. For example, E. Lambert and Son, *Special List of Domestic and Surgical Specialities* (n.p., 1900), p. 5. For the wider expansion of mail order in Britain, see R. Coopey, S. O'Connor and D. Porter, *Mail Order Retailing in Britain: A Business and Social History* (Oxford: Oxford University Press, 2005). For the mail-order trade in medical and surgical instruments, see C. L. Jones, *The Medical Trade Catalogue in Britain, 1880–1914* (London: Pickering and Chatto, 2013).

10 Cook, *The Long Sexual Revolution*, pp. 60–1.

11 C. J. Welton's *Marriage and Its Mysteries, Being an Enquiry into the Great Social Evil of Overpopulation*, first published in 1900, contained sixteen pages of advertising, while Holmes's *True Morality*, first published in 1890, contained ten pages.

12 Lambert, [*Catalogue*] (1897), pp. 89–103.

13 Bull, 'Managing the "Obscene M.D."', 719.

14 S. Jones, *The Illustrated Police News: London's Court Cases and Sensational Stories* (Nottingham: Wicked Publications, 2002), p. 1.

15 See also L. Z. Sigel, 'Censorship in inter-war Britain: obscenity, spectacle, and the workings of the liberal state', *Journal of Social History*, 45:1 (2011), 73; Sigel, *Making Modern Love*, p. 24.
16 Old Bailey Proceedings Online, 'October 1906, trial of MARNEY, Edward de (journalist) (t19061022-58)', www.oldbaileyonline.org/browse.jsp?id=t19061022-58&div=t19061022-58&terms=de_marney#highlight [accessed 20 July 2019]. See also, Cocks, 'Saucy stories', 468, 476.
17 McLaren, *Birth Control*, p. 229 n. 27.
18 Indeed, in the 1920s the circulation of the provincial morning and evening papers alone, without weekly papers, was still one-third greater than the London dailies. Hobbs, *A Fleet Street in Every Town*, pp. 4–5; R. Matthews, *The History of the Provincial Press in England* (London: Bloomsbury, 2017), p. 86.
19 L. Brake and M. Demoor, *Dictionary of Nineteenth-Century Journalism in Great Britain and Ireland* (Ghent: Academia Press, 2009), pp. 817, 1674.
20 Cocks, 'Saucy stories', 476.
21 Bingham, *Family Newspapers?*, pp. 11, 23.
22 For example, an article by Gerald Gould (1885–1936) in 1916 reviewing Adelyne More's *Fecundity versus Civilisation* argued that there was 'no doubt about the urgent social necessity for extending the use of contraceptives'. 'Adelyne More' was a pseudonym of Charles Kay Ogden, linguist, philosopher and writer. Gould used his review of Ogden's book to encourage readers to adopt neo-Malthusian perspectives and argued, 'I wish some of the bland and wealthy and celibate ecclesiastics who preach the virtue of large families could be made to read "Maternity", that heart-searching collection of letters from working-class mothers'. G. Gould, 'Fecundity versus Civilisation', *Daily Herald* (18 November 1916), p. 15; (2 December 1916), pp. 26–7. Brake and Demoor, *Dictionary of Nineteenth-Century Journalism*, p. 423; Himes, *Medical History of Contraception*, p. 326.
23 Bingham, *Family Newspapers?*, p. 57; Soloway, *Birth Control*, p. 191.
24 A. Leathard, *The Fight for Family Planning* (London: Palgrave Macmillan, 1980), pp. 13, 15; A. C. T. Geppert, 'Divine sex, happy marriage, regenerated nation: Marie Stopes's marital manual Married Love and the making of a best-seller, 1918–1955', *Journal of the History of Sexuality*, 8:3 (1998), 420.
25 A. Bingham, 'The British popular press and venereal disease during the Second World War', *Historical Journal*, 48:4 (2005), 1059.
26 Porter and Hall, *The Facts of Life*, p. 238; M. Ferguson, *Forever Feminine: Women's Magazines and the Cult of Femininity* (Aldershot: Gower, 1983); P. Tinkler, *Constructing Girlhood: Popular Magazines*

for Girls Growing up in England, 1920–1950 (London: Taylor and Francis, 1995), pp. 162–3.

27 Rendell's advertisements appeared in over twenty nursing and women's journals and general health magazines including *Nursing Mirror*; *Nursing World*; *Parents*; *Health and Beauty*; *Weldon's Home Dressmaker*; *Home Fashions*; *Woman and Home*; *Woman's Magazine*; *Woman's World*; *The Queen*; *New Knitting*; *Ballet*; *Dorette Designs*; *Householders*; and *Home Review*. The firm kept cut-outs. Rendell (uncatalogued papers), [Advertisement folder].

28 For example, *Nursing Mirror* (1 November 1947); (15 November 1947); (13 December 1947); *Householder* (December 1947). For similar forms of advertising in interwar North America, see A. Sarch, 'Those dirty ads! Birth control advertising in the 1920s and 1930s', *Critical Studies in Mass Communication*, 14:1 (1997), 31–48.

29 WL, SA/FPA/A7/100, letter by Prentif to advertising manager, *Illustrated London News* and *Sketch*, 12 October 1937; letter by *Illustrated London News* to Prentif, 18 October 1937; letter by Prentif to *Illustrated London News*, 21 October 1937; letter by the Amalgamated Press to Prentif, 19 November 1937.

30 Jütte, *Contraception*, pp. 117–34.

31 For lending libraries, see Porter and Hall, *The Facts of Life*, p. 259; 'Medico-Legal', *British Medical Journal*, 2 (1934), p. 95. Readers could borrow works by Norman Haire, Stopes and Rennie MacAndrew alongside cheap and popular romantic fiction.

32 Hall, *Sex, Gender and Social Change*, pp. 96–7.

33 Solidol Chemical Ltd., *Woman's Guide to Intimate Hygiene* (London: Solidol, 1930).

34 For example, Walton Rubber Goods Co., *Revised Price List of Rubber Goods and Contraceptive Appliances* (1937), pp. 11–16; S. Seymour, *Catalogue* (c.1935), p. 3; Hancock, *Shadow of the Stork*, pp. 9–12; London Rubber Company, *Price List*, pp. 4–5.

35 Cook, *The Long Sexual Revolution*, pp. 341–6; Cook, 'Sex and the doctors', p. 193.

36 Geppert, 'Divine sex', 402.

37 Lamberts Prorace Ltd, *Revised Price List* (1933), pp. 13, 20, 23, 26; *Revised List of Up-to-Date Contraceptive Appliances* (1941), p. 13.

38 Walton, *Revised Price List*, pp. 2, 4.

39 Kait Pharmacies Ltd, *An Open Book on the Mysteries of the Sex Life* (London: Kait Pharmacies, 1934), pp. 12–14.

40 Cocks, 'Saucy stories', 472.

41 Hall, *Sex, Gender and Social Change*, p. 92.

42 'Medico-Legal', *BMJ*, 95.

43 BL, Add. MS 58638, letter by Stopes to Lambert, 10 April 1922;

letter by Lambert to Stopes, 24 April 1922; 27 April 1922; 11 July 1923; 'Surgical appliances of all kinds', *Chemist and Druggist* (22 April 1922), p. xxviii.
44   Prentif, *Contraceptive Practice*, 2 (1938); WL SA/FPA/A7/99, letter by Prentif to Pyke, 22 February 1936.
45   Himes, *Medical History of Contraception*, p. 327.
46   Bona fide books that contained this warning included I. Bloch, *The Sexual Life of Our Time, in Its Relations to Modern Civilisations* (London: Rebman, 1909), p. v, and G. Ryley Scott, *Scott's Encyclopaedia of Sex* (London: T. Warner Laurie Ltd, 1939), p. vi.
47   Seymour, *Catalogue*, pp. 34–6.
48   Le Brasseur, *Revised List of Surgical Rubber Specialties* (1931), pp. 35–8; *Sporting Times* (21 March 1925).
49   Himes, *Medical History of Contraception*, p. 326; WL, SA/FPA/A7/100, letter by Prentif to advertising manager, *Illustrated London News* and *Sketch*, 12 October 1937; letter by *Illustrated London News* to Prentif, 18 October 1937; letter by Prentif to *Illustrated London News*, 21 October 1937; the Amalgamated Press to Prentif, 19 November 1937.
50   Geppert, 'Divine sex', 415.
51   L. A. Hall, *Hidden Anxieties: Male Sexuality, 1900–1950* (Boston, MA: Polity Press, 1991), p. 67.
52   BL, Add. MS 58638, letter by Lambert to Stopes, 2 February 1926.
53   Himes, *Medical History of Contraception*, p. 326; WL, SA/FPA/A13/46, Marie Stopes Memorial Trust and Clinic, 1936–1966, Birth control advertisement; *Sporting Times* (21 February 1925), p. 7; (15 August 1925), p. 1; (7 November 1925), p. 10. See also, P. Fryer, *British Birth Control Ephemera, 1870–1947* (London: The Barracuda Press, 1969), pp. 18, 24, 25.
54   St Clair Maurice, *Advice to Married Women* (London: The Medical and Surgical Supply Co., 1938), p. 1.
55   B. Goodman, *My Views on Birth Control* (London: The London Manufacturing Co., 1948).
56   St Clair Maurice, *Advice to Married Women* (1938), p. 14.
57   S. Warren, *The Wife's Guide and Friend* (London: A. Lambert, 1904); Fryer, *British Birth Control Ephemera*, p. 34.
58   O. Mann, *Birth Control (The Husband and Wife's Handbook)* (London: The Hygienic Stores, 1926); D. R. Payne, *Private Words to Women* (London: The Hygienic Stores, 1934); Fryer, *British Birth Control Ephemera*, pp. 24, 26.
59   O. Mann, *Birth Control* (1926, 1927), pp. 5–6.
60   O. Mann, *Birth Control* (1926, 1927), p. 8.
61   The Hygienic Stores Ltd, *The Popular Herbal Family Medical Guide*

and Husband's and Wife's Handbook (London: The Hygienic Stores, [between 1910 and 1919?]).
62 Graham, M., *A Common-Sense Treatise on Birth Control* (London: Bale, 1926). See also Himes, *Medical History of Contraception*, p. 326.
63 BL, Add. MS 58640, 1, letter by Medical Trading Co. to Stopes, 24 September 1923; 97, 15 October 1930; Neushul, 'Marie C. Stopes', 260.
64 BL, Add. MS 58640, 11, letter by Medical Trading Co. to Stopes, 13 December 1923; 14, 17 December 1923; 97, 15 October 1930.
65 Bingham, *Family Newspapers?*, p. 31.
66 BL, Add. MS 58640, 42, letter by Medical Trading Co to Stopes, 5 November 1925; 49, 17, November 1925; 51, letter by Stopes to Medical Trading Co., 18 November 1925.
67 M. Fielding, *Parenthood: Design or Accident? A Manual of Birth Control* (1934; London: Noel Douglas, 1928); Cook, *The Long Sexual Revolution*, p. 122.
68 BL, Add. MS 58639, letter by Lambert to Stopes, 22 March 1928; letter by Stopes to Lambert, 8 July 1929; letter by Lambert to Stopes, 16 July 1929; letter by Stopes to Lambert, 18 July 1928; 2 December 1929.
69 BL, Add. MS 58639, letter by Lambert to Stopes, 3 December 1929; letter by Lambert to Mrs B., Chadwell Heath, 25 April 1934; Lamberts Prorace Ltd, *Revised Price List* (1933), back cover; *Revised List of Up-to-Date Contraceptive Appliances* (1941), back cover.
70 Fielding, *Parenthood*, p. 11.
71 BL, Add. MS 58639, letter by Stopes to Lambert, 15 January 1935.
72 BL, Add. MS 58639, letter by Lambert to Stopes, 22 March 1928.
73 BL, Add. MS 58639, letter by Stopes to Lambert, 18 July 1929.
74 Fielding, *Parenthood*, p. 1.
75 BL, Add. MS 58640, 33, letter by Medical Trading Company to Stopes, 27 March 1925.
76 BL, Add. MS 58640, 32, letter by G. A. Roberts to Stopes, 27 March 1925.
77 BL, Add. MS 58639, letter by Lambert to Stopes, 6 August 1930.
78 D. Neale, *Guide for Husbands and Wives or A Manual of Wisdom* (Birmingham: Le Brasseur, 1937); B. Goodman, *My Views on Birth Control* (London: The Medical Publishing Company, 1937); G. Stewart, *Wedlock and Birth Control: A Straightforward Talk on a Momentous and Delicate Subject* (London: The London Medical Manufacturing Company, 1948). Porter and Hall, *The Facts of Life*, p. 263. M-O, A9 16/A, Topic Collection, 'Advertising and Publications: Published Material on Sex'. 12 16/A, Topic Collection, 'Contraceptives and surgical products'.

79 M-O, 12 16/B, Topic Collection, 'Publications on Sex', the London Medical Manufacturing Co. Ltd to Mrs V., Westbourne Grove, 4 August 1949.
80 T. H. Reynolds, *Birth Control: Its Use and Abuse* (London: The Hygienic Stores, 1933); Payne, *Private Words to Women: Containing Wisdom for Wives* (1937); Mann, *Birth Control (Husband and Wife's Handbook)* (London: The Hygienic Stores, 1938); *Illustrated Police News* (13 November 1930); (14 November 1935); (3 March 1938). Fryer, *British Birth Control Ephemera*, pp. 24, 26, 31.
81 M-O, 12 16/B.
82 Hansard, 'Contraceptives (Regulation) Bill', HC vol. 342, cols. 2429–33, 2435–8 (16 December 1938).
83 Latham, *Regulating Reproduction*, p. 25.
84 Contraceptives Bill, no. 110, clause d.; Contraceptives (Regulation) Bill, no. 115, clause c.
85 The literature on public morality movements is extensive. See, for example, Bristow, *Vice and Vigilance*; N. A. Drehler, 'The virtuous and the verminous: turn-of-the-century moral panics in London's public parks', *Albion*, 29:2 (1997), 246–67; Soloway, *Birth Control*, p. 54; J. R. Walkowitz, *City of Dreadful Delight: Narratives of Sexual Danger in Late-Victorian London* (Chicago: Chicago University Press, 1992).
86 Hall, *Sex, Gender and Social Change*, p. 44.
87 Elderton, *Report on the English Birth-Rate*, pp. 79, 105.
88 National Archives, London (hereafter NA), HO45/10932/157111, letter by Chief Constable, Birmingham to Home Office, 13 September 1907.
89 Porter and Hall, *The Facts of Life*, p. 258.
90 Seymour, *Catalogue*, p. 2; Le Brasseur, *Revised List of Medical Goods 1925: Catalogue 'C'* (1925), frontispiece; Lamberts Prorace Ltd, *Revised Price List* (1936), p. 2.
91 'A Father', *The Times* (21 September 1937), p. 10.
92 Cocks, 'Saucy stories', 477.
93 NA HO45/24761, Obscene publications, 1939; WL SA/FPA/A14/91.1. Stopes, 'A mistake about birth control', *Leeds Mercury* (28 January 1932).
94 Cocks, 'Saucy stories', 480; H. G. Cocks, '"The social picture of our own times": reading obscene magazines in mid-twentieth-century Britain', *Twentieth Century British History*, 27:2 (2016), 183; Cook, *The Long Sexual Revolution*, p. 342; 'Medico-Legal', *BMJ*, 95.
95 WL, PP/BED/B.2, letter by Tyrer to Dawson, 4 December 1933; LMA, A/PMC/067; Hansard, 'Contraceptives Bill', HL vol. 90, cols. 963–4 (27 February 1934).

96 Hansard, 'Contraceptives (Regulation) Bill', HC vol. 342, col. 2423 (16 December 1938).
97 WL, PP/MCS/A.6, letter by Stopes to Mrs A, 15 July 1938; WL, PP/BED/B.2, letter by Linstead to Dawson, 7 April 1933.
98 WL, PP/BED/B.2, misc. papers.
99 WL, PP/BED/B.2, letter by Linstead to Dawson, 26 June 1933.
100 Le Brasseur, *Revised List of Medical Goods 1925*, p. 1; Seymour, *Catalogue*, p. 2.
101 WL, PP/BED/B.2, [Scribbled note], Dawson, n.d.
102 WL, SA/FPA/A7/75, letter by Reid to Clifford Smith, 29 June 1956.

4

'As honest as business permits': medical practitioners, birth control clinics and contraceptive efficacy

Following the passing of Dawson's Contraceptives (Regulation) Bill in the House of Lords in 1934, Dr Edward F. Griffith (1895–1987), member of the medical committee of the National Birth Control Association and medical officer at the Aldershot birth control clinic, wrote a statement to help medical practitioners navigate the contraceptive market. As the Association medical committee's proposed response to the Bill, Griffith's statement aimed to provide practitioners with guidance on the many contraceptive brands available from chemists, 'rubber shops', garages and slot machines and enable them to distinguish between those that were reliable and those that were not. It was often quite impossible, Griffith argued, 'for the medical practitioner to decide on the relative merits of these different articles, unless he has considerable knowledge of contraceptive technique, and it is even more impossible for the ordinary member of the public to make any satisfactory decision whatsoever'. While stating that it was not the function of the committee to determine whether legislation was the most appropriate way to remedy the 'most unsatisfactory' state of the market, Griffith was explicit about the fact that 'some authoritative action is necessary'. To Griffith, 'authoritative action' meant that medical practitioners needed to be more proactive in seeking out education and training in contraceptive technique, so they could replace businesses in dominating contraceptive supply. In the absence of any formal medical education in birth control, such education and training could only be obtained at the growing number of clinics operating under the National Birth Control Association.[1]

Although seemingly never published or circulated beyond the committee, Griffith's statement encapsulates how the National Birth Control Association (and the Family Planning Association, as it became from 1939), and the increasing numbers of medical practitioners interested in birth control, sought to incorporate birth control into the profession by the mid-1930s and in so doing, how they sought to dominate the contraceptive market. The medicalisation of birth control had been the aim of some individuals since at least the late nineteenth century, but it was only from the interwar period that medical practitioners and nurses were more openly able to disseminate birth control information and contraceptives through face to face consultation.[2] While most medical practitioners in the early 1920s were far from convinced that birth control was within the realm of their expertise, Dawson stated to Stopes that 'knowledge as to the applications of birth control should be conveyed by doctors to their patients'.[3] With the amalgamation of all five clinic-running organisations under the National Birth Control Council (which became the National Birth Control Association) and implementation of the Ministry of Health's sanction 153/MCW in 1930, medical provision of contraceptive advice to women whose health would be at risk from pregnancy expanded to local authority mother and infant welfare clinics, where married women who typically already had children could access contraceptives to prevent further pregnancies.[4] Nurses, medical practitioners and other clinic workers increasingly became seen as gatekeepers of birth control knowledge and as important intermediary distributors of contraceptives between suppliers and consumers. For contraceptive manufacturers, it was of course highly beneficial to supply medical practitioners, nurses and clinics, not only because of the increased profit provided by sales but also because the medicalisation of contraception transformed contraceptives into respectable commodities.

As this chapter will outline, the growth of birth control clinics and attempts at birth control medicalisation in the interwar period and post-Second World War disrupted the contraceptive marketplace. This disruption was most obvious in the mid-1930s as contraceptive commercialisation was being publicly challenged by the Contraceptives (Regulation) Bill, but also as the introduction of new standards of contraceptive testing sought to shift the burden of proof of reliability and efficacy from the clinic to the laboratory. Yet, while such changes disrupted supply, they did not succeed in replacing older products and their suppliers with those that were 'scientifically' sanctioned. Indeed, this replacement did not take place until well into the 1950s, and even then it was only partially successful. Despite Griffith's and the wider profession's aim, the claims of medical science over what was and was not an effective and reliable contraceptive did not quickly replace preferences among individual clinicians for contraceptives produced by certain firms. These individual preferences were not only based on practitioner education and training but also on important commercial elements, such as company reputation and brand goodwill that had built up over the proceeding decades. The relationship between practitioners, clinics and companies then was key and had a profound and long-lasting effect on the continued reliance on certain firms and their products.

Manufacturers' necessary involvement in clinic supply and clinics' concomitant reliance on their contraceptives, both new and old, also demonstrates a wider point relevant to histories of birth control clinics and the medical profession. Not only were manufacturers an integral but hitherto neglected part of the philanthropic birth control clinic movement, but clinics were sites of commerce. Established by and with support from prominent medical authorities, clinics set themselves apart from the marketplace; but their continual reliance on trade knowledge, as well as materials and technologies, meant that clinics and commerce were never separate. Commerce was embedded in the very running of the clinic through the financial transactions between clinicians, companies and clients that took place in the buying and selling of contraceptives. Indeed, a key purpose of clinics was that they distributed contraceptives to married women more cheaply than chemists' shops. Outwardly, the birth control movement downplayed its marketplace connection in its efforts to portray itself as commercially disinterested, an image that historians (with a few recent exceptions) have subsequently accepted without question.[5] But, as we will see in this chapter, clinicians and medical practitioners worked together to develop, test and disseminate contraceptives through this medicalised distribution method, blurring the boundaries between charity, medicine and commerce. As Holz has argued in her study of interwar birth control clinics in America, because the clinic sought at the 'most fundamental level to make available what were undeniably commercial products, it could never quite break free from this marketplace connection'.[6] In what follows then, we will see that chronological continuities in clinic contraceptive supply were just as important as changes.

Caps, clinics and companies

Before the National Birth Control Association's introduction of contraceptive testing in the mid-1930s, clinics, medical practitioners and the birth control movement relied on contraceptive manufacturers with good reputations to supply reliable products. Amid the many surgical store imitators, wholesalers and contraceptive entrepreneurs, it was primarily Lamberts and its long-standing reputation for manufacturing the most reliable rubber and chemical contraceptives available that led to its domination of clinic supply from the early 1920s. As we saw in Chapter 1, the firm's successful supply of all sixty-five birth control clinics across the country by the outbreak of the Second World War meant that it maintained its sheet rubber production, rather than transform itself into a manufacturer of latex goods. While Lamberts supplied the first clinics with a variety of its contraceptives, the prevailing belief in the female barrier method meant that the products it most commonly supplied were split into two main lines: the cervical cap in combination with an oil-based chemical pessary, pioneered by Marie Stopes and fitted by nurses qualified and trained at her clinics for Constructive Birth Control and Racial Progress, and the Dutch cap (or diaphragm) with a spermicidal jelly followed by douching, pioneered by Norman Haire, a physician and first medical officer of the Malthusian League's Women's Welfare Centre in Walworth from 1921. Other methods and contraceptives were recommended if for any reason women could not or would not use these barrier methods. Lamberts' reputation meant that it not only dominated clinic supply with products associated with these methods but also worked with clinicians to improve existing contraceptive designs.

Working with Lamberts to supply clinics in the 1920s seemed to Stopes and Haire to be the most effective and efficient way to supply safe and reliable contraceptives to women. But Stopes and Haire differed in how they presented their relationship with the firm. As we have seen in Chapter 2, Stopes's relationship with Lamberts was tense and inconsistent. While claiming to want no commercial involvement, Stopes instructed the firm to develop the 'Pro-Race' cervical cap, its quinine pessaries, as well as the 'Racial' cap and 'Chinosol' pessaries under the Constructive Birth Control name, and sold these products to mainly middle-class patients via clinics.[7] Her relationship with the firm was largely cemented through its ability to defend the 'Pro-Race' from imitation by disreputable surgical stores and extended even further into clinic supply, as we will see. Yet Haire risked his professional reputation by working with Lamberts. Convinced that women users of the cervical cap of the Stopes variety were inadequately protected from pregnancy and that only qualified medical practitioners should advise women in birth control methods, Haire requested that Lamberts make for him a Dutch cap and a spermicidal jelly according to his design and specifications. Accordingly, the 'Lam-butt' Dutch cap and 'Contraceptalene' spermicidal jelly became Haire's preferred method.[8]

While Henry Allbutt's relationship with Rendell and his more general promotion of contraceptive goods had led to his expulsion from the medical profession in the 1880s, Haire was similarly required to justify his 1922 revision of the Malthusian League's publication *Hygienic Methods of Family Limitation* to the General Medical Council.[9] Within this revision, Haire recommended Lamberts' products, stating that the firm would only supply 'bona fide hygienic devices for preventing conception'.[10] Ten thousand copies of the pamphlet circulated by 1927.[11] In his letter to the council, Haire stated that he had 'always respected the authority of the General Medical Council and endeavoured to conform to its regulations', even when this prevented him from involvement in activities that he felt were vitally important for the welfare of patients. The letter was seemingly enough to appease the council. Indeed, unlike Stopes, Haire had kept his name out of the press and had only permitted Lamberts to refer to his medical status in its promotion of the Dutch cap and 'Contraceptalene' providing his name was not mentioned. Accordingly, Lamberts' 1933 catalogue stated that 'Contraceptalene' was made 'according to a formula by a well-known Harley Street doctor'.[12] Haire thus fitted the 'Lam-butt' Dutch cap with 'Contraceptalene' at the Walworth clinic. Unlike Stopes's clinic, the Walworth clinic charged for all consultations (a shilling), but sold the Dutch cap for 2s 6d, a much lower price than the 7s 6d it would cost to buy from a retailer.[13]

After leaving the Walworth clinic and parting ways with the Malthusian League in 1923, Haire continued to supply Lamberts' contraceptives from his rented private practice in Harley Street, and from October 1927 from his clinic, Cromer Welfare and Sunlight Centre at King's Cross, which was attended primarily by mothers looking for a more reliable contraceptive. Haire also introduced Norman Himes to Edward W. Lambert after Himes enquired about the firm's contraceptive supply.[14] In a 1934 lecture to medical students, Haire highlighted that the 'Lam-butt' Dutch cap was the 'most satisfactory method', while demonstrating that the 'Lam-butt Quinine Pessaries' and Lamberts' 'Pro-Race' supplied to Stopes's clinics failed in 70 and 86 per cent of cases, respectively, statistics that invoked Stopes's wrath.[15] Haire continued to refer to the quality of Lamberts' contraceptives within *Birth Control Methods*, his 1936 book, along with LRC's condoms and Rendell's pessaries, by which time the General Medical Council was no longer concerned about practitioners' involvement in birth control.

As more voluntary clinics opened throughout the 1920s and as increasing numbers of medical practitioners began to prescribe and fit female barrier contraceptives, Lamberts' supply grew. Most doctors followed Haire's lead and, preferring the diaphragm-jelly method, ordered and prescribed 'Lam-butt' Dutch caps, 'Contraceptalene' and its whirling sprays and syringes in order to wash out a patient a week after fitting. Clinics that followed this method included those established by the Society for the Provision of Birth Control clinics in Wolverhampton, Cambridge, Manchester and Salford, Glasgow, East London, Oxford and Birmingham, Rotherham, Liverpool and Newcastle-upon-Tyne. Dr Alice Robson, medical officer at the Cambridge clinic, stated that 'we were all brought up on the Walworth methods', while Dr Winter of Wolverhampton stated that 'we do the same as the Walworth clinic'.[16] Non-Society clinics that also followed this method included the one established in Crouch End, North London, by Nurse Elizabeth Daniels, following her dismissal from Edmonton District Council for providing contraceptive advice in 1922. Eric Pritchard, medical director of the Infant's Hospital, Westminster, also became convinced that the Dutch cap was the best, safest and most reliable, while Anne Louise McIlroy's fitting of these caps in the out-patients clinic of the Royal Free Hospital famously invoked the wrath of Stopes after McIlroy testified against Stopes in the Halliday Sutherland trial.[17] During the trial, McIlroy had suggested that caps were harmful, but thereafter reluctantly began to accept that the growing uptake of contraception meant that it was necessary for the medical profession to bring it under its control, and had started fitting women with caps.

In contrast, Constructive Birth Control clinics beyond London, including those in Aberdeen, Leeds, Belfast and Cardiff, of course followed Stopes's method of prescribing Lamberts' 'Pro-Race' or 'Racial' caps with its quinine or Chinosol pessaries. Other clinicians with a close relationship to Stopes or who had relied on her advice followed her methods too. Dr Jane Hawthorne, who had a practice at 150 Harley Street and attended Stopes's the Mothers' Clinic on a Friday to deal with any abnormal cases detected by the midwife nurses, adopted Stopes's method.[18] Victor Roberts too had turned to Stopes for contraceptive advice before establishing a clinic at Abertillery District Hospital in Wales in 1924. Stopes recommended Chinosol pessaries to Roberts because, at 6d per packet, they would be affordable to very poor women.[19] Before establishing her own clinic, also in 1924, Nurse Rosina Thompson had fitted and prescribed Lamberts' caps and pessaries at Stopes's clinic, where she had worked for a year, and took her training and the methods and supplies she used with her. Stopes found Thompson disloyal for establishing her own clinic a year after joining the Mothers' Clinic, but acknowledged to Lamberts that she had 'no right to object' to the firm supplying her and, in fact, 'probably the advice she gives will be quite useful to the poor people'.[20]

The emulation of the contraceptive methods and technologies of either Haire and Stopes among medical practitioners and nurses grew as clinics became central sites of contraceptive education as well as distribution. Stopes and Haire opened their clinics for general training in 1925 and 1927, respectively. At Stopes's clinic, extra contraceptive supplies were required to train midwives qualified with the Central Midwife Board in physical examinations and fittings during four weeks' practical clinic experience. From 1931 this opportunity was also opened to doctors, although again it is unclear how many attended this training. A 'very large number' of Guy's medical students were seemingly keen to attend as early as 1923, although Stopes warned them of the crowded conditions of the clinic.[21] Written and oral examinations tested candidates on the anatomy and physiology of the female reproductive tract, contraceptive methods and conditions which required special consideration when fitting and on their preference for various types of cap.[22] The correct answer for cap preference was, of course, Lamberts' 'Pro-Race' or the increasingly popular 'Racial'. Medical practitioners also began to study Haire's work and undertook practical training at his clinic for a small fee. Their practical training and early clinical experience with Lamberts' products meant that medical professionals continued to use and recommend these products to patients in their private practices and subsequent hospital and clinic positions, and thus provided Lamberts with more custom.

Stopes did not always approve of the clinics Lamberts supplied. Indeed, she considered several clinics it supplied to be thoroughly disreputable. Again, revealing her anti-Semitism and political conservatism, she complained to Lamberts about its supply of two London-based clinics established by Rose Witcop (originally Rachel Vitkopski), a Jewish Russian anarchist, libertarian communist and founding member of the Workers' Birth Control Group. Famed for her arrest for publishing and distributing Sanger's *Family Limitation* with Guy Aldred, Witcop established the Parents' Clinic for Discretionary Birth Control and Social Welfare in 1924 at Plashet Lane, a poor street in the working-class district of East Ham, and the People's Clinic for Birth Control and Social Welfare in Fulham in 1925. There was clear animosity between Witcop and Stopes. Witcop's connection to the Workers' Birth Control Group was discreet, and as a lobbying group fronted by respectable married women agitating for the provision of contraceptive advice in local authority maternal welfare clinics, the group aimed to distance itself from Stopes's Society for Constructive Birth Control and Racial Progress and its connections to eugenics. Stopes viewed the nurses of Witcop's clinic as incompetent and Witcop's running of the clinic on overtly commercial, rather than charitable, grounds as scandalous. The women attending the Plashet Lane clinic, many of whom only existed on an income of 27s a week to support often large families, were charged 5s, plus the cost of the appliances fitted. Stopes also noted that at least three women who had visited the clinic had become pregnant following a nurse's poor fitting of a 'Pro-Race' cap; another nurse had even tried to fit a cap on a pregnant woman. Stopes also accused Witcop of producing and distributing a pamphlet that was 'a badly distorted crib' of her own work. Stopes thus warned Lamberts that 'it would be very advisable in the interests of the movement that she should not be able to get her caps from you … I think it would be much better and probably safer for you to cease to supply her.'[23] Witcop sold the Plashet Lane clinic in 1925, a year after it had opened, and in 1928 the Fulham clinic moved to Shepherd's Bush, where Lamberts continued to supply it; Witcop ran this clinic until her death in 1932.²⁴ Suspicious of another clinic that had opened in Notting Hill Gate in the late 1920s, Stopes found that a Mr Carpenter, the clinic proprietor, was willing to supply pills that appeared to be abortifacients. Stopes handed pills she had purchased from Carpenter to the police, who then charged Carpenter with fifteen offences including the supply of noxious substances.²⁵ Stopes informed Lamberts that the police had found a note of Carpenter's payments to Mr Watkins of the firm for rubber goods, but because the firm had done nothing but supply him, Stopes promised to keep the firm out of the court case.²⁶

While it is clear that Lamberts dominated clinic supply, the number of products distributed to patients from each clinic, or even from all clinics, is difficult to determine, not least because attendance, contraceptive fitting and follow-up cases were not methodically recorded; figures that were recorded were often exaggerated to present a narrative of success.²⁷ As historians have long suggested, clinics were only attended by a very small proportion of the population, particularly in the early years of the clinic movement, and thus the distribution of contraceptive goods was also likely to have been small. Most people limiting their families were doing so without any assistance from either clinics or doctors. Clinic supply was almost certainly smaller than distribution via the retail sector, a figure that itself was small in any case. As Chapter 1 outlined, Lamberts was selling at least 250,000 condoms annually by the 1890s. Clinics struggled to attract patients, not solely because of the cost of a consultation or contraceptive, but also amid widespread sexual ignorance and embarrassment. Indeed, during its first year of operation, only an average of three women a day visited Stopes's clinic, while *The Malthusian's* claim that 150 women were instructed in contraceptive techniques at the Walworth clinic in its first week seems unlikely.²⁸ The Abertillery clinic closed in 1927 following poor attendance and a subsequent withdrawal of hospital support, and Witcop sold her Plashet Lane clinic in 1925, as mentioned above. Neither does clinic supply mean that patients were satisfied with the contraceptives prescribed to them. Some women were reluctant to have caps fitted, viewing them as improper, harmful or difficult to use. More than half of women fitted with a Dutch cap failed to show up to renew their jelly prescription; many others abandoned this method after a couple of months. But Stopes assumed that if a woman did not return, she was probably satisfied with her contraceptive prescription and was having no difficulty. The best estimate then suggests that approximately twenty-one thousand women had attended the sixteen existing clinics and two private consultants in the country by 1930.[29] Whether all of these women were fitted with a rubber and chemical pessary is unclear, but just three years later Lamberts was supplying almost 12,000 boxes of its Chinosol pessaries and almost 1,200 cervical caps to Stopes annually.[30]

Yet, clinic distribution figures aside, such was the potential for clinics and medical practitioners to act as a legitimising force for contraceptives that Lamberts established its own clinic. Seeking to take advantage of the changing social and medical climate towards clinics as a new and respectable method of practical birth control instruction, Lamberts had attempted to purchase Witcop's clinic on Plashet Lane when it came up for sale in 1925. The firm was outbid by a retired bank manager from South Africa named Brown, who purchased it for the considerable sum of £2,500 and seemingly still ran the clinic as a commercial enterprise until at least 1936.[31] Much to the disgust of Stopes, the clinic was seemingly no better run under Brown than Witcop; Brown had sold a local married (and probably pregnant) woman a rubber cap and soluble pessaries for 10s 6d and this woman had complained to Stopes.[32] Lamberts' close relationship with Stopes, however, meant that she sold her first clinic on Marlborough Road in Holloway to the firm in 1925 for between £3,000 and £3,800, following her relocation to Whitfield Street, near Tottenham Court Road. A Deed of Covenant meant Stopes retained the 'Mothers' Clinic' name and guaranteed that Lamberts would make its commercial running of the clinic clear through its display of a sign indicating: 'This clinic is no longer connected with the Society for Constructive Birth Control and Racial Progress nor with Dr Marie Stopes'.[33] Initially calling its new clinic 'The Wives' Clinic' and then 'The Birth Control Advisory Bureau', the firm explained in its catalogues that 'in July 1925, Stopes handed this [the clinic] over to Lamberts Prorace Ltd (who are the makers of the Prorace Caps), whom she considered the most reliable firm manufacturing contraceptives'. It also explained that the clinic was 'for the benefit of customers seeking first-hand information and advice on the subject of Birth Control'.[34]

Lamberts' clinic blended medical and commercial services. Like the Stopes clinic, it was designed to put patients at their ease; but instead of a separate waiting room and examination room, Lamberts'

Figure 14 Lamberts' clinic – 'A Consulting-Fitting Room at the Birth Control Advisory Bureau'.

clinic merely consisted of a single room used for examinations and fittings (fig. 14).[35] It also ensured that women in attendance were seen by a nurse who had received Constructive Birth Control training and could give 'advice on matters relating to birth control and to wives desiring children'. Nurses would fit the firm's 'Pro-Race' or, in special circumstances, the 'Lam-butt' Dutch cap, advising a check-up three months after marriage and other checks every nineteen months to two years. In fact, trained Constructive Birth Control nurses worked across Stopes's and Lamberts' clinics: Lamberts employed those who had unsuccessfully applied to the Mothers' Clinic via advertisements in the *Nursing Mirror* and similar nursing publications. Four midwife nurses, Lilian Scannell, Maude N. Hargreaves, Alice M. Wallingford and E. G. Davies, were offered posts in the Lamberts clinic by this process, with Hargreaves as the nurse in charge who was responsible for ordering supplies, requesting contraceptives on behalf of clinic patients and testing new Lamberts contraceptives.[36] The firm even lent Hargreaves and a clinic clerk to Stopes's clinic during busy periods. The clerk answered a wealth of correspondence that Stopes received on the back of the publicity surrounding her series of articles in *John Bull* in 1926, and addressed wrappers for new editions of the

Society's *Birth Control News*.³⁷ While attending the Mothers' Clinic on a Friday, Dr Hawthorne attended Lamberts' Bureau on the last Wednesday of every month. Following Hawthorne's departure from the clinic, the Lambert clinic relied on Drs Joan Malleson, medical officer at the Society for the Provision of Birth Control Clinics' North Kensington clinic, and then Rosalie Taylor for medical advice.³⁸ Like Stopes's clinic, Lamberts' clinic also offered a letter answering and a visiting nurse service, emulating Stopes's caravan clinic which toured the country from 1927.

Yet, of course, Lamberts' clinic was also a retail outlet for the firm's contraceptive supplies.³⁹ The firm charged what it called 'a small fee' for fitting and for the appliances at prices stated in its catalogues. This 'small fee', however, was the considerable sum of one guinea. The husband of a woman from Goodmayes, Essex, who had visited Lamberts' clinic for the first time in 1932, complained to Margaret Pyke, secretary of the National Birth Control Association, that his wife felt she had 'been had' after paying 10 to 12s for a cap and tablets, plus one guinea for a consultation and fitting.⁴⁰ The nurse in charge at the Lamberts clinic replied to letters without any financial cost to correspondents, but the travelling nurses also charged the high price of two guineas. While the Association was concerned about the practices of Lamberts' Bureau, the commercial ownership of the clinic meant that there was little it could do to intervene.⁴¹ Unlike Stopes's clinic, Lamberts' clinic aimed to appeal to middle-class women who, 'while not wishing to attend one of the free clinics for poor women, at the same time do not wish to pay a Harley Street fee, but wish to get expert advice on practical birth control'.⁴²

The clinic was also a promotional method; through the clinic, Lamberts not only distributed a large quantity of Stopes's *A Letter to Working Mothers* but also its own publication, *The Wife's Adviser*. It is through its clinic that Lamberts distributed over two hundred thousand copies of the publication by 1927. Himes stated that 'though it is a commercial tract designed to advertise the clinic, it does not seem in bad taste. The pamphlet has an excellent picture of the interior of the clinic'.⁴³ From 1938 the clinic also distributed a pamphlet titled *The Voice of Experience* as an updated version of *The Wife's Adviser*, which outlined 'practical birth control instruction' and promoted the firm's products. It is not clear whether Nurse M. R. Hooper, author of the pamphlet, was a genuine nurse at the clinic or another company pseudonym. The pamphlet, an attempt to exploit the increasing involvement of nurses in providing contraceptive advice and care, was explicit that Hooper had been the nurse in charge at the clinic since March 1928, but there seem to be no records confirming this and it is undermined by the fact that the Association argued that Hooper sounded illiterate.[44] 'Hooper' emphasised the benefits of having 'Messrs. Lamberts (Dalston) behind us, willing to carry out to the letter everything we ask in the way of special requirements and alterations'. Lamberts' clinic was heavily bombed in 1940, but Eleanor Mears, Medical Secretary of the Family Planning Association, noted that it was still operational and run along the same lines as Stopes's clinic in 1960.[45]

Despite Himes's 1936 claim that it was 'a rather unique case of the commercial diffusion of contraceptive information in England', Lamberts' clinic was not the only firm-run clinic in the country.[46] Other contraceptive appliance sellers established their own clinics after Himes had published his *Medical History of Contraception*. Surgical stores, in particular, such as the Stockwell Hygiene Company Ltd and W. George, replicated clinics and established 'modern fitting rooms' for rubber caps within their premises, while Rendell and Hancock offered medical advice to mail-order correspondents and invoked the rhetoric of the importance of family planning and family values.[47] Collating and analysing the intimate data it collected from readers in order to develop products and its advertising, Rendell claimed that its advice service had aided marriage issues. The firm also paid for readers to see William Charles Wallace Nixon, a well-known professor of gynaecology, as private patients.[48] George established a consulting service in its store in Leicester Square. Supplied by Prentif's goods, the new service included 'the fitting of contraceptive appliances of all kinds by a fully experienced, qualified Nurse'. Similar to Lamberts' pricing, the service cost a fee of 10s 6d, which covered 'all necessary instruction and the cost of the appliance supplied'. The firm also offered its consulting rooms 'freely at the disposal of any member of the medical professional who would prefer to make use of our special facilities when interviewing his patient'.

Before the mid-1930s then, Lamberts was intimately involved in the establishment and running of the early clinics. Clinics, and the nurses and practitioners who worked and were trained within them, relied on the firm to supply and develop the most effective rubber and chemical pessaries available. Efficacy was based on company reputation and practitioners' clinical experience. Such was the distribution potential of clinics to both practitioners and consumers that the firm developed its own clinic, making the distinction between commerce and charity difficult for general consumers and patients.

The introduction of scientific standards

The increasing efforts of the National Birth Control Association and its predecessors to transform birth control into a legitimate subject of scientific inquiry from the late 1920s began to challenge Lamberts' monopoly on the supply of contraceptives to clinics and medical practitioners. The Birth Control Investigation Committee, as the Association's research branch, had been drawing attention to the lack of scientific knowledge on contraceptive efficiency and the need for systematic collection of statistical data since the mid-1920s. Indeed, committee members, such as Enid Charles, had explicitly stressed the importance of finding common standards of contraceptive assessment and uniformity to establish contraceptive 'reliability'.[49] Accordingly, the committee established an ambitious programme of scientific research. Ilana Löwy has demonstrated how the committee worked with John Baker, the University of Oxford eugenicist and cytologist, and the commercial firm British Drug Houses to transform chemical contraceptives from secret proprietary products sold over the counter into 'ethical drugs' of known composition and physiological effects. The joint efforts resulted in the launch of Volpar (for Voluntary Parenthood) in 1937, as the first scientifically sanctioned chemical spermicide.[50] The committee invested in chemical contraceptives because they had practical and applied benefits. It was biological science that legitimised birth control and in this tablet form, chemical contraceptives held the key to a new efficient, easy-to-apply and pleasant product, which would overcome the problems of rubber caps experienced in the 1920s with patients not being able to fit them and their interference in the spontaneity of the sexual act.

But concern over legitimisation and standardisation of contraceptives through scientific measurement and management extended to rubber goods too. Indeed, sole reliance on clinical experience in the 1920s meant that it was difficult for the National Birth Control Association to distinguish between poor product quality and patient's incorrect appliance use. Staff at individual association clinics had long reported problems with the quality of Lamberts' rubber products – Walworth, for example, had seen sixty 'failures' with Lamberts' 'Pro-Race' cap by 1924, while other clinics complained about minute holes in its cervical caps – but such problems were often dismissed by clinicians and by the firm as the result of patients' improper use.[51] Stopes's Constructive Birth Control clinics similarly experienced this ambiguity between poor quality goods and improper use. In 1931 Stopes told the firm that 'it is difficult to express adequately the annoyance caused to our Society by the repeated failure of your firm to supply our Racial goods to standard', but at the same time, she frequently complained about the appalling ignorance of the women who visited the clinic, who were unable to fit caps properly themselves.[52] Stopes's withdrawal of the Constructive Birth Control clinics from the Association in 1933 meant that its programme of research did not apply to these clinics. Constructive Birth Control's own medical research committee seemingly made little headway with a scientific research programme, and despite ongoing and frequent complaints to Lamberts, these clinics continued to rely on the firm for cervical caps. In contrast, the Association's ambitious programme of scientific research not only sought to standardise contraceptive production (as we saw in Chapter 1) but also broadened the clinic market for firms other than Lamberts.

Aware of the growing numbers of clinics and the National Birth Control Association's increasing attempts to transform birth control into a legitimate subject of scientific inquiry, other firms quickly begun to inundate the Association with soliciting letters, product samples and contraceptives at special discounted rates (normally around 10 per cent normal retail price). LRC was among the first to solicit the Association. Conscious of the Association's search for a 'perfect' chemical contraceptive and knowledgeable about its latest research, LRC sent samples of its 'Bircon' antiseptic and prophylactic tablets under a subsidiary firm called the Bircon Laboratories in 1931, claiming that it was prescribed by over two thousand medical practitioners and that John Baker considered it among the best chemical contraceptives. The Association responded that 'Bircon' would have to be subjected to a clinical trial.[53] Attempting to profit from Enid Charles's 1932 report into clinic contraceptive methods that stated sheaths were the most reliable of the forms available, LRC also sent the Association and the Workers' Birth Control Group samples of its 'Durex' and 'Ona' condoms in 1933, although the Association's response to such samples is unrecorded. By 1937 the firm offered a discount of 50 per cent to medical professionals on its 'Durex' condoms. The Association quickly became overwhelmed with samples from other firms, but keen not to rely on solicitation, they persuaded Prentif to begin manufacturing its own Dutch and Dumas rubber caps in 1934, modelled on those of Lamberts, and sheaths and latex condoms in 1936.[54] Prentif also began to manufacture Stopes's 'Racial' cap. Until 1934 the firm had relied on imports, particularly Holland-Rantos 'Koromex' coil spring latex dome diaphragms from the United States. The 'Koromex' met with the approval of several Association doctors, but was outright mocked by Stopes when the firm sent samples to her in the hope of gaining her custom.[55]

The National Birth Control Association's introduction of laboratory-based product testing in 1935 meant that it could rely on the standardised results of outsourced biomedical scientists and rubber experts to gauge whether contraceptives received from companies should be distributed via clinics, instead of relying on subjective clinician and patient experience. The Association's laboratory tests for inflation, ageing, elongation, tensile strength, dating and visual assessment for rubber goods, which shaped contraceptive manufactories, were supplemented by spermicidal efficiency (using the 'Baker test') and harmlessness tests for chemical contraceptives. Tests revealed, for example, that many of the cocoa butter and quinine pessaries on the market, including Chinosol and Rendell's 'Wife's Friend', had no spermicidal efficacy and cocoa butter deteriorated rubber; the outcome of tests thus had the potential to change the market. Only products that passed these tests were meant to be supplied to Association clinics. A list of products that had passed the tests and were now scientifically approved replaced Griffith's draft recommendations for practitioners and was circulated to clinics and to the many enquirers who wrote to the Association seeking contraceptive information. Regularly updated, the list aimed to circumvent company advertising to provide guidance 'to those who have practically no other source of independent information on all the various contraceptives on the market'. It informed readers that goods were available at reputable chemists and at 'special prices' to clinics and doctors; from the 1940s the list detailed retail, wholesale and clinic pricing and quantities, demonstrating not only the Association's aim of keeping the price of contraceptives affordable so that clinics, doctors and end consumers could benefit from discounts, but also the notion that clinics could invest turnover from contraceptive sales back into clinic management, a vitally important part of clinics' income stream that was otherwise largely made up of donations and subscriptions.[56] For example, Dumas and Dutch caps retailed at 5s each and condoms at 4s per dozen, but clinics could obtain each cap and a dozen condoms at 1s 5d and 1s 10d, respectively, in bulk orders. Crucially, prices for products of the same type but from different manufacturers were generally standardised so that one firm was not unfairly advantaged. Equating it with the introduction of anaesthesia, asepsis and vaccination, Griffith attempted to convince general medical practitioners that the Association's sanction of reliable contraceptives embodied in the approved list was an example of the pioneering work of medical science that is initially opposed but then 'relieves much needless suffering'. 'The era of acceptance is approaching', he continued, 'contraception is here, and has come to stay'.[57]

Initially, firms pushed back at these new testing standards. Some refused to pay the testing fee, which amounted to approximately two guineas per product and thus could be a considerable sum if a number of products were tested simultaneously; some claimed the tests were unnecessary, impractical or inadequate for ensuring that a contraceptive was reliable.[58] LRC claimed that elongation to nine times its length was practically impossible for any sheath and that there was no need to give goods a three-year guarantee because products sold quickly. Lamberts sought to rely on its own in-house tests instead, claiming that only a few of its products had ever failed its own stringent standards. Chemical contraceptive producers, such as Gilmont, took issue with the National Birth Control Association's adoption of the Baker test for spermicidal efficiency, claiming that it was not the only reliable testing method.[59] After all, such tests were only newly developed; proprietary tablets and suppositories were only tested four times each.[60] But firms wishing to supply the Association's clinics had no choice but to comply and submit product samples for testing; consequently, the number of firms supplying clinics expanded. Indeed, while Natasha Szuhan has suggested that the content of the list embodied the commercial nature of the Association, firms recognised that it was also a powerful promotional tool for their products. Stopes was critical of the list because she felt it gave firms too much valuable publicity. Indeed, on reading the list, patients wrote to the Association to find out more about approved products and their manufacturers.[61]

Despite Lamberts' protest and earlier clinic issues with the quality of its rubber products, the firm's Dutch and cervical caps and sheaths appeared on the National Birth Control Association's first approved product list in October 1936. Its goods were now officially sanctioned and continued to be supplied to clinics, along with eleven other products manufactured by five other firms.[62] Lamberts proudly included details of the tests in its catalogues but without mentioning the Association: 'sheaths are tested by air pressure under microscopic examination and every one is dated. Every condom and sheath is guaranteed to have been subjected to these tests on the actual day of sale, which is important'. In fact, the firm began to include the approved status in the titles of its catalogues; its catalogue of 1941, for example, was titled *Latest Price List of Approved Catalogue Appliances*. Lamberts also highlighted the fact that the report of the medical committee appointed in connection with the investigations of the National Birth-Rate Commission in 1927 mentioned Dutch caps, which were 'fitted at all the birth control clinics throughout the UK', but again neglected to point out that the report had not mentioned any firm names in order to avoid promotion.[63] In addition, Prentif, with its Dumas caps, sheaths, condoms, lubricating jelly and soluble pessaries on the approved list, quickly became an Association favourite too, challenging Lamberts' monopoly.

From the late 1920s then, contraceptive firms found themselves negotiating their way around the National Birth Control/Family Planning Association's introduction of new scientific standards. Where once Lamberts' contraceptives, and its caps in particular, had been an industry standard, the Association began to increasingly accept the products of other manufacturers in its quest to legitimise birth control. Its new tests of the mid-1930s expanded the definition of product quality and reliability so that products had to satisfy laboratory standards, and not just clinical experience, and in doing so, helped to level the market.

Beyond laboratory testing: favoured suppliers in the clinic

Beyond expanding the number of clinic suppliers, the immediate effects of the National Birth Control Association's research programme on clinic supply were not as transformative as Griffith expected. Inclusion on one of the Association's lists did not mean automatic inclusion on subsequent versions; products were continually retested and the list revised accordingly. More significantly, laboratory testing and the circulation of an approved product list did not mean that contraceptives were reliable or that problems with failures and patient use were overcome. Indeed, Griffith admitted when the tests were introduced that they were 'somewhat experimental'; post-Second World War, Margaret Jackson, medical officer of the Exeter clinic, acknowledged the limitations of the list by stating that it 'was produced very hurriedly and without proper supervision'.[64]

The first indication that laboratory tests did not quickly become the Association's gold standard was the continued inclusion of products on the list that had failed some part of the tests. During the 1940s, Dutch caps made by Prentif and Lamberts failed the Association's ageing tests, while Dutch caps and condoms by LRC failed dating standards. In part, the continual inclusion of these products on the approved list was due to the Association's more relaxed standards towards supply during wartime. Indeed, the Association accepted that the rubber supply and storage issues experienced by Lamberts and Prentif meant that, after ageing, their caps 'had acquired a somewhat pronounced odour, and that the adhesion of the rubber plies round the rings was rather weak'.[65] Individual clinics became accustomed to caps splitting at the edges, bubbles appearing between the layers of latex and each cap having a more shallow dome than was normally required. The Association even accepted Lamberts' claims that a wartime price increase for caps from 24s per dozen to 27s was necessary in 1943 in order to cover rising wages and price increases of raw materials. Accordingly, the Association amended the wording on the approved list to state 'these have all passed clinical and/or laboratory tests'.[66] The Association also recognised that LRC's failure to include the date of manufacture on its packaging of condoms resulted from its fear of not being able to sell goods made from wartime rubber, although it was less accepting of this reason than rubber supply issues and crossed its caps and condoms from the lists until it altered its packaging to include a three-year guarantee at the end of the 1940s. Derisively, Miss Holland, secretary of the Bournemouth clinic, wrote to Margaret Pyke, chair and general secretary of the Family Planning Association, to suggest that the lack of dating might suit the 'more casual' clinics of Marie Stopes, who had not adopted the same definition of efficacy, but would not suit the Association.[67] Moreover, many Association members were involved in urgent wartime activities and clinic buildings were bombed in air raids; the Association thus prioritised keeping the service running rather than strictly adhering to the newly established standards.[68]

Yet, the retention of both Lamberts' and Prentif's caps on the list, despite so many failures and price increases, was not only due to the declining quantity and quality of wartime rubber, but was also dictated by 'the strength of many years of successful clinical experience' with the products and a sense of loyalty to the firms that had worked closely with clinic pioneers.[69] Certainly, some clinicians were confused that the Association continued to sanction as reliable and effective products that they themselves had seen fail. Some clinic doctors were afraid that the continued prescription of Lamberts' caps would result in a growing abortion rate and continually sent back faulty caps, while others sent back Prentif's faulty condoms, despite the fact that all tests in the laboratory had demonstrated that the rubber was of very good quality.[70] But for numerous clinicians who had dedicated much of their careers to advancing medical birth control, the list of approved products was not as meaningful as their many years of clinical experience with a firm and its goods. Haire argued in 1928 that the medical profession's limited acceptance of birth control was a generational issue, with the most vocal enemies over 62 years of age having never studied it or considered it as an area of professional treatment; but Haire's own generation were similarly blinded by their own preferences.[71] In response to an Association survey in 1945, a large number of Association doctors and at least sixteen non-Association doctors stated that they continued to supply caps by Prentif and Lamberts; many of these doctors had long been involved in the birth control movement and in the running of the first clinics.[72] Lamberts supplied almost 120 municipal, hospital and Association clinics by 1945.[73] Loyalty to Lamberts resulted from its reputation as the country's oldest cap manufacturer, but the Association also recognised Prentif as 'one of the first to try and meet the needs of clinics' and its goods were among the first tested.[74] Indeed, unlike other firms, Prentif explicitly expressed its delight at the Association's introduction of stringent testing as part of its wider push for rigorous industry standards. Clinician loyalty to these two firms in particular and trust in the efficacy of their goods was key to maintaining their clinic and medical supply, regardless of the approved list.

Gladys Cox, the author of *Clinical Contraception* (first published in 1933 and republished in 1937), medical officer to the Association and member of the Birth Control Investigation Committee that had approved the laboratory tests, continued to prefer the caps of Lamberts and Prentif. In her book, Cox was careful not to recommend one company over another, stating: 'I feel it wise to state that I have no commercial or other interests in any of the proprietary contraceptives mentioned in this book'; she also listed a comprehensive range of contraceptive products and manufacturers, including the disreputable Le Brasseur.[75] But in private correspondence to Association members, Cox emphasised the fact that Lamberts had supplied clinics for the past twenty years; she herself had prescribed them during her time as medical officer of Walworth and East London clinics in the 1920s, and the Prentif cap when it began supplying the Walworth clinic in 1934.

Cox's trust in Lamberts had developed following a visit to the firm's factory by some members of the Association's medical committee in 1934. The visit had been prompted by clinic reports of faulty products, but inspection of production resulted in the committee's defence of the firm. The compiler of the report after the visit, presumably Margaret Pyke, stated that she liked the company's two directors, who were 'well-intentioned, as honest as business permits' and 'genuinely anxious to please us'. The report also revealed that the committee trusted the two directors despite their shocking revelation that the firm had bought out another 'where the standards of works had never been as high ... and the firm continued to sell inferior stock to shops "who want a cheaper quality"'.[76] This revelation, that Lamberts supplied its inferior goods to shops, made Cox and the other doctors wary and suggested that there may be 'a double standard of honesty', but it was not enough to dent the Association's relationship with the firm. Pyke expressed her disappointment in the failure of Lamberts' cap to pass the ageing test in 1940 by exclaiming 'Blast!'[77] Meanwhile, doctors from the Walworth and East London clinics, who were not bound by the approved list, were reportedly 'most impressed with the care which is taken in the manufacture of the goods' following a visit to Lamberts' factory in 1935; they emphasised that the lasting quality of the rubber Lamberts used 'has been shown in practice. It is not uncommon for patients to return having used the pessaries for several years, the pessaries still being in very good condition'.[78]

Drs Marjorie Edwards at the Royal Free Hospital and Helena Wright, Cecile Booysen and Dorothea Sinton at Women's Welfare centres in North Kensington, Goswell and Newcastle were among doctors that became reliant on Prentif's approved goods following its supply of Dutch caps to the Association in 1934.[79] Prentif had welcomed the Association's medical committee to its factory in 1937, and the firm and the Association developed a close and informal relationship, as suggested by the light and jovial tone of the correspondence between Mr R. Harrison and Margaret Pyke, and then between Harrison and Holland once she took over from Pyke as Association chair.[80] The secretaries of both the Association and the firm wrote informal letters to each other, enquiring about each other's families. Indeed, the Association began to rely on Harrison from Prentif as gatekeeper between them and disreputable rubber stores, just as Stopes had relied on Lamberts for the same purpose ten years earlier. Holland reported that Joan Malleson had stated in 1945 that 'there was definitely a place for' Prentif's caps, and that Lamberts' ordinary caps were essential – nothing could take their place.[81] In her 1935 clinical textbook for general practitioners, *The Principles of Contraception*, Malleson referenced Lamberts' caps and Prentif's condoms as the best available. This book was explicitly based 'on her own observations, own preferences and own instructional technique'.[82] As Caroline Rusterholz has argued, Malleson's private practical experience was a source of scientific legitimacy, as much as laboratory testing.[83] As we saw in Chapter 1, Malleson had made a case for the production of more of Lamberts' caps to the Director of Medical Supplies at the Ministry of Supply during the war, but her preference for the firm's caps was rooted in her use and prescription of them while medical officer to Stopes's Constructive Birth Control clinic in London.

Helena Wright (1887–1982) similarly continued to prescribe caps of both Lamberts and Prentif at the North Kensington clinic. Wright was impressed by Harrison's attempts to challenge unethical advertising of contraceptives in the general and medical press between 1937 and the early 1940s.[84] The firm's launch of its own medical journal, *Contraceptive Practice*, not only circulated to thirty thousand medical practitioners, as we saw in Chapter 3, but was approved by the Association and contained contributions from medical practitioners. The first edition of Prentif's journal referenced Cox's *Clinical Contraception*, Himes's *Medical History of Contraception* and Booysen's 'Quinine as a Contraceptive'.[85] Griffith, the physician keen for 'authoritative action' on medical education in birth control, not only made explicit reference to the quality of Prentif's products within his 1937 textbook *Voluntary Parenthood* but also wrote four anonymous articles for the firm's journal.[86] Griffith's first article gave detailed directions and a series of five black-and-white sketches of how its various caps should look when correctly inserted into the vagina. It received criticism from Norman Haire in the journal's correspondence pages. Haire disagreed with Griffith's method for fitting the diaphragm and his letter appeared along with an extract of his *Birth Control Methods* (1936). In the following pages, Griffith responded: 'I am sure Dr Haire will realise that individual variances in technique could not be dealt with in the space of a short article'.[87] Demonstrating their technical authority, Prentif also commented that Haire's book failed to mention the vault cap, as a form of cap distinct from the diaphragm, which it suggested was 'a serious omission'. Under Griffith's instruction, the Association also provided the Admiralty with a reference for Prentif in 1938, stating that its goods were among the most reliable.[88]

Clinician preference for and long experience with these contraceptives was also continually replicated through instruction, in both lecture and print form. In addition to *Contraceptive Practice*, Prentif instructed medical practitioners on cap fitting in another publication, *Clinical Notes on the Fitting of Vaginal Diaphragms (Dutch Cap)*, which provided more detailed diagrams of the correct method of inserting Prentif's diaphragm into the vagina and contained detailed text outlining how practitioners should explain to patients 'the theory of the diaphragm method' in simple terms. The firm also produced anatomical models that demonstrated how to fit a cervical cap or diaphragm in 1948, although the Association pointed out that its first model was anatomically incorrect and thus 'may be exceedingly misleading if used for demonstrating for patients'.[89] If these products continued to hold favour with clinic doctors, they were also more likely to be accepted by their patients, with whom they developed a relationship of trust.

In contrast, the Association and its doctors did not respond well to LRC's aggressive marketing tactics. According to Borge, one of LRC's employees recalled of the early years of clinic supply that 'we didn't like the Family Planning Association any more than they liked us. It was pretty cold and had arisen from their side'.[90] Hostility from the Association towards LRC seemingly followed the firm's initial distribution of its samples of 'Bircon' pessaries in 1931. Gladys

Cox was outraged at the firm's claim that she had tested 'Bircon' with 'guinea pig sperms' in her role as member of the Birth Control Investigation Committee. The firm claimed that Dr Ethel Browning was preparing a 'medical book' for them and, accordingly, a number of the firm's travelling salesmen attempted to obtain from clinic staff information that presumably fed back into their product development. Chas F. Cullingham, one of the firm's travelling salesmen, wrote to Holland in 1934 requesting 'suitable authoritative data for the purpose of compiling a pamphlet'. Another, noted as a 'medical propagandist for LRC', requested information on where he could obtain supplies of the Gräfenburg ring and notices of lectures on birth control. A note in the Association's archive states: 'I disliked him ... I gave him papers of North Kensington and Walworth ... and said I could do nothing more to help him'.[91]

Following LRC's complaints about product testing in 1936, the Association also noted that the firm 'made rather extravagant claims altogether'.[92] Philip Schidrowitz, rubber tester for the Association, stated that LRC's condoms were 'perhaps less reliable on the whole' than Prentif's condoms.[93] After discovering Lamberts and Prentif were also on the approved list, LRC attempted to smear the reputation of the two firms in 1937. Calling LRC 'unnecessarily critical', the Association defended Prentif after LRC warned it that Prentif obtained its goods from German manufacturers and was thus unlikely to overcome Hitler's plan to make German rubber industries independent of imports; it also largely ignored LRC's criticism of Lamberts' products.[94] Even LRC's offer in 1939 to give six months' credit to clinics was not accepted, but instead made Pyke wonder if 'we could put our cards on the table with Prentif and Lamberts and see if they could make their prices compete'.[95]

Naturally, neither Lamberts nor Prentif were supportive of LRC. Prentif continued to place the firm in the same disreputable category as surgical stores, stating to the Association that the firm's trading methods were 'deplorable' and that it supplied garages, rather than reputable chemists.[96] Harrison also complained to the Association about the quality of LRC's condoms and expressed disbelief at inclusion of these products on its 1940 approved list. Unaware that they had already failed the dating test, Harrison reported that LRC's condoms had failed Prentif's own in-house testing. Harrison had purchased a bulk of LRC's ivory and transparent latex condoms from a chemist wholesaler, and concluded that almost one-third of the

3,312 he tested at the Prentif manufactory were faulty: 10 per cent had tiny holes, 5 per cent large holes and 15 per cent had burst. Harrison considered it 'rather unfair' to have Prentif's products associated with those of such 'extremely bad quality' and recommended that the Association purchase a batch in the same way in order to conduct their own tests.[97] The Association did as Harrison suggested, but its batch satisfied in-house tests and thus the appliances remained on the approved list, much to Harrison's dismay. Of course, Harrison may well have exaggerated claims of faulty products in order to deter the Association from his competition, particularly when Prentif's own caps had failed Association tests; but regardless, Reid of LRC was furious when he discovered Harrison's actions. In what the Association described as a revenge tactic, LRC began to inform chemists that end consumers were able to purchase Prentif sheaths and condoms from the Association at prices far lower than it charged. Indeed, as demonstrated by the approved list, the Association charged on average 50 per cent, but occasionally up to 65 per cent, less for products than chemists.

While the Association had aimed for its contraceptive supply to complement that of chemists' shops under one united contraceptive standard, clinics and chemists ended up competing for sales. Chemists responded badly to this news of clinic price undercutting and Prentif claimed that LRC's 'fifth column propaganda' had done considerable damage to its business with the chemists' trade.[98] Prentif was forced to change the packaging of its condoms and sheaths so that its clinic supplies were no longer branded and could be distinguished from chemists' supplies. The Association admitted that 'there is a lot of commercial jealousy latent among pharmacists', a fear that was seemingly confirmed when an unhappy Walsall-based chemist queried why patients at the Birmingham clinic could mail order Volpar gels and paste more cheaply than he could supply.[99] In correspondence to Holland, Pyke rhetorically asked 'Aren't the LRC charming people?!' and noted that 'it is true that Prentif tried to do them a bad turn, but at least it was on the quality of their goods – not in this shady sort of way'.[100] Cullingham, LRC's representative who had been keen to obtain information from the Association in the mid-1930s, contacted Prentif directly in 1940 attempting to procure the firm's products under the guise of an individual wishing to establish his own philanthropic health centre called 'Cunningham'. Suspicious, Harrison asked the Association to verify the status of Cunningham and his clinic, to which it responded that he had been in contact previously but it had 'never felt he was someone whom we could recognise and I do not think he would come under the heading of those to whom you would supply your products'. Prentif decided to 'act in accordance with' the views of the Family Planning Association, and did not supply Cunningham.[101]

Sustained clinical preference for Lamberts and Prentif and their products, resulting from the Association's perception of ethical business practices and a development of goodwill and loyalty, meant that not only did clinicians continue to recommend the two firms and prescribe such products over LRC's but they also recommended and sold them to their non-clinic practitioners and to clinic correspondents. Daisy Stewart-Matthews, a consulting gynaecologist in Liverpool, ordered Prentif's goods through the clinic at clinic prices in order to sell them on to her patients in her private practice, thus allowing her to make a profit. Similarly, a doctor based in Wallingford, near Oxford, ordered Prentif's 'best condoms' at the clinic's discounted rate in 1941 for his own personal use. Colin Barnes, Prentif's sales director, did not think the practice of medical practitioners selling on its discounted products for profit or taking advantage of discounted products for personal use was 'ethically sound' but saw 'no way of proving that it happens or of stopping it'. Despite having clear evidence of this practice, the Association assured Prentif that it had never supplied doctors with caps to prescribe to their own private patients.[102] But this practice continued in Liverpool into the 1950s, as well as at branches in Edinburgh, Newcastle, Middlesbrough and Birkenhead.[103] Many of the Association's correspondents during the early 1940s were military personnel seeking advice or prophylactics at wholesale prices. The Association recommended Prentif's condoms over LRC's, despite LRC being the official supplier to the armed forces during the war. For example, in September 1940, the Association recommended Prentif's condoms to a captain of the Somerset Light Infantry, who wanted them for his troops.[104] The Association recommended Prentif because 'the firm hoped to build up a reputation for specially tested high-class contraceptives and for an ethical standard of doing business'. Prentif supplied the captain under its general policy of supplying condoms to medical officers attached to battalions with a discount of 10 per cent, asking him to be discreet about getting a price lower than chemists could offer. Similarly, in June 1944, the

Association referred a lieutenant to Prentif for nearly six hundred sheaths costing £7 5s. The lieutenant stated that he felt able to write to the Association because he had previously obtained supplies from its clinics 'as a husband and feels that the help which we gave him should be shared with his men'; this suggests it was the lieutenant's home sex life that had exposed him to contraceptives, rather than the military, as was the case for some soldiers.[105] The lieutenant stated: 'I, personally in the past have received valuable assistance and advice from you [the Association] and I feel now that in the interests of my men I should carry a quantity of rubber sheaths'. While Prentif was reluctant to supply this lieutenant with this order because he was not a medical officer, the firm did so to maintain a good relationship with the Association, to which Holland stated: 'I am so glad that you feel you can carry out this order'. Accordingly, such orders enabled Prentif to claim that over 85 per cent of its condom output, certainly those branded 'Servicepax', went to the armed forces. The continued supply of products that doctors both within and beyond the Association knew had not passed all new laboratory tests, but from firms it trusted, not only demonstrates a preference for clinical experience over laboratory testing but also highlights the infancy of universal standards in birth control in mid-twentieth-century Britain.

The decline of favoured suppliers in the post-war clinic

Amid increasing post-war stability and the rapid expansion of Family Planning Association clinics to 179 in 1955 and 276 in 1960, the dominance of Lamberts and Prentif over the birth control clinic market began to decline. Conversely, LRC's near monopoly was just beginning. The firm were able to provide its diaphragms, a method prescribed to nearly 98 per cent of female clinic patients by 1959, and 'Durex' branded condoms, a contraceptive that clinics began to prescribe more frequently, at a quality and at a price with which its competitors could not compete.[106] From 1950, goods were required to pass more stringent standardised clinical testing, alongside laboratory testing. Growing numbers of Association clinics turned to LRC's products as they found serious faults with the contraceptives of Lamberts and Prentif, in part resulting from their inability to recover from material and staff shortages experienced during the war. The Swindon clinic found Lamberts' caps 'hopelessly split', describing them as 'very shoddy', North Staffordshire stated that they were 'very disappointed' and a staff member at Sheffield had put her finger through twenty-four of Lamberts' caps. The Richmond clinic discarded fifty of Lamberts' caps in just two months in 1950, while Islington rejected almost eight hundred new caps in 1949 and nearly five hundred in 1950. Complaints from clinics continued into the 1960s.[107]

Clinic costs for LRC products were significantly lower too. Prentif's diaphragms were 5s 5d each, while LRC's cost 3s 6d. Another attraction of LRC was its provision of discounts, free start-up kits of products to new clinics and its supply of practice diaphragms to aid the teaching of the 250 medical students and practitioners that attended courses at Association clinics.[108] LRC's offer to new Family Planning Association clinics included six dozen boxes of both 'Duracreme' and diaphragms, and clinic discounts of 15 per cent for 'Elarcreme', its branded spermicidal cream, 20 per cent for condoms and between 40 and 50 per cent for diaphragms.[109] Lamberts, in contrast, could not initially offer any goods and reported to the Association that it thought LRC's free offer to be 'not altogether reputable'; Prentif could only provide discounts on diaphragms for orders exceeding one gross (144 units).[110] Supplying better quality goods at a lower discounted price than its competitors meant that LRC was able to claim 75 per cent of diaphragm market by 1952, a figure similar to that quoted by Lamberts in the 1920s for its cervical caps.[111] By the end of the 1950s, LRC supplied 186 of the Association's clinics with its diaphragms, while Prentif only supplied 24.[112]

Yet, amid their declining popularity, the contraceptives of Lamberts and Prentif continued to hold favour with some clinicians. Unsurprisingly, these clinicians tended to be those who had long prescribed them. Those at some of the first clinics established, such as Manchester in 1926, certainly remained loyal to Lamberts; some patients also continued to insist on only being fitted with 'Pro-Race' caps.[113] Indeed, Lamberts were still supplying clinics with 20 per cent of its total product output by 1953, 2 per cent of which went to former Constructive Birth Control clinics where Stopes's influence and preference for the cervical cap remained strong.[114] Following Pyke's announcement that the Association would be removing Lamberts' 'Racial' cap from its approved list in 1956, Stopes's Whitfield Street clinic not only made a case for the product to remain on the list but was also extremely worried about the fact that proposed price increases associated with the popularity of LRC's goods, from 3s 5d for its red cap and 4s 2d for its black cap to 5s, would deter working-class women from attending.[115] Malleson also continued to order Prentif's caps for the patients she saw in private practice right up until her untimely death in 1956. Others also highlighted the high quality of Prentif diaphragms, while some complained that LRC's products, particularly those under its 'Durex' brand, were too expensive.[116] Some clinicians also still found fault with the rubber of LRC diaphragms and expressed annoyance and dismay at the Association's increasing reliance on them.[117] But the Association seemed to dismiss complaints from individual clinics, and LRC came to dominate clinic supply.

While the quality and price of LRC's diaphragms led to the Association's new reliance on the firm, it was the inflexibility of Lamberts and Prentif on these two key issues that played a key role in their growing unpopularity among clinicians. Indeed, doctors implored Lamberts and Prentif to catch up with the technical knowledge that had changed so rapidly since the war. Lamberts refused to accept the declining popularity of its 'Pro-Race' and 'Racial' caps. Watkins of the firm emphasised that the 'Pro-Race' had 'proved very popular and most satisfactory' for many years and presented the Association with a wide assortment of example testimonials from women located across the country to highlight customer satisfaction.[118] Lamberts continued to blame faults with caps on patients' incorrect use rather than its own production processes. It blamed rubber erosion, for example, on patients' use of Volpar instead of 'Contraceptalene', the spermicide the firm had made for Haire in the 1920s. It ignored Association pleas to become more efficient by producing just one type of cervical cap, rather than the four almost identical designs it was still producing in 1950. In denial about its declining popularity, the firm continued to revel in its history. In correspondence with the Association and in its catalogue, the firm continually drew on the fact that its Dutch caps were manufactured in the same manner as they were fifty years previously and had thus 'stood the test of time'.[119] The Association began to find the firm's reluctance to technologically adapt problematic and expressed annoyance with its apparent lack of understanding of the quality expected. Margaret Jackson stated: 'I am very tired of their letters about caps ... the fact that we are trying to get into their thick heads is that the "average" quality of their caps has deteriorated in the last few years; whereas one could expect a Lamberts cap to last 1–5 or even 7 years now we are quite surprised if they last more than 1 year (common range I would say – 2 months to 2 years)'.[120] The Association also tried to encourage Lamberts to submit its sheaths for approval as they were becoming a more popular clinic contraceptive but the firm simply stated it did not supply its sheaths to clinics, while simultaneously revelling in the fact that it pioneered the cement process of rubber sheath manufacture in the 1880s. In fact, Lamberts admitted to the Association that it was no longer concerned with supplying clinics, and only did so because being on the approved list was 'useful for retail sales'.[121]

Similarly, Prentif lost patience with the Association. Exasperated at its lack of communication on changing details of its laboratory and clinical tests, Barnes of the firm claimed that there were no standardised tests at all, a fact he suggested was confirmed by the failure of other firms to gain details of the tests too. The whole process, Barnes claimed, was an 'extremely dark mystery'.[122] Reasserting Harrison's earlier condemnation of LRC's products and as an attempt to reaffirm Prentif's authority in birth control clinic supply, Barnes reiterated that many products would not have been accepted on the approved list if they had been properly tested. Barnes's tirade seems to have been a tactic to persuade the Association to invite manufacturers with the appropriate technical knowledge onto its medical sub-committee. In response, however, the Association sent Prentif a schedule of testing. Barnes had also discussed with the Association the option of centralised buying to bring down product prices and to aid branches with their accounts; his continued receipt of vague orders and letters from different branches led him to state 'don't they need it'.[123] The Association's eventual adoption of a recommended selling price in 1956 for clinics, pricing the firm's caps at 6s and LRC's at 5s, ironically priced Prentif out of the market.

As the Association became increasingly reliant on LRC for its diaphragm supplies, promotional advice and expertise, its relationship with the firm vastly improved. As we saw in Chapter 3, LRC began to publish and promote its *Planned Families* booklet in the national media from the mid-1950s, but it also provided the Association with financial and practical support in public relations. Such support included a £1,000 contribution to the production of *Birthright*, an Association propaganda film, in 1957, and the services of Dai Hayward, LRC's public relations professional, between 1959 and 1961.[124] This changed relationship meant that the Association was more willing to accept the aggressive marketing tactics that it had previously dismissed. For example, the Association accepted Reid's suggestion that it 'put a little gentle pressure on clinics to purchase more LRC products'.[125] With Association approval, the firm also established its own clinic opposite Selfridges on Oxford Street in 1960. LRC's Family Planning Clinic offered birth control advice and contraceptive fitting and prescription, and later the contraceptive Pill. Beryl Northage, the Association's assistant secretary of five years and employee of twelve years, became the clinic's medical secretary. While Reid claimed this was a new type of clinic, run along 'fully ethical lines' and under the banner of 'family planning', there was seemingly little to distinguish it from Lamberts' clinic that was still operating in Marlborough Street. Clients at both the clinics of Lamberts and LRC were charged a consultation fee and prescribed a suitable product from the corresponding firm's range.

Conclusion

From the 1920s, clinics became important sites of distribution for contraceptive goods. As charitable or municipal organisations that were simultaneously sites of medical authority and of commercial exchange, clinics were vital to exposing largely married middle-class women to cervical caps, diaphragms and chemical pessaries, foams and creams, and their husbands to sheaths and condoms, as well as the birth control knowledge that underpinned their use. Yet, while only a small proportion of the population ever attended a clinic – even in 1960, only 8 per cent of women went to a Family Planning Association clinic – and supplies were never on a grand scale, clinics were a vital gateway to exposing a medical profession increasingly interested in birth control, along with their patients, to contraceptive knowledge. Clinics acted as legitimising institutions not only for birth control as a practice but also for the associated technologies and their manufacturers. Untold numbers of practitioners were instructed at a clinic and their patients may have been exposed to birth control and contraceptives in this way, particularly as the Family Planning Association was increasingly mentioned in the media from the 1950s.

Lamberts was the first to draw on the opportunity to supply clinics. The firm's belief in the legitimisation of its products through the clinic setting led to its establishment of its own clinic in 1925, an initiative that LRC followed thirty-five years later. Lamberts held an almost near monopoly on clinic supply of cervical caps and spermicides until the mid-1930s when Prentif established its own 'ethical standards' and aligned itself to the increasing medicalisation of contraception. With the Association's growing embrace of laboratory medicine and the standardisation of 'reliability' as a way to legitimise birth control, clinic supply broadened to include Lamberts' competitors and, as a result, LRC held the near monopolising position in the 1950s that Lamberts had held some thirty years earlier. Yet, what is so striking about interwar and post-war clinic supply is not the fact that the technologically superior rubber contraceptives dominated clinic supply by the end of the period under study. Indeed, this is unsurprising and confirms the picture presented by recent histories of birth control. What is striking is the fact that contraceptives scientifically proven to be inferior endured; products that had failed the Association's laboratory and clinical tests but had long been supplied to clinics were preferred by clinicians of long standing and patients alike. These clinicians and patients had had many years of successful experiences with these contraceptives and their manufacturers. It took thirty years for the increasing authority of scientific testing to challenge clinical experience and brand loyalty, thus demonstrating that medical science's authority over birth control was neither as wholesale or complete as its practitioners and subsequent historians deemed it to be. Practical experience, as well as commercial concerns, including trade goodwill and price, were also vitally important in shaping clinic supply before the contraceptive Pill.

Notes

1 WL, SA/FPA/A14/32, Griffith, Medical sub-committee – the present position with regard to the sale and distribution of contraceptives, c.1936.
2 The Ministry of Health Act of 1918, for example, permitted local authorities to give birth control advice on gynaecological grounds to women, although few local authorities initially gave such advice. The Act was followed by the opening of birth control clinics, not by local

authorities, but by charitable bodies and through private enterprise. The first of these were opened by Marie Stopes and the Malthusian League in opposite ends of London in 1921. Stopes argued that the Mothers' Clinic was to be the first clinic in the Empire and/or the world, both of which claims can be disputed. Aletta Jacobs is credited with opening the first clinic in the world in the Netherlands in 1882 while the American nurse Margaret Sanger opened her clinic in New York in 1916. The claim to be first in the Empire is also open to doubt as Alice Vickery is reputed to have been operating a clinic in Rotherhithe in 1910, although the evidence as to its purpose is unclear.

3   BL, Add. MS 59567, 11, Dawson to Stopes, 24 February 1922.
4   The five clinic-running organisations were the Provision of Birth Control Clinics, the Birth Control International Information Centre, the National Birth Control Association, the Workers' Birth Control Group and Birth Control Investigation Committee.
5   Leathard, *The Fight for Family Planning*; B. Evans, *Freedom to Choose: The Life and Work of Dr. Helena Wright, Pioneer of Contraception* (London: Bodley Head, 1984), p. 146; Löwy, '"Sexual chemistry" before the Pill'. Recent exceptions include Borge '"Wanting it Both Ways"'; Neushul, 'Marie C. Stopes'.
6   Holz, *The Birth Control Clinic*, p. 2.
7   Stopes also asked Lambert to supply some rubber ('Racial') and sea sponges of each size, BL, Add. MS 58638, letter by Stopes to Lamberts 20 April 1928; MS 58639, 24 February 1931. Stopes also imported 'Clinocaps' from a German firm before 1939, BL, Add. MS 58640, Notes on contents of this box.
8   J. Peel and M. Potts, *Textbook of Contraceptive Practice* (Cambridge: Cambridge University Press, 1969), p. 63; Fryer, *The Birth Controllers*, pp. 250–1.
9   D. Wyndham, *Norman Haire and the Study of Sex* (Sydney: Sydney University Press, 2012), p. 81.
10 N. Haire, *Hygienic Methods of Family Limitation* (London: G. Standring, 1922), p. 18.
11 Fryer, *The Birth Controllers*, p. 239.
12 Lamberts Prorace, *Revised Price List* (1933), p. 22.
13 'Statements and Evidence Submitted to the Committee: IV. Mrs G. M. Cox, M. B., B. S.', *Medical Aspects of Contraception*, p. 72.
14 Wyndham, *Norman Haire and the Study of Sex*, p. 145.
15 BL, Add. MS 58567, 65, Reports of lectures at Cromer Street centre, 'Practical methods of birth control'. See also, Haire, *Birth Control Methods* (1936), p. 104.
16 *Medical Aspects of Contraception*, pp. 84, 90.

17 Soloway, *Birth Control*, pp. 258, 261, 268; Neushul, 'Marie C. Stopes', p. 265.
18 P. Brand, 'Birth Control Nursing in the Marie Stopes' Mothers' Clinics, 1921–1931' (PhD thesis, De Montfort University, 2007), p. 149; Fryer, *The Birth Controllers*, p. 229.
19 WL, PP/MCS/C15, letter by Stopes to Victor Roberts, 7 May 1925; 12 May 1925.
20 BL, Add. MS 58638, letter by Stopes to Lambert, 19 December 1924.
21 Hall, *Marie Stopes*, p. 105.
22 Brand, 'Birth Control Nursing', p. 222.
23 BL, Add. MS 58638, letter by Stopes to Lambert, 6 January 1926.
24 Soloway, *Birth Control*, p. 301.
25 Brand, 'Birth Control Nursing', p. 242.
26 BL, Add. MS 58638, letter by Stopes to Lambert, 2 December 1929.
27 Soloway, *Birth Control*, p. 277.
28 *The Malthusian* (15 July 1921), p. 53. Fryer, *The Birth Controllers*, p. 251.
29 Fryer and Leathard have tended to rely on exaggerated figures: Fryer, *The Birth Controllers*, pp. 255, 256; Leathard, *The Fight for Family Planning*, p. 39. See Soloway, *Birth Control*, p. 277; D. A. Cohen, 'Private lives in public spaces: Marie Stopes, the Mothers' Clinics and the practice of contraception', *History Workshop Journal*, 35 (1993), 95–7.
30 BL, Add. MS 58639, letter by Stopes to Lambert, 21 May 1931; letter by Lambert to Stopes, 31 January 1933.
31 BL, Add. MS 58638, letter by Lambert to Stopes, 19 May 1925; 22 June 1925.
32 WL, PP/MCS/A.14, letter by Stopes to Mrs A, 16 November 1925.
33 Brand, 'Birth Control Nursing', p. 164; BL Add. MS 58638, letter by Lambert to Stopes, 19 May 1925. Stopes left the Whitfield Street clinic to the Eugenics Society.
34 Lamberts Prorace Ltd, *Revised Price List* (1933; 1936), p. 4; Lamberts (Dalston) Ltd, *Revised List* (1941), p. 5; *Latest Price List* (c.1950), pp. 4–5.
35 Cohen, 'Private lives in public spaces', 97.
36 Brand, 'Birth Control Nursing', p. 167.
37 BL, Add. MS 58638, letter by Stopes to Lambert, 21 February 1926.
38 WL, SA/FPA/A7/68, letter by E. Mears to M. Blair, 27 June 1960.
39 Wood and Suitters, *The Fight for Acceptance*, p. 166.
40 WL, SA/FPA/A7/66, letter by Mr G. to Pike, 9 September 1932.
41 WL, SA/FPA/A7/66, letter by Dr M. B. Savory to Pike, 21 May 1936.
42 WL, SA/FPA/A7/68, M. R. Hooper, *The Voice of Experience* (London: The Birth Control Advisory Bureau, 1938, 1960), p. 9.
43 Himes, *Medical History of Contraception*, p. 328.

44 WL, SA/FPA/A7/68, Hooper, *Voice of Experience*, p. 7; WL, SA/FPA/A14/58.1, letter by General Secretary to Malleson, 4 January 1950.
45 WL, SA/FPA/A7/68, letter by E. Mears to M. Blair, 27 June 1960. See also, WL, SA/FPA/A7/68, Discussion with Mr Watkins of Lamberts, 9 June 1960.
46 Himes, *Medical History of Contraception*, p. 328.
47 WL, SA/FPA/A7/99, George's Consulting Service, c.1935; Hancock and Co. Ltd, *The Shadow of the Stork: A Text Book of Birth Control Methods* (London: 1933), p. 26; A. Phelps, *Children by Desire: A Treatise on Sex Problems and Modern Methods of Birth Control* (London: Phelps Contraceptives Ltd, 1940), pp. 2–3.
48 Rendell (uncatalogued papers), History of the company.
49 Charles, *The Practice of Birth Control* (1932).
50 Löwy, '"Sexual chemistry" before the Pill'.
51 WL, SA/FPA/A13/85B, 348, Walworth papers.
52 BL, Add. MS 58639, letter by Stopes to Lambert, 8 October 1931.
53 WL, SA/FPA/A7/71, letter by LRC to FPA, March 1931; 1 September 1936.
54 WL, SA/FPA/A7/99, letter by Prentif to Holland, 29 August 1934; 22 September 1934; 19 October 1934; 19 November 1934; letter by Holland to Prentif, 16 November 1934.
55 BL, Add. MS 58641, 15, letter by Stopes to Prentif, 26 January 1935.
56 WL, SA/FPA/A7/1, SA/FPA/A7/A3; SA/FPA/A7/5, Approved Lists. See also, Szuhan, 'Sex in the laboratory', 494.
57 E. F. Griffith, *Contraception in General Practice* (London: Eyre and Spottiswoode, 1936), pp. 3–4. Reprinted from *The Practitioner*, 136 (1936), 767–76.
58 WL, SA/FPA/A7/116, letter by Winchester Manufacturing Company to Holland, 18 March 1938; SA/FPA/A7/61, letter by International Latex Products Ltd to Holland, 16 March 1937. The fee increased to four guineas after the Second World War. See Borge, '"Wanting it Both Ways"', p. 203.
59 WL, SA/FPA/A7/71, letter by LRC to Holland, 9 November 1936. Szuhan, 'Sex in the laboratory', 499.
60 Cox, *Clinical Contraception*, pp. 53–4.
61 For example, WL, SA/FPA/A7/50, letter by J. W. of Skegby to FPA, 24 June 1949; letter by FPA to J. W., 30 June 1949.
62 WL, SA/FPA/A7/5, October 1936.
63 Lamberts Prorace, *Revised Price List* (1936), pp. 5, 13, 14.
64 Griffith, *Contraceptives in General Practice*, p. 12; WL SA/FPA/A7/103, Dr Jackson's comments on Mrs Arnold's notes on Prentif's letter, 27 November 1950.

65 WL, SA/FPA/A7/101, letter by Holland to Prentif, 23 April 1940.
66 WL, SA/FPA/A7/5, agenda of the medical committee, May 1940; Approved list, October 1940.
67 WL, SA/FPA/A7/71, letter by Holland to Pyke to 26 March 1941; Memo by Pyke, 3 April 1941.
68 Hall, *Sex, Gender and Social Change*, p. 123.
69 WL, SA/FPA/A7/101, letter by Holland to Prentif, 7 June 1940.
70 WL, SA/FPA/A7/102, letter by Holland to Pyke, 12 February 1945; letter by Pyke to K. Jinks, 22 August 1947; letter by Pyke to Prentif, 22 August 1947; SA/FPA/A7/67, letter by General Secretary to Lamberts, 1 November 1949.
71 Soloway, *Birth Control*, p. 273.
72 WL, SA/FPA/A7/102, letter by Holland to Pyke, 12 February 1945.
73 WL, SA/FPA/A7/66, memo titled 'Schedule of the clinics we are supplying', c.1940.
74 WL, SA/FPA/A7/71, letter by General Secretary to LRC, 8 April 1937.
75 Cox, *Clinical Contraception*, preface.
76 WL, SA/FPA/A7/66, [complaints of faulty products], 30 November 1934.
77 WL, SA/FPA/A7/101, letter by Pyke to Holland, 5 August 1940.
78 WL, SA/FPA/A7/66, letter by Society for the Provision of Birth Control Clinics to FPA, 14 January 1935.
79 WL, SA/FPA/A7/99, [doctors' orders], 3 November 1936.
80 For example, see SA/FPA/A7/100, memo on factory visit [c.1937]; Memo on Prentif, 8 October 1937; letter by Prentif to Pyke, 20 October 1937.
81 WL, SA/FPA/A7/102, letter Holland to Pyke, 12 February 1945.
82 J. Malleson, *The Principles of Contraception* (London: V. Gollancz, 1935), p. 1. See also, 'Contraceptive technique: *The Principles of Contraception: A Handbook for General Practitioners* by Joan Malleson', *British Medical Journal*, 2:3905 (1935), 901.
83 C. Rusterholz, 'English women doctors, contraception and family planning in transnational perspective (1930–1970)', *Medical History*, 63:2 (2019), 162.
84 WL, SA/FPA/A7/138, miscellaneous advertisements, 1935–43; SA/FPA/A7/99, letter by Stewart to Pyke, 10 October 1936.
85 C. Booysen, 'Quinine as a contraceptive', *Marriage Hygiene*, 2:1 (1935).
86 Prentif, *Contraceptive Practice* (November 1937), pp. 1–4; E. F. Griffith, *Voluntary Parenthood* (London: Heinemann, 1937), pp. 43, 47; SA/FPA/A14/32, letter by Griffith to Pyke, 21 July 1938; SA/FPA/A7/100, Memo of telephone call from Harrison, 8 October 1937.

87   N. Haire, 'The fitting of vaginal diaphragms', in Prentif, *Contraceptive Practice*, 2 (February 1938), pp. 4–5.
88   WL, SA/FPA/A14/32, letter by General Secretary to Griffith, 10 February 1938.
89   WL, SA/FPA/A7/102, letter by General Secretary to C. A. Barnes, 29 June 1948. Helena Wright also developed anatomical models in the 1950s. See Rusterholz, 'English women doctors', 165.
90   Borge, '"Wanting it Both Ways"', p. 205.
91   WL, SA/FPA/A7/71, letter by Cullingham to Holland, 26 July 1934; letter by LRC to medical committee, 6 November 1934; letter by medical committee to LRC, 15 November 1934; 10 January 1935; Memo, 15 May 1936; Note, 9 Sept 1935.
92   WL, SA/FPA/A7/71, telephone memo, 8 November 1936.
93   In his book *Birth Control Methods* (1936), Haire referred to LRC's condoms as among the best available, p. 91; SA/FPA/A7/71, telephone memo, 17 October 1935.
94   WL, SA/FPA/A7/71, 8 April 1937.
95   WL, SA/FPA/A7/71, letter by Holland to Pyke, 26 March 1941.
96   WL, SA/FPA/A7/101, memo, 'Confidential. London Rubber Company', 14 June 1938.
97   WL, SA/FPA/A7/101, letter by Prentif to Holland, 31 May 1940; 'Confidential report on telephone conversation with Mr Harrison of Prentif's re tests made by them of condoms manufactured by LRC (ivory and transparent – latex)', Spring 1940.
98   WL, SA/FPA/A7/101, letter by Prentif to Holland, 2 August 1940.
99   WL, SA/FPA/A4/1, letter by British Drug Houses Ltd to FPA, 3 February 1954; letter by General Secretary to Mrs Court, 5 February 1954.
100 WL, SA/FPA/A7/101, letter by Pyke to Holland, 5 August 1940.
101 WL, SA/FPA/A7/101, letter by Prentif to Holland, 14 May 1940; Holland to Prentif, 16 May 1940; Prentif to Holland, 20 May 1940.
102 WL, SA/FPA/A7/101, letter by Dr R. to FPA, 13 May 1941; SA/FPA/A7/103, telephone conversation with Prentif, 19 December 1951.
103 WL, SA/FPA/A1/40, memo of clinic sales to private patients, c.1956.
104 WL, SA/FPA/A7/101, letter by Captain C. H., RAMC, c/o GPO, Bonnington, Ashford, Kent to FPA, 26 September 1940.
105 WL, SA/FPA/A7/101, letter by Prentif to Holland, 22 June 1944.
106 Borge, '"Wanting it Both Ways"', p, 192.
107 WL, SA/FPA/A7/67, Memo, 26 February 1951; letter by General Secretary to Mrs Rusby, Sheffield, 6 November 1950.
108 Leathard, *The Fight for Family Planning*, p. 92.

109 Borge, '"Wanting it Both Ways'", p. 206.
110 SA/FPA/A7/68, telephone Conversation between P. Cripps and Mr Lambert, 16 April 1951; 'Alterations to Price List', 19 Dec 1957.
111 Borge, '"Wanting it Both Ways'", p. 134.
112 WL, SA/FPA/A1/40, Note on Selling Prices, *c.*1956.
113 Others include Bolton, Burnley, Castleford, Hounslow, East Ham, Bangor, Bristol, Wigan.
114 WL, SA/FPA/A1/40, telephone conversation between Mrs Northage and the Constructive Birth Control Society, 29 June 1956.
115 WL, SA/FPA/A1/40, telephone conversation between Mrs Northage and the Constructive Birth Control Society, 29 June 1956.
116 WL, SA/FPA/A1/40, telephone conversation with Mrs O' Neil of Surbiton branch and General Secretary, 4 October 1961.
117 WL, SA/FPA/A7/75, letter by Clay to Clifford Smith, 15 February 1956; Clay to Northage, 2 March 1956; Cripps to Northage, 23 March 1956; Howard to Northage, 3 May 1956.
118 WL, SA/FPA/A7/67, letter by Lamberts to General Secretary, 9 March 1950; Interview by James with Watkins, 14 November 1950.
119 WL, SA/FPA/A7/67, letter by Lamberts to James, 4 November 1953.
120 WL, SA/FPA/A7/103, letter by Jackson to James, 6 February 1951.
121 WL, SA/FPA/A7/68, telephone conversation between P. Cripps and Watkins, 29 June 1956.
122 WL, SA/FPA/A7/103, letter by Prentif to FPA, 17 December 1952.
123 WL, SA/FPA/A7/103, telephone conversation between Howard and Barnes, 26 November 1952.
124 Borge, '"Wanting it Both Ways'", pp. 216–17.
125 WL, SA/FPA/A7/75, letter by Reid to Clifford Smith, 4 February 1957.

5

Over the counter and on the high street: contraceptive retailing in the urban landscape

Of all the concerns surrounding interwar contraceptive commercialisation, it was the growing visual presence of branded contraceptives on the high street that was the most pronounced. While packaging, print promotion, mail order and clinic supply were viewed by some as problematic to varying degrees, it was the growth in the unmediated retail sale and overt display of contraceptives, and the potential these strategies had to corrupt innocent unmarried adolescents, on which the Contraceptives (Regulation) Bill and surrounding debates focused most heavily. It was contraceptive display within the changing urban consumer landscape that attracted most attention and the aspect of retailing in which contraceptives became most visible. As Margot Finn has remarked, urban consumer culture has become central to revisionist histories of sexual prudery that view the city as a place 'of social, sexual, and spatial emancipation', rather than as a place of conservative repression.[1] Some of the most recent of these histories have explored the city as a queer space.[2] As yet, however, we have not attended to the growing visual presence and availability of contraceptives on the high street.

Chemists, as increasingly important urban contraceptive retailers throughout the interwar period, played a prominent part in such debates. As we will see in this chapter, growing contraceptive visibility on the high street sat uncomfortably alongside chemists' adherence to professional codes of conduct. It was chemists' dual medical-commercial status that not only led to ambiguity and confusion around legitimate contraceptive retailing and the most appropriate ways to regulate it but also fed directly into concerns about the role of the chemist in the new world of modern retailing. Just as clinics grappled with the tensions between medical and commercial provision, so too did chemists. As the boundaries between acceptable and non-acceptable commercialisation of contraceptives in retail were being established, so too were similar boundaries being drawn between the profession of pharmacy and the retail chemist, and who had – and who should have – expertise in contraceptive prescribing, sales and the giving of contraceptive advice. Distinguishing chemists from surgical stores, the other main contraceptive retailer in this period, and establishing what contraceptives were appropriate for a chemist to sell and how, formed a distinct part of mid-twentieth-century chemist professionalisation.

Shopping before the Contraceptives (Regulation) Bill

For retailers of rubber contraceptives established in the mid-nineteenth century, being visible to the small market of knowing consumers while being inconspicuous to the unknowing was the key to success. Consumers in urban shopping centres had long taken advantage of the barber's ability to discreetly disseminate rubber sheaths and condoms to his clients with the subtle enquiry 'something for the weekend, sir?'; but tobacconists, herbalists and booksellers were also retailers that successfully but discreetly sold contraceptives to shoppers.[3] Indeed, it was in his father's hairdressing and tobacconist shop that Lionel A. Jackson, the founder of LRC, first became exposed to sheath selling. His experiences within his father's shop encouraged him to set up his own importing business in 1915.

But as the acceptability of birth control increased after the First World War, place became even more central to contraceptive retailing.[4] Retailers, particularly the growing number of surgical stores, began to prize a more visible urban centre location in order to promote and sell all manner of contraceptives alongside 'serious', 'scientific' and medical works on birth control and cures for sexual disorders. Many surgical stores located themselves in (or relocated to) Soho, alongside new theatres, second-hand bookstores and shops selling pornography, in order to benefit from the area's commercialised cultural tourism consisting of theatre, prostitution, dining, drinking and dancing; by the interwar period, Soho became the centre of Britain's specialist birth control retail trade.[5] Constantine and Jackson, the firm established in 1850 with a dubious reputation for imitations of both contraceptives and birth control manuals, had relocated to the newly constructed Charing Cross Road (connecting Leicester Square to Oxford Street and the Strand), while W. George, established in 1840, relocated to Green Street, near Leicester Square, following the demolition of Wych Street and Holywell Street and the modernisation of the Strand. These stores sat alongside new specialist birth control shops often established by Eastern European emigre Jews, including Ray's Surgical Appliance and Book Store, Johnnie's Rubber Stores and Robert's Surgical Stores. By the 1930s there were reportedly twenty-two specialist birth control shops in the wider Soho district, fourteen of which only sold contraceptives.[6] The Hygienic Stores Ltd alone claimed to have twelve London outlets, including seven within a one-mile radius of its flagship store on Charing Cross Road.

Demand for contraceptive goods was almost certainly driven by Soho's sex industry and was higher in this London district than elsewhere in the country.[7] Indeed, it was Soho's reputation that attracted consumers from other parts of the country; consumers travelled to this area *because* of its reputation, not despite it. The area's improved and cheaper transport links and the fact that surgical stores were open between 10 a.m. and 12 a.m. also provided greater access to consumers from the surrounding counties and beyond.[8] Fisher and Szreter's oral history evidence suggests that both middle- and working-class men in Hertfordshire and Oxford were more likely to use the sheath than those in Blackburn partly due to the close proximity of Hertfordshire and Oxford to London and the range of sheaths available from numerous vendors in the city.[9] Even the police's targeted clean-up of Charing Cross Road in May 1937, which resulted in the widespread confiscation of forms of obscene print, did not limit the contraceptive trade in this area.[10] Surgical stores located beyond Soho, from Camden to West Kensington, and beyond London, from Cambridge to Winchester, similarly began to locate themselves in urban locations accessible to knowing consumers. Located a few streets away from Birmingham's New Street station, Curtis's Surgical Store, for example, aimed to attract consumers going to and from the city's main transport hub. One store even opened opposite Stopes's Whitfield clinic in London, as its proprietor, a Dr Nikola, attempted to profit from sales to women attending the clinic, but also from the passing trade of nearby Tottenham Court Road.[11]

Alongside shop location, a key part of the increasing contraceptive visibility in urban centres in the interwar period was the increasing display of pre-packaged and branded contraceptive goods inside shops and in shop windows.[12] Brightly coloured branded goods began to replace those that were unpackaged and unbranded and those of the kind described by Elderton as appearing on the counters of chemists' shops in the working-class textile manufacturing districts of Lancashire; such branded goods also began to replace the unbranded products that featured in the early displays of department stores and chain chemists, including the Army and Navy Co-Operative Society, Timothy Whites, and John Bell and Croydon.[13] In shop displays before the First World War, unpacked and unbranded enemas, syringes and rubber pessaries blended alongside hot-water bottles and rubber tubing, presenting an often chaotic and excessive aesthetic that signified values of abundance, prosperity and plenty to middle- and working-class consumers, particularly women already eager to consume other medical goods. Such displays, which presented contraceptives as medical hygiene appliances, rarely attracted attention beyond knowing consumers.[14] Even Boots and Co., one of Britain's most successful high-street chemists and renowned for refusing to sell caps and pessaries without prescription until 1949 and sheaths until 1965, openly sold Higginson's syringe alongside other 'hygienic' enemas and promoted them as 'nurse's requisites'.[15] But the growing public discourse on contraception after the war meant displays could be more overt. Like the contraceptive branding and packaging discussed in Chapter 2, the new practice of displaying pre-packaged and branded contraceptive goods was underpinned by the professionalisation of retail salesmanship and aimed at attracting consumer attention, provoking interest and creating desire.[16] Contraceptive manufacturers sent chemists what Rendell called 'dignified counter show cards' to aid promotional display, while Boots openly sold Stopes's 'Racial' soluble pessaries.[17] Yet, while these brightly coloured packages aimed to attract custom, they were rarely explicit about the intended uses for the products contained therein, thus allowing unknowing consumers to browse unencumbered by concerns about respectability.

While shop display was important, window display developed into its own retail specialism inaugurated by the first National Association of Window Display meeting in London in 1921. Business professionals like Herbert Casson argued that window display design was becoming the most 'powerful selling force in modern sales promotion' for its potential not only to encourage consumers to purchase certain goods but to attract into the shop the ubiquitous and anonymous passer-by and convert them into a consumer.[18] Casson stated that 'the truth is that most people walk like automata. If they are thinking at all, they are thinking of their destination or of their own private affairs. Very few go out for the sole purpose of looking at windows. It is only the window with a PULL that can be sure to attract their attention'.[19] The significance of an effective display was the fact it made 'seeing' unavoidable. The visual display facing the world through the window became synonymous with a verbal sales pitch, resulting in contemporary retailers describing the 1920s and 1930s window display as the 'silent salesman'.[20] Chemists and department stores largely considered overt contraceptive window displays offensive, but among the chemists that did invest in contraceptive window display was Hancock of Fleet Street. Hancock claimed his window was tactful and that the contraceptives were displayed 'in a manner which cannot offend the most sensitive or fastidious person'. With his emphasis on the importance of physically inspecting goods before purchase, Hancock invited its catalogue readers to 'call and inspect our goods, see what you are buying', aiming to convert mail-order customers into retail ones too.[21] Rendell was among the manufacturers attempting to convince more chemists to display contraceptives in their windows by providing them with four lithographed showcards in ten colours that purported to be 'A Customer Magnet for Your Window'. Highlighting the continued importance of married mothers as end consumers, these showcards encouraged female consumers to 'be fair to your baby and to yourself! Adopt the Rendell method'. The firm incentivised chemists to display its show cards by stating that it would provide a bonus of one dozen boxes of pessaries if the showcards were displayed in the window for two weeks.[22]

It was the surgical stores of Soho that fully embraced the retail mantra of window display; their windows featured brightly coloured packaged and branded contraceptives with ranges of highly decorative showcards. Displays of the Hygienic Stores Ltd in Cambridge Circus, Soho, and Euston Road in North London, and one of Sims in Praed Street in West London near Paddington were reportedly packed with piles of boxes of 'Hygeolene' contraceptive ointment, 'the Poor Man's Friend' (combined pessary and sheath), 'Pro-Race' and 'Anti-Geniture' rubber caps (Lamberts' or imitations), 'Dr Paterson's Pills', 'Dr Osterman's Pessaries' and a variety of washable sheaths, syringes and enemas alongside showcards announcing the availability of 'Hygienic Rubber Goods', 'Surgical Appliances', 'Medical Books on Birth Control' and 'Whirling Spray Syringes'.[23] If the firm's half-tone image within its catalogue of the mid-1930s is accurate, the Hygienic Stores' flagship store on Charing Cross Road contained no less than fifteen signs spanning along the full height of the building, including those announcing that it was a 'Chemist', 'Pharmacy,' 'Birth Control Specialist', 'French and American druggist' and that it sold a wide range of brands, including 'Damaroids' (for male virility), 'Dr Paterson's Famous Pills' and contraceptive manuals, including Stopes's *Married Love*, Payne's *Wisdom for Wives* and Ostermann's *Birth Control* (fig. 15).[24] Several Soho stores also began to invest in illuminated signs announcing the availability of birth control requisites to attract even greater attention from passers-by. The illuminated sign of one store was over three feet long.[25] Such illuminated

Figure 15 The Hygienic Surgical Store, 95 Charing Cross Road.

signs would not have looked out of place among the bright lights and illuminated advertisements that dominated the area around Piccadilly Circus by the interwar period; they formed part of the artificial lighting of Soho, which represented a technology vital to the local atmospherics and cultural production of the area's nightlife.

Chain surgical stores replicated their window displays beyond Soho. The Camberwell branch of the Hygienic Stores, three miles south-east of the firm's flagship store on Charing Cross Road, for example, reportedly had 'a striking appearance' and its window display was similar in form to its Cambridge Circus and Leicester Square branches, containing both a wealth of contraceptive advertisements and packaged and branded contraceptives ranging from sheaths to chemical pessaries.[26] In other cities, window displays of surgical stores were similarly explicit. Birmingham's Curtis's Surgical Store, for example, displayed a two-foot sign stating 'surgical rubber goods' on the first floor of the building.[27] Yet, the window display of some surgical stores, particularly in provincial towns, were more modest. Window displays of the Stockwell Hygienic Company of Tooting and Croydon, and Phelps (Contraceptives) Ltd of Tottenham still displayed rubber contraceptives unpackaged and unbranded alongside other rubber goods, trusses and hosiery in a manner similar to the interior displays of chemists' and department stores of the pre-war period.[28]

Also forming part of the growing visibility of branded condoms in urban centres was the slot machine. Corresponding with the growth of the railway network across Britain, slot machines retailing tickets and confectionary, such as Nestle's and Fry's chocolate, could be found at many London stations by 1900, and were viewed as a convenient and quick way of making purchases en route. But it was in the late 1920s that new specialist slot machines vending LRC's 'Ona' branded condoms and stating 'Surgical Rubber Ware, Finest Quality, Guaranteed' began to appear outside and within chemists, rubber stores, hairdressers, barbers, tobacconists, garages, public houses and new sites of leisure common among adolescents: the cinema, the dance hall, and the amusement and shopping arcade, thus transforming the condom into a modern commodity like any other.[29] As another form of 'silent salesman', slot machines provided retail chemists, barbers, hairdressers, tobacconists and surgical stores with a new profitable way to sell contraceptives. Manufacturers of weighing machines, a similar form of slot machine, quoted that slot machines would reduce selling expenses, such as marketing and staff costs, by 50 to 75 per cent.[30] Consumers could access goods from machines at all times of the day, including when the shop was closed, and no form of personal interaction between seller and buyer was necessary. Machines might also appeal to passers-by who made unplanned purchasing decisions. While there is little accurate information on how many slot machines vending condoms were installed, at least 166 machines were placed all over London between 1929 and 1950, providing a new conspicuous method of contraceptive commercialisation. The first machines were installed outside surgical stores in Soho and aimed to attract the custom of passers-by who were partaking in the area's cosmopolitan pleasures. The machine of Sid J. Siger of Siger Products Ltd, was located in the heart of Soho on Archer Street, a five-minute walk away from the Hygienic Stores' flagship outlet on Charing Cross Road. It stood in a hatch closed between two folding doors in the centre of the shop window, bearing a sign that stated 'open Monday, Tuesday, Wednesday, Friday, Saturday at 7.30 p.m.' and was accessible when the doors were open.[31]

Beyond Soho, machines were erected outside surgical stores in Hackney, Paddington and outside the shops of barbers, chemists and tobacconists in Battersea, Clerkenwell, Islington and Camden. Indeed, approximately one-third of the 166 slot machines erected in London were located outside barber's shops, most in easy reach of main railway and underground stations, extending the long tradition of barbers selling sheaths. Three, for example, were located on Eversholt Street and Drummond Street, next to Euston station, an area acquiring a reputation for the sale of obscene literature and prostitution. Beyond London, machines were established across Kent, Surrey, Sussex and the more populous cities of Scotland.[32] A number of machines were also installed in Leeds and the wider West Riding of Yorkshire, and in Leicester. Given the West Riding's status as a traditional textile manufacturing region and one long considered a hub of 'neo-Malthusian literature and appliances' for its low birth rate, it is perhaps unsurprising that machines were popular here. Leeds' improved transport network of trams and trains in the first half of the twentieth century also made it easy for consumers to travel into the city from the surrounding towns and villages.[33] The first machine in this region was erected outside Dunsby's Chemists on North Street in the heart of the city centre in 1932 (fig. 16). Providing an insight into the novel and entrepreneurial nature of this

Figure 16 A slot machine vending condoms outside Dunsby's Chemists, Leeds, 1932.

interwar industry, Autovendors, a Leeds-based firm consisting of two car mechanics, supplied the machine to Dunsby. Spotting an opportunity to make profit, the partners purchased one hundred disused Fry's chocolate slot machines and used their mechanical knowledge to convert them into machines vending contraceptives. Autovendors installed the machines wherever they could, including outside another Leeds chemist's shop and one in Bradford, a nearby textile city with a similar, long-established reputation for birth control propaganda, while seven others were erected inside shops in the wider West Yorkshire region.[34] Machines made by other firms were also erected outside three other chemists' in Bradford.[35] The Belgrave Pharmacy in Leicester installed a more conspicuous bright red machine, over six feet tall and three feet wide, outside its shop in 1933. The machine, with the words 'Belgrave Pharmacy' at the top and 'Take what you want 6d and 1/1' at the bottom, covered the doorway when the shop was closed. The machine had forty-four compartments with glass fronts, half were 1s slots and the other half 6d slots. The 6d side contained Aspros, Iodine and cough tablets, while the 1s side contained small packets of LRC's 'Durex' condoms, with 'Guaranteed Absolutely Perfect' written on their side. The machine was apparently in frequent use by the men and boys employed in the nearby factory. The transformation of the contraceptive retailing sector from invisible to visible provided greater access to unknowing and knowing consumers alike.

The adolescent, the shy consumer and the professional chemist

Of course, increasing the visibility of contraceptives on the high street was far from universally popular. The shift to new, modern forms of contraceptive retailing – prominent showcards on shop counters, crowded displays of packaged products in windows and bright slot machines – resulted in intense drafting of and debate over the Contraceptives (Regulation) Bill. Indeed, the first three of the Bill's four clauses prohibited the sale of contraceptives on the street by slot machine and overt promotional shop displays, mandating a penalty of up to £20 for a first offence and £50 for a second offence, while the remaining clause addressed unsolicited print advertising.[36] Like the final clause of the Bill, the first three clauses were primarily aimed at protecting unknowing, unmarried adolescents, whose uncontrollable sexual desires were thought likely to be enflamed by such displays. Interwar concerns about the corrupting influence of contraceptive advertising were rooted in nineteenth-century repressive discourse on print culture and pornography, as we saw in Chapter 3; modern forms of display and the mechanisation of distribution not only altered the focus of such fears, but enhanced them.

The Bill's supporters provided Dawson with evidence that the young and unmarried were attracted to brightly decorated stores and slot machines. Popular American drug stores, such as Heppell's on the Strand, actively sold and promoted Lamberts' 'Pro-Race' pessaries from the mid-1920s and enticed adolescents with their window displays and soda fountains.[37] The morally conservative Public Morality Council, chaired by Arthur Winnington-Ingram, Lord Bishop of London, and supported by purity organisations that had been integral to the passing of the Criminal Amendment Act, including the Mothers' Unions, the White Cross League and the

Salvation Army, compiled its evidence of contraceptive sales and promotion in a six-page booklet titled *To Protect Lives: The Menace of Unchecked Advertisement and Display of Contraceptives*. The Council's other similar publications included *Advertisement and Exposure of Birth Prevention Accessories* and *Typical Incidents Regarding the Use of Contraceptives by Young Persons*.[38] In 1939 the Council claimed to have observed 182 young males and 112 young females inspecting five London-based shop windows on three nights between 6 p.m. and 8 p.m.; 35 of the 294 were attracted enough, they concluded, by the contents in the window to enter the shops.[39] The fervent opposition of such organisations to contraceptive display, however, means that the accuracy of their reporting is difficult to verify. Indeed, some of the Council's claims were so far-fetched – contraceptive firms were using 'the medium of air' to fly aeroplanes with advertising banners across the sky, for example – that it also brings their other claims into doubt.[40] Moreover, there is no evidence to suggest whether those observed entering the shops purchased goods. Independent testimony, however, confirms that surgical stores did play a considerable and valuable role in the dissemination of sexual information to adolescents, who had little opportunity to gain practical, matter-of-fact information elsewhere. Surgical store proprietors asked few questions and gave no moral lectures.[41] For example, Stan Hall's family ran the surgical store in Chesterfield between the early 1920s and 1950s and recalled answering lots of questions from 'grammar school types and high school females'. He recalled allowing them to peruse the various caps and condoms on display, as well as the leaflets and catalogues produced by contraceptive firms and birth control manuals. He even remembered loaning some books from the store to a young couple to read in the local park. The concerns of moralists then were seemingly more justified than their own evidence suggested.

Slot machines that provided adolescents with unrestricted access to condoms caused greater alarm than shop windows. Introducing the Contraceptives (Regulation) Bill in the House of Commons in 1938, Oliver Simmonds, Conservative MP for Duddeston in Birmingham, who had already expressed his concern about the corrupting influence of unsolicited print advertising, stated that 'there has been none on which a stronger feeling has existed among honourable members than on the question of slot machines for the sale of contraceptives'. Simmonds argued that machines in his constituency had been contributing 'very largely' to an increase in 'amateur prostitution'. He argued that girls working in the local factories, who otherwise had been unable to procure contraceptive devices, were now easily able to carry them in their handbags. He also relayed the case of a social worker in an industrial district of Birmingham who had found that a group of 'youngsters had obtained contraceptives or sheaths by manipulating a slot machine, and were playing with them. When he asked them if they knew what they were, the boys replied that they did, and that the girls did and carried them in their bags ready for any boys who wanted them. These were children not yet in their teens'.[42] Simmonds impressed to the House that the corrupting influence of these machines would prevent adolescents from developing into happy and well-functioning adults. While in favour of expanding the provision of sexual education to adolescents, the British Social Hygiene Council was also prompted to support the Bill after it was horrified to receive an offer from the Cigarette Automatic Supply Company of Green Street, Leicester Square, to include Council leaflets in the condom packets it dispensed from its slot machines.[43] Indeed, the Council's vision for youth sexual education did not include industry provision of commercial information, but centred on lectures in sexual instruction. But those within the birth control movement generally opposed the outlawing of slot machines on the basis that any restriction placed on contraceptive access would afflict those with a licit need. Stopes was the most vocal on this: 'I approve of slot machines and I think every chemist should have one. If you knew the appalling increase in abortion which is caused by the absence of slot machines, I am sure you would be on my side and not allow any law against them'.[44] Stopes's argument, that improved contraception and its wider use would reduce the resort to abortion, was a widely used rhetorical strategy in the birth control movement, although of course Stopes remained firmly against distribution by disreputable surgical stores.

Considering the available evidence, Dawson was keen to stress that the Bill was not designed to attack birth control as a moral issue, as the Public Morality Council seemed to suggest, but to set a new standard of contraceptive retailing, one that would permit access to married adults seeking birth control, while restricting the access of adolescents. Yet, as with contraceptive print culture, the question was how to achieve such a standard. Dawson feared that an overly prohibitive Bill – one that outlawed window displays, for example – would deter shy married women from making their contraceptive purchases because they would no longer be able to point out to the shop assistant the goods they required. As Dawson argued, married women, who were shy and/or uneducated, were still too embarrassed to ask for sanitary towels and could only make purchases by pointing to them on display, but their embarrassment over contraceptive purchasing was much more profound. Embarrassment, and even shame, was also reportedly felt by male consumers attempting to purchase condoms from chemists. Brian Hebert, an apprentice in a chemist's shop in Portsmouth in 1939, recalled that all shop staff knew that sheepish-looking customers who entered asking for the pharmacist wanted to buy 'Durex'.[45] While Leslie from Pontypridd never used condoms because he did not like to go into the chemist's shop to ask, Fred procured them from a chemist in a town where no one knew him.[46] Instead of asking for condoms, Jack Backer, a youth in Devon, remembered summoning all his courage to hand a chemist a note asking 'Please could you supply me half a dozen contraceptives that gentlemen use?' After his first successful purchase, Backer took in an empty packet to another chemist and stated 'I'll have half a dozen of these, please'. Embarrassment could also prevent customers buying contraceptives altogether. A number of consumers seemed to have emerged from the chemist's shop with new toothbrushes rather than the contraceptives they had aimed to purchase.[47] These experiences then suggest that window and shop display were vital modern retailing practices that could help subvert consumer embarrassment and assist chemists' legitimate sales.

Dawson was similarly keen for the Bill not to hinder the legitimate business of chemists to sell contraceptive goods. Given their expansion into retailing, chemists had an important role to play in setting the new contraceptive standard. Stopes agreed and stated in the *Leeds Mercury* that 'first class chemists' were vital in the 'open and decent sale of medically and scientifically approved necessities'.[48] Proposals by the House of Lords to introduce a new monitoring role for chemists – to check the age of contraceptive consumers by asking for a birth certificate and checking their hands for a wedding ring – were quickly thrown out for their impracticability. But advice from Hugh Linstead, president of the Royal Pharmaceutical Society, suggested to Dawson just how difficult it would be to introduce statutes aimed at regulating the display and vending activities of the Society's members. Linstead claimed that the problem was 'not chemists' shops in the ordinary sense of the term', but was surgical stores and other retail hybrids, such as druggists and drug stores, for which the Society had no jurisdiction and which were perfectly free to sell contraceptive goods. Indeed, the surgical stores of Soho used the 'chemist' and 'pharmacist' descriptor with little recourse. But Linstead also admitted that there was very little the Society could do to regulate the activities of its extremely diverse membership either.[49] The Pharmacy and Poisons Act 1933 (and updated Pharmacy and Medicines Act 1941) brought together all chemists, ranging from the qualified pharmacist to the wholesale druggist, under the disciplinary control of the Society for the first time through a common register, but until the Society included an explicit clause on the prohibition of contraceptive display in its formal code of professional conduct in 1944, there was little the Society could do to stop its members from displaying contraceptives if they chose to do so.[50]

The Pharmacy Acts only stipulated that a retail chemist required a qualified pharmaceutical chemist on its board of directors in order to use the word 'chemist' in its title and to dispense poisons; however, the Acts did not provide guidance on whether or how such chemists should sell contraceptives. In the expectation that the Contraceptives (Regulation) Bill would become law, the Society's first formal professional code of conduct of 1939 did not address contraceptive display but merely prohibited chemists from enclosing unsolicited contraceptive advertisements in the packaging of other products and from selling medicines with claims to cure sexual weakness.[51] Indeed, it was contravening these clauses that resulted in the expulsion of Abraham Nathan Hancock, the registered chemist and director of Hancock's of Fleet Street, from the Society's register in 1942. Dawson had confirmed that Hancock, along with W. George, had been distributing contraceptive advertising unsolicited through the post since his venture into birth control in the 1920s; he was also responsible for displaying contraceptives in his shop window. But Hancock's use of the 'chemist' title and his promotion of the firm's long history as a chemist since 1760 within his advertising was not only a clear tactic aimed at establishing medical authority and legitimacy within the medical marketplace, but also a clear contravention of the Pharmacy Acts. Hancock's expulsion from the chemist's register prohibited his use of the 'chemist' descriptor, although it did nothing to stop him from operating as a birth control business.[52]

But of course, the abandonment of the Contraceptives (Regulation) Bill before the war meant that the Society's members had no guidance on contraceptive display. Before the Royal Pharmaceutical Society's establishment of its contraceptive display clause in 1944 then, chemists were forced to use their own judgement on whether to overtly display contraceptives and hire slot machines to vend condoms. The lack of clarity on this topic left some chemists questioning their professional role and status. While figures are wanting, it is clear that many chemists continued not to sell, never mind display, contraceptives. Some thought there was already a professional prohibition of their sale. A Lincoln chemist, for example, stated that 'we weren't allowed to advertise or display them'.[53] Others who were against the chemist sale of contraceptives were qualified pharmacists who had been affiliated to the Society long before the establishment of a common register in 1933. Such pharmacists not only opposed the sale of contraceptives from chemists' shops but also opposed methods of modern retail salesmanship in general because they viewed such sales tactics as a cause in the decline of the business of the traditional pharmacy. For example, a 47-year-old pharmacist of Finchley, touting for work in the *Chemist and Druggist* in 1935, explicitly stated in his advertisement that he was 'not in sympathy with modern developments of the chemist's business, particularly with regard to contraceptives'.[54]

Since the late nineteenth century, such pharmaceutical chemists had bewailed that the emerging intensively competitive retail market of pre-packaged and branded goods undermined their expertise in prescribing and dispensing medicines and represented a threat to their very livelihood and the pharmaceutical profession. They feared that the skill, knowledge and qualification of the pharmacist that had once been integral to the art of medicine dispensing were being replaced by the new business technique of displaying the pre-formulated and packaged medicines and appliances that modern consumers demanded. As early as 1898, the *Chemist and Druggist* quoted the President of the Pharmaceutical Society who described company pharmacists as 'Judas-like' traitors, degrading pharmacy 'to the lowest depths of mere commercialism'.[55] By the interwar period, such chemists assisted the Public Morality Council with the collection of evidence highlighting the dangerous effects of contraceptive display on adolescents. The eventual development of the display clause in the code of conduct in 1944 was prompted by a chemist in Exeter, who had suggested that the association between 'surgical goods' and pharmacy was damaging the profession.[56]

Some chemists disliked modern methods of retail salesmanship but felt they had no choice but to stock popular pre-packaged and branded goods (including contraceptives) as demand for counter dispensing declined and they were forced to compete with department stores, co-operatives and other retailers for custom. Large chain chemists, department stores and co-operatives were unlike small independent chemists and could afford to offer low prices as they profited from discounts and bulk purchasing from manufacturers. Chemists complained that such price undercutting reduced their profits from the sale of proprietary goods to almost nothing.[57] The Proprietary Articles Trade Association (PATA), founded in 1896, aimed to protect its chemist members from price cutting by setting agreed retail prices, and refused to supply non-members. Rendell had been a proud member of the PATA since the 1920s, along with nearly five hundred other manufacturers, and thus the price of its pessaries remained at 2s 6d across the entire retail sector.[58] Contraceptives, however, were not eligible under the National Pharmacists Union's Chemists' Friends Scheme. This scheme, launched in 1936, was a new price-cutting rival to PATA that sought to professionalise chemists' business practices and restrict sales to appropriate pharmaceutical outlets, boycotting the products of manufacturers who supplied them to non-chemists.[59] The scheme's chairman refused to listen to continual petitions from Harrison of Prentif and stated that the movement was not intended to protect contraceptive manufacturers.[60]

But other chemists continued to accept and even embrace contraceptive selling and display as part of their role as modern retailers.[61] Numerous chemist customers of Lamberts, for example, reassured Stopes that the Pharmacy and Medicines Act 1941 would not mean that Lamberts would be forced to reveal the formula of its 'Racial' soluble pessaries and thus be open to imitation.[62] A correspondent in the *Chemist and Druggist* in 1941 further confirmed that the Act placed 'no restriction on the sale of contraceptives, mechanical or chemical, which do not contain poisons, by drug stores which have no qualified chemist in charge, patent medicine dealers, hygiene stores, herbalists, hairdressers etc.'[63] Feedback from three Manchester-based chemists following consultation with the Royal Pharmaceutical Society's members on the new code in 1943 suggested that the clause prohibiting contraceptive display was unwelcome because it raised moral, rather than professional issues. Arguing that the clause was reactionary, presumably in the face of increasing wartime sales of condoms, the three chemists stated that the clause should be deleted because it was an unwelcome interference in the chemist's personal freedom. Moreover, like Dawson, these chemists suggested that such a clause would deter the shy consumer.[64] In this uncertain, unregulated and increasingly competitive market, such chemists appreciated the high returns contraceptives provided. Recognising the importance of chemist profits and how profitable contraceptives were for the chemists' trade, contraceptive manufacturers provided chemists with what they described as 'very generous trade terms', which aimed to match those offered to birth control clinics. As early as 1922, Lamberts offered chemists profit of one-third of the net price paid for its 'Pro-Race' caps.[65] Both Herbert Fromm, the German firm that had established a British base in the 1930s (and that Prentif accused of imitating its products and literature) and F. W. Cassell, a new contraceptive supplier established in 1935 in Nottingham, promised chemists 300 per cent profit on their branded condoms.[66] The Public Morality Council estimated that profits from the retail sale of contraceptives averaged between 375 to 500 per cent, although the Monopolies and Mergers Commission's investigation into LRC suggest that such figures are a gross exaggeration.[67] Retailers could make up to 75 per cent profit on 'Durex' sales until 1953, when they dropped to 67.5 per cent.[68]

Chemists were also receptive to manufacturers' growing fleet of travelling salesmen. Travelling salesmanship was becoming a low-cost but increasingly efficient way to establish the reputation of contraceptive manufacturers and the quality of their products in the 1930s modern retail market, particularly among smaller and rural chemists.[69] It cut printing costs, allowed firms to circumvent the difficulty of advertising in the professional press as well as aided the development of informal, personal relationships between chemists and firms' representatives. With their entry into latex production in the 1930s, LRC and International Latex Ltd were quick to employ travelling salesmen, advertising positions for travelling representatives in the *Chemist and Druggist*.[70] It may have been through the journal's classified advertisements that Frank Rickman came to work for LRC. From the late 1930s Rickman canvassed chemists' shops in North West England, and as LRC's sales grew into the 1940s he concentrated solely on Lancashire. While it is difficult to estimate how many salesmen were employed in contraceptive distribution, it was almost certainly considerably fewer than similarly sized firms in other industries with around 130 travelling representatives.[71] However, the sales force of LRC was certainly large enough to target both retail outlets and birth control clinics within specific geographical areas of the country from 8 a.m. to 6 p.m., six days a week.[72] With wages based on commission, each representative took two weeks to visit all the relevant retail outlets in his area before starting again.

Manufacturers also appealed to chemists' professional sensibilities by promoting the fact that they only supplied qualified chemists. Stating as much to Dawson, Angus Reid, LRC's managing director, suggested that he believed that the law should confine contraceptive sales to chemists, with around eight hundred of which LRC did business (although the firm claimed to the Family Planning Association that the figure was more like eight thousand).[73] Supplying about five thousand of the fourteen thousand registered pharmacists, Prentif claimed in its catalogues that

> in the firm belief that it is in the best interests of the user, the retail sale of 'Prentif' contraceptive products is confined to chemists. By virtue of his professional training and sense of responsibility the chemist, who is in the habit of handling surgical supplies, fall naturally into the position of one capable of advising and recommending in those cases where a Doctor's assistance is not called for.[74]

Indeed, Prentif claimed to only supply chemists that agreed to supply its goods by doctor's prescription only.[75] There is certainly evidence to verify Prentif's assertion that some chemists did feel a sense of responsibility to sell and prescribe contraceptives, valuing their expertise as vital to the purchasing process.

While other modern commodities freely on display encouraged consumer browsing and reduced the need for shop assistance, the chemist still needed to produce the condom from under the counter.[76] Some chemists were self-conscious about this particular aspect of their business and reluctantly stocked contraceptives as demand increased, but many were more knowledgeable about contraceptives than doctors and, like surgical store proprietors, could also play an important role in imparting sexual knowledge to the unmarried and ignorant.[77] The chemists located in popular honeymoon spots and seaside resorts sometimes had to guide newly married couples on sexual matters. Ronald Crisp, a newly qualified pharmacist in the early 1930s who worked in a chemist's shop in Torquay, Devon, recalled that couples would ask the pharmacist all sorts of questions about sex.[78] Indeed, chemists in the British seaside resort, as a central site of extra-marital affairs in the early twentieth century, commonly stocked and sold contraceptives. Interwar Brighton, for example, was at the height of its reputation for promiscuity during this period of sexual geographic ghettoisation.[79] Chemists' experience with products meant that they were also able to recommend certain brands on request. One chemist in Earlsfield, south-west London, recommended Rendell's pessaries to a female consumer and showed her the firm's pamphlets on birth control, while another from Llanelly informed a male customer that Rendell's pessaries were 'the best out there', suggesting that both men and women purchased Rendell's pessaries from chemists' shops with useful assistance.[80]

Yet of course, while presenting themselves as solely supplying chemists, contraceptive manufacturers simultaneously continued to supply surgical stores, barbers, tobacconists and slot machines with other brands. Reid denied Dawson's allegations that it was LRC's 'Ona' and 'Durex' brand condoms that were commonly stocked in slot machines, downplaying the extent of the surgical store trade and the fact that chemists sold condoms to adolescents, but his testimony is difficult to verify. Chemists, surgical stores, tobacconists, hairdressers and barbers could certainly have purchased the firm's condoms in bulk and stocked slot machines themselves, but Reid was nonetheless aware of the machine vending of his condoms. As Jessica Borge's study of LRC has suggested, LRC would often say 'one thing whilst doing another' in order to conceal from competitors the workings of the company's practical operation and retailing agreements.[81] Reid seemed fearful that the success of machine vending would open up to competitors the contraceptive market from which it had generated much of its profits, but his denial of involvement to Dawson also reveals his desire to maintain a veneer of professional respectability. LRC's involvement in machine vending is all the more likely given that Reid admitted to Dawson that the company had tried vending machine sales in the past: 'we did, as a matter of fact, try out one dozen a considerable time ago, although not without misgiving and the experiment was an utter failure'.[82] Portraying the attempt as a failure was seemingly an attempt to distract Dawson, but Dawson's handwritten notes of the company's extensive trade with surgical stores, tobacconists and hairdressers suggest that Dawson was aware of Reid's duplicitousness, although it is unclear whether he realised that the practice of British manufacturers offloading their inferior rubber goods to surgical stores was commonplace.

By the time the Royal Pharmaceutical Society had introduced its professional code prohibiting contraceptive display in 1944, some chemists had long been supplying and promoting contraceptive goods and had been guided by their own discretion, moral compass and profit requirements to do so. While the 'chemist' descriptor carried with it respectability and professionalism, the average consumer was unlikely to have been aware of the different professional permutations and the varying chemist stances on contraceptive sale and promotion. Indeed, consumers were not always able to differentiate between product brands, as we saw with the imitations of Rendell's 'Wife's Friend' and Lamberts' 'Pro-Race' in Chapter 2, never mind types of retailer. The flooding of the market with all manner of prepacked and branded proprietary medicines and appliances (including contraceptives) had not only made it much more competitive for chemists but it also resulted in the increasing homogenisation of the retail sector. Some consumers would purchase from the store that supplied their preferred product at the cheapest price or was the most conveniently located on the high street. An observer in the *Chemist and Druggist* in 1924 stated that

> the unregistered persons who delight to call their places of business pharmacies benefit by the submerging of the professional side of our business. That any body of traders who are not pharmacists can legally style their businesses pharmacies is an abnormity which is bound to confuse in the public mind the distinction between us and them. Between their windows and ours the difference is often *nil*, and between our general spirit and behaviour and theirs it is not always discernible.[83]

Slot machines and post-war retailing

Immediately after the Second World War, it was slot machines and their continued potential to corrupt adolescents that became the target of a renewed moral panic on contraceptive commercialisation. The rising number of slot machines on Britain's streets aligned with post-war economic, social and moral anxieties linked to the rise of a secular, consumerist, mass-democratic society. But the revival of parliamentary discussion on contraceptive regulation in 1949 was a direct result of a new policy under the Labour government of granting licences for slot machine manufacture 'without limiting the range of articles to be vended'. The newly created Ministry of Supply incorporated this policy into its measures for bringing much-needed investment into the post-war economy. A number of MPs (including Labour MPs) questioned the morality of granting licences for machines that the government knew would vend contraceptives, but George Strauss, the Minister of Supply, stated that it was not the government's role to dictate the kinds of goods licensed companies should be stocking in machines. Strauss deemed stimulating the economy more important than any moral argument.[84] Accordingly, the Public Morality Council and its supporters sought to gather more data on the damage caused to adolescents by this unmonitored and unregulated form of contraceptive supply; they switched from monitoring window displays to monitoring slot machine sales, reporting high sales from machines in London, Leeds, Birmingham and Denbighshire.[85] A member of the National Council of Women reported being approached by a mother much distressed who said that she had found a contraceptive in the pocket of her 14-year-old son, who had obtained it from a machine in Leeds.[86] Further opposition to machines in Leeds and the West Riding came from two hundred representatives of the West Riding Federation of Councils of Free Church Women.[87] In Birmingham, Reverend Bryan Green urged readers of the *Birmingham Gazette* to write to their local MP to urge them to ban such machines in their local district.[88] Henry Morris-Jones, doctor and Liberal MP for Denbigh, reported receiving one hundred letters a day from constituents about the sale of contraceptives from slot machines.[89] While content for consumers to purchase condoms from men's hairdressers directly, the Hackney branch of the National Hairdressers' Federation also unanimously agreed that hairdressers in the vicinity should not have machines for the sale of contraceptives outside their shops.[90]

Basil Henriques, vice-president of the National Association of Boys' Clubs and chairman of East London Juvenile Court, and Cynthia Colville, Lady in Waiting to Queen Mary and a magistrate at the Toynbee Hall Juvenile Court, wrote to *The Times* to express their anger at the government's promotion of slot machines at the expense of 'today's youth'.[91] Convinced that such machines encouraged delinquent behaviour and juvenile crime in the fragile post-war years, Henriques and Colville outlined a case of two boys, aged 13 and 16, who attempted to break into a machine fixed to the wall outside a tobacconist's and confectioner's shop. Further evidence of juvenile delinquency was presented by chemists, who reported that a number of machines across London had been stolen over the Christmas holidays when they had not been present and their shops had been closed.[92] The Ministry of Supply's blasé response to such reports further infuriated Henriques and Colville, who fumed that encouraging promiscuous intercourse between adolescent boys and girls was tantamount to selling England's birth right simply to get dollars.[93]

Increasing opposition to slot machines, however, did not result in the revival of the Contraceptives (Regulation) Bill, but it did lead to the introduction of a local byelaw that prohibited the sale of contraceptives from such machines and decreed the dismantling of those in operation. The Archbishop of Canterbury, Geoffrey Fisher, along with his wife, Rosamond, who was president of the Mothers' Union, urged the early adoption and vigorous enforcement of the byelaw: 'all Christians should make quite sure that their local authorities do not delay in adopting it', while York Convocation appealed to its local council to quickly adopt it.[94] Supported by the Association of Municipal Councils, the byelaw was adopted by 90 per cent of local authorities across the country and hailed as 'a victory for decency' by *Christian World*.[95] Yet, evoking fears of the 1930s debates, chemists and surgical stores were concerned about the damage this byelaw would do to their business. Both Sid J. Siger, who ran Siger Products on Archer Street where the first contraceptive vending machine had been established in 1929, and Dunsby, the chemist in Leeds, insisted that the machines outside their shops allowed them to do legitimate contraceptive business and argued that they had received no complaints about the machines in the twenty years they had been there.[96] In fact, Siger stated that many customers had thanked him for the fact that they were able to obtain contraceptives from the machine late into the evening.

Other retailers also resented this form of State interference into their trade, and opposition to the byelaw came from prominent individuals and organisations, as well as individual consumers. Oxford University Labour Group viewed the byelaw as 'intolerant and narrow-minded', while Norman Haire, by now a renowned gynaecologist and sex reformer with first-hand experience of censorship laws (as we saw in Chapter 3), stated that the byelaw only served to advertise contraceptives further.[97] In the *Freethinker*, the secular and anti-Christian publication, J. H. D. Butler compared the byelaw to the Contagious Diseases Acts of the 1860s and aligned the Public Morality Council with the religious fanatics who saw venereal disease as a righteous punishment from God for promiscuity.[98] Individual consumers complained in national and local newspapers. A number wrote to the *Sunday Pictorial*, a newspaper known for its liberal stance on contraceptives and, at times, daring sexual content.[99] A Navy wife and ex-Wren of Wimbledon wrote to the newspaper to express her amusement at the concern that contraceptives could get into the hands of adolescents and children, given that 'lads on service in the Navy' had already been given such products. A man from Pinner, Middlesex, stated that he was disappointed to see the *Sunday Pictorial* supporting the plea to abolish the free sale of contraceptives from machines because they diminished the likelihood of illegitimate births to young girls and checked the spread of venereal disease to young men. A woman from Bournemouth expressed surprise that there was no other alternative to prevent these machines from being displayed for 'the curious and natural interest of children'.[100] A correspondent identified only as 'J. C.' felt obliged to write to the *Willesden Chronicle* not to defend the use of contraceptives, but to condemn the condemnation of the slot machine: 'If the automatic vending machines had been selling commodities such as cigarettes or chewing gum, then there would have been no complaints, but because the machines sell contraceptives – some people had their dirty little narrow minds stimulated'. 'J. C.' noted that opponents to contraceptive slot machines were of 'the older generation, who tend to see dirt where there is no dirt, and who tend to judge other people's behaviour as sinful only because it is different from their own', observing that they were also 'churchgoers or those with a strict religious upbringing'.[101]

Examples of protest against the byelaw notwithstanding, a report by R. J. B. McDowell, the Chief Officer of the Public Control Department, noted that there was only one machine left working in his district of London in January 1950, and this had been moved inside the shop and was not visible from outside the premises. Of the other 165 machines in London, 122 machines were being removed, 41 had been adapted to sell other products (notably razor blades) with all branding of contraceptive products removed and 2 were empty.[102] By June 1950 there were only fifteen machines still in use in London, twelve of those vending razors and three Aspirin; by June 1951 there were only six left, four of which were empty with no indication of contents while the other two contained Aspirin.

By 1951 the slot machine method of promotion and distribution had disappeared from the country's high streets.[103] But did the removal of these machines solve the risk of exposure of contraceptives to adolescents? While hailed as a victory for decency by the Church and indeed Henriques himself, adolescents were still able to access contraceptives by other means, not least by pointing at contraceptives in the windows of surgical stores or asking chemists to retrieve condoms from under the counter. Indeed, the retail sale of contraceptives increased. The four hundred or so surgical stores across Britain continued to display contraceptives in their windows unabashed, offering sexual advice to adolescents and adults alike, and barbers, hairdressers and other retailers continued to freely supply contraceptive goods, displaying advertisements and showcards in their premises and windows.[104] Henriques recalled talking to a boy of 15 who was seen going off with a well-known prostitute to whom, it turned out, he had arranged to pay 7s 6d. He asked the boy if he was feeling annoyed with him for having been instrumental in removing slot machines from the streets. "'Not particularly", he casually replied, "I can always get one when I want from my father's shop."' His father was a barber.[105]

However, tensions between professionalism and commercialism within the pharmacy trade over contraceptive sales and display remained. Contraceptive manufacturers stepped up their efforts to supply chemists with their ready-made attractive counter displays and by increasing their workforce of travelling salesmen.[106] Aligned with its print marketing campaign, W. J. Rendell encouraged chemists to purchase new bright shop displays and show cards claiming that they would give confidence to regular purchasers and would 'attract new customers who, seeing our advertisements, have become interested in the problems of feminine hygiene'; LRC, meanwhile, provided chemists with plastic shelf strips displaying the 'Durex' brand name.[107] While by no means all chemists were receptive to visits from manufacturers' sales representatives, LRC was able to build a sales department formed of travelling representatives. By 1965 it employed 33 salesmen to look after 1,200 accounts.[108] Joe Buxton, one of LRC's salesmen employed by the firm from 1951, had built up a customer base of a thousand chemist's shops in Central and East London by 1965. Chemists remained attractive customers; they not only accounted for 80 per cent of the overall contraceptive retail trade by 1965 but also continued to provide medical legitimacy and respectability to their goods.[109] Yet, at the same time, manufacturers were fighting against the Pharmaceutical Society's more restrictive and explicit 1953 Statement Upon Matters of Professional Conduct, developed in collaboration with the increasingly authoritative Family Planning Association. The Society's new statement prohibited all exhibition and advertisement of contraceptives within stores and windows, the only exception being 'a notice approved by the Council [of the Pharmaceutical Society] bearing the words "Family Planning Requisites"'.[110] The Association had imposed the use of this notice on manufacturers with contraceptives on its approved list since the mid-1930s with the aim of curbing its association with commercial displays, but the 1953 clause meant that it now applied to all contraceptives sold by chemists.[111]

The effects of the 1953 statement on chemist displays, and indeed the clauses in those in 1944 and 1939 before it, are difficult to establish because not only did company supply of display material to chemists increase but, again, the Society's disciplinary mechanisms were unlikely to be able to extend to all chemists across the country. Chemists continued to hold diverse views on contraceptives and their own role in their dissemination and display. Moreover, it is clear that chemists on both sides of the debate initially called for the removal of the contraceptive display clause from the statement, arguing either that contraceptives had nothing to do with the work of a pharmacist or that it was right for chemists to display contraceptives because if they did not, sales would fall back into the hands of the 'undesirable types of shops'. This, again, highlighted the value of chemist professionalism and expertise.[112] The clause remained in place until 1970; it did at least provide chemists with definitive guidance on professional practice and acted as a rhetorical device for promoting pharmacy as a bona fide profession to the public. Certainly, other attempts by the Society to enhance its professional image and disassociate itself from the business practices of other forms of retailer were unsuccessful. For example, it failed in its attempt to prosecute Boots in 1953 for introducing self-service in one of its stores; self-service was a business practice increasingly adopted by other forms of retailer but one which the Society claimed contravened Pharmacy Acts. The Society's failure to prosecute Boots meant that the firm subsequently applied self-service to all branches, although many other chemists retained counter service into the 1960s because they valued the pharmaceutical and retailing expertise of the chemist.[113] Overall then, the post-war slot machine byelaw and the Royal Pharmaceutical Society's statement of conduct had some effect in restricting overt commercialism by chemists and contraceptive access to unknowing and impulsive consumers, but they did little to prevent retail sales to the knowing consumer, adolescent or otherwise.

Conclusion

The growing presence of contraceptives in the urban commercial landscape from the First World War onwards not only formed part of the increasing liberation of sexual attitudes and the rising acceptability of birth control but also formed part of the modernisation of retailing. In the new interwar retail market, specialists in birth control like surgical stores competed with new and old general retailers alike, including department stores, chemists, barbers and tobacconists, to supply contraceptives. The new retail practices of displaying contraceptives in brightly coloured and branded boxes within attractive shop and window displays and slot machines became increasingly important in attracting both knowing consumers and passers-by, although the explicit nature of such displays varied between types of retailer. In particular, the window displays of the birth control shops of 1930s Soho, with brightly coloured packages, signs and lights, and slot machines including the words 'surgical rubber ware' left nothing to be desired in aiming to attract both male and female passers-by already partaking in the consumer pleasures of the urban environment. It was this growth in contraceptive retailing and its potential to attract unmarried adolescents that prompted attempts at legal regulation in the form of the Contraceptives (Regulation) Bill in the 1930s with the aim of setting a new contraceptive retailing standard.

Chemists, in the process of a professional transition from qualified dispenser and compounder of medicines to a retailer adhering to modern retail practices, held a difficult and unique position in setting this new standard. Aligning with the Public Morality Council and other opposition groups, the Royal Pharmaceutical Society, in its role as statutory body for all chemists from 1933, sought to prohibit its members from overtly displaying contraceptives in their shops and windows and from providing consumer access to condoms via slot machines. Yet, without specific Society guidance until at least 1944, chemists were free to supply and display contraceptives, resulting in a diverse trade. Some chemists stocked contraceptives, incorporating the business into their professional practice of providing consumers with advice and valuing the high profit margins such goods provided in an increasingly competitive market. Some were vocal in their disagreement with any professional prohibition on contraceptive sale or display, arguing that it confused commercial issues with moral ones and interfered with freedom of choice. Others outright rejected contraceptives as part of the modernisation of retail pharmacy and refused to sell them, never mind display them. But even the introduction of the slot machine byelaw in 1949 and the Royal Pharmaceutical Society's more restrictive clause on contraceptive display in its statement of conduct in 1953 did not succeed in repressing the trade among its members and, judging from the opposition to the byelaw, did not seem to reflect public opinion on contraceptive retailing. While surgical stores, barbers and other retailers were still overtly displaying contraceptives, manufacturers of soluble pessaries, rubber pessaries and condoms continued to supply chemists with shop display material to promote their goods. The disappearance of slot machines and restrictions on chemists' displays may have limited purchases by unknowing consumers and passers-by, but did not restrict the retail trade in contraceptives to any significant extent.

Notes

1. M. Finn, 'Sex and the city: metropolitan modernities in English history', *Victorian Studies*, 44 (2001/2), 25.
2. M. Cook, *London and the Culture of Homosexuality, 1885–1914* (Cambridge: Cambridge University Press, 2008); M. Houlbrook, *Queer London: Perils and Pleasures in the Sexual Metropolis, 1918–1957* (Chicago: University of Chicago Press, 2005); H. Smith, *Masculinity and Same-Sex Desire in Industrial England, 1895–1957* (Basingstoke: Palgrave Macmillan, 2015).
3. See, for example, Sutton, *We Didn't Know Aught*, p. 89; Szreter and Fisher, *Sex Before the Sexual Revolution*, pp. 240–1. There were approximately four hundred thousand tobacconists in Britain by the 1930s. WL, PP/BED/B.2, Note on National Retail Union of Tobacconists. c.1933.
4. For example, L. Nead, *Victorian Babylon: People, Streets and Images in Nineteenth-Century London* (New Haven and London: Yale University Press, 2005); Rappaport, *Shopping for Pleasure*.

5 J. R. Walkowitz, *Nights Out: Life in Cosmopolitan London* (New Haven and London: Yale University Press, 2012). See also, P. Bailey, 'Fats Waller meets Harry Champion: Americanization, national identity and sexual politics in inter-war British music hall', *Cultural and Social History*, 4:4 (2007), 495–509.
6 LMA, A/PMC/067, report on the growth of contraceptives.
7 S. A. Slater, 'Containment: Managing street prostitution in London, 1918–1959', *Journal of British Studies*, 49:2 (2010), 346.
8 M. Ogburn, *Spaces of Modernity: London's Geographies 1680–1780* (New York and London: Guilford Press, 1998); Trentmann, *Empire of Things*, p. 174; B. Edwards, 'West End Shopping with *Vogue*: 1930s geographies of metropolitan consumption', in Benson and Ugolini (eds), *Cultures of Selling: Perspectives on Consumption and Society since 1700* (Abingdon: Ashgate, 2006), pp. 29–58.
9 K. Fisher, '"She was quite satisfied with the arrangements I made": gender and birth control in Britain, 1920–1950', *Past and Present*, 169 (2000), 170; Fisher, *Birth Control, Sex, and Marriage*, p. 127; Szreter and Fisher, *Sex Before the Sexual Revolution*, pp. 239, 259.
10 Sigel, *Making Modern Love*, pp. 23–4.
11 Brand, 'Birth Control Nursing', p. 242.
12 *Business Methods for Chemists* (London: Retail Pharmacists' Union, 1932), p. 38. Fraser, *The Coming of the Mass Market*, p. 7; WL, PP/MCS/A.7, letter by Stopes to anon, 6 April 1920.
13 Elderton, *Report on the English Birth-Rate*, p. 35; Army and Navy Co-Operative Society, *Yesterday's Shopping: The Army and Navy Stores Catalogue, 1907* (London: David and Charles, 1969); Army and Navy, *General Catalogue* (n.p.: 1883), p. 593.
14 Parker, 'Sign consumption', 353, 360–5; P. Wallis, 'Consumption, retailing and medicine in early modern London', *Economic History Review*, 61 (2008), 26–53.
15 Monopolies and Mergers Commission, *Contraceptive Sheaths* (1975), p. 12; Boots Company PLC Records Centre, Nottingham (hereafter Boots), WBA/BT/11/37/3/6, *Catalogue* (n.p., 1911), p. 123; Boots, 'The Bee', 1, 5 December 1924.
16 Bowlby, *Carried Away*, pp. 40, 56. Trentmann, *Empire of Things*.
17 WL, SA/FPA/A13/46.2, Advertisement for Racial Solubles, 1 March 1930.
18 G. L. Timmins, *Window Dressing: The Principles of 'Display'* (London: Sir I. Pitman and Sons, 1922); L. M. Feery, *Modern Window Display: A Practical Guide for the Shopkeeper* (London: Cassell's Business Handbooks, 1922); H. Casson, *Twelve Tips on Window Display* (London: The Efficiency Magazine, 1924); W. N. Taft, *Handbook of Window Display* (New York: McGraw-Hill, 1926). For a broader

perspective on window displays in 1930s London, see B. Edwards, 'Making the West End Modern: Space, Architecture and Shopping in 1930s London' (PhD thesis, University of the Arts, London, 2004).
19 H. Casson, *Window Display Above All* (London: The Efficiency Magazine, [1934]), p. 78.
20 Bowlby, *Carried Away*, p. 35.
21 Hancock, *Shadow of the Stork* (1933; 1934), p. 8.
22 'A customer magnet for your window,' *Chemist and Druggist* (2 January 1932), p. 19.
23 LMA, A/PMC/067, report on the growth of contraceptives.
24 The Hygienic Stores Ltd, *Revised Catalogue of Birth Control and Surgical Rubber Goods* (n.p., 1937).
25 Hansard, 'Contraceptives Bill', HL vol. 90, col. 962 (27 February 1934).
26 WL, PP/BED/B.2, PMC report on shops selling contraceptives and certain books, Camberwell Green, 11 December 1933.
27 Curtis's Surgical Store Ltd., *Revised Catalogue of Surgical Rubber Goods, Pro-Race Appliances and Medical Sundries* (n.p., 1925), p. 1.
28 A. Willis, *How to Limit Your Family* (London: Stockwell Hygienic Co. Ltd, 1940), p. 64; A. Phelps, *Children by Desire* (1940; 1948), p. 1.
29 WL, PP/BED/B.2, 'Report by Chief Officer of the Public Control Department, R. J. B. McDowell', 30 January 1950. 'This Contraceptive Business', *Lancet* (9 April 1938), p. 852.
30 See, for example, *Chemist and Druggist* (12 January 1929), p. 25; (2 February 1929), p. 47; (9 March 1929), p. 16; (12 April 1929), p. 35; (8 December 1928), p. 27; (23 November 1929), p. 27. By 1929, Super-Automatic Aspro Machine Company claimed that hundreds of pharmaceutical chemists had already installed its machine. Weighing machine manufacturers, including W. and T. Avery of Birmingham, also targeted chemists with their new penny-in-the-slot weighing machines.
31 LMA, LCC/PC/SHO/1/048, Shops Act – Sale of Contraceptives from Automatic Machines, Inspectors' Reports, Correspondence, etc., 1949–51, General papers, number 32b, Correspondence with Metropolitan Borough Council, June 1950.
32 Hansard, 'Contraceptives (Regulation) Bill', HC vol. 342, col. 2428 (16 December 1938).
33 Fisher, *Birth Control, Sex, and Marriage*, p. 127 from Elderton, *Report on the English Birth-Rate*, p. 107. WL, PP/BED/B.2, letter from Chief Constable to Carlton Oldfield, Leeds, 2 December 1932.
34 Ittmann, 'Family limitation'.
35 WL, PP/BED/B.2, letter from Fred Webster, superintendent to Chief Constable, Leeds City Police, 6 April 1933.

36 Contraceptives Bill, no. 110; no. 115.
37 BL, Add. MS 58638, letter by Lambert to Stopes, 27 October 1922. Heppell's took over many British pharmacies from 1924.
38 LMA, A/PMC/067, report on the growth of contraceptives.
39 LMA, A/PMC/067, report on the growth of contraceptives.
40 LMA, A/PMC/067, grave contraceptive scandal, *c*.1937.
41 Humphries, *Secret World of Sex*, p. 60.
42 Hansard, 'Contraceptives (Regulation) Bill', HC vol. 342, cols. 2421–2 (16 December 1938).
43 WL, PP/BED/B.2, distribution of contraceptives through automatic machines, June–July 1930.
44 WL, SA/FPA/A13/46.1, letter by Stopes to Lt Col. The Right Hon Sir Samuel Hoare, Home Office, 15 December 1938.
45 Anderson and Berridge, 'The role of the community pharmacist', p. 66.
46 Fisher, *Birth Control, Sex, and Marriage*, pp. 147–8.
47 Humphries, *Secret World of Sex*, p. 112; Fisher, *Birth Control, Sex, and Marriage*, pp. 143–9.
48 WL, SA/FPA/A14/91.1, Stopes, 'A mistake about birth control', *Leeds Mercury* (28 January 1932).
49 WL, PP/BED/B.2, letter by Linstead to Dawson, 7 April 1933.
50 A Bill to Amend the Pharmacy and Poisons Act 1933, to prohibit certain advertisements relating to medical matters, and to amend the law relating to medicines, no. 41 (London: The Stationery Office, 1941).
51 Borge, '"Wanting it Both Ways"', pp. 170–3.
52 'Statutory committee meeting', *Chemist and Druggist* (11 July 1942), p. 34–7; (18 July 1942), p. 58–9; 'Removed from the register' (1 August 1942), p. 1.
53 Sutton, *We Didn't Know Aught*, p. 88.
54 [classified advertisements], *Chemist and Druggist* (2 March 1935), p. xxviii.
55 Brownfield-Pope, 'From Chemist Shop to Community Pharmacy', p. 32.
56 'Branch representatives' meetings – a code of ethics', *Chemist and Druggist* (1 October 1938), p. 363; LMA, A/PMC/067, Typical incidents regarding the use of contraceptives by young persons, 15 December 1938.
57 'Manchester essays – what should be the attitude of the Pharmacist in respect of Proprietary Medicines advertised to the Public?', *Chemist and Druggist* (3 February 1923), pp. 164–5.
58 'Price protection problems', *Chemist and Druggist* (2 October 1926), p. 540.

59 Brownfield-Pope, 'From Chemist Shop to Community Pharmacy', p. 109.
60 'National Pharmacists Union Secretary at Greenwich', *Chemist and Druggist* (30 April 1938), p. 491; 'Chemists Friend Scheme' (4 February 1939), p. 117.
61 S. Anderson, 'Community pharmacy and sexual health in twentieth century Britain', *Pharmaceutical Journal*, 266:7129 (2001), 23–9.
62 BL, Add. MS 58639, Lambert to Stopes, 9 May 1942.
63 'Miscellaneous inquiries – contraceptives', *Chemist and Druggist* (27 September 1941), p. 172.
64 'Correspondence – professional conduct', *Chemist and Druggist* (3 April 1943), p. 362.
65 BL, Add. MS 58638, letter by Lambert to Stopes, 20 March 1922.
66 'Morfi – Known the whole world over!', *Chemist and Druggist* (supplement) (1 September 1934), p. xx; WL, FPA/A7/100, memo of telephone call with Mr Harrison, 1 October and 8 October 1937; 'Natex contraceptives', *Chemist and Druggist* (5 January 1935), p. 23.
67 LMA, A/PMC/067, Letter to Mr Tyrer, 14 December 1938.
68 Monopolies and Mergers Commission, *Contraceptive Sheaths* (1975), p. 49.
69 M. French, 'Commercials, careers, and culture: travelling salesmen in Britain, 1890s–1930s', *Economic History Review*, 58:2 (2005), 353–4.
70 [classified advertisements], *Chemist and Druggist* (supplement) (4 January 1936), pp. xxi–ii; 'We seek travellers' sundriesmen agents', *Chemist and Druggist* (supplement) (5 December 1936), p. xxi.
71 French, 'Commercials, careers and culture', 355.
72 WL, SA/FPA/A7/71, Chas F. Cullingham to Holland, 26 July 1934.
73 WL, PP/BED/B.2, letter by Reid to Dawson, 19 May 1933; WL, SA/FPA/A7/71, letter by Reid to Holland, 1 September 1936.
74 Prentif, *'Prentif: The Approved Standard in Contraceptives* (n.p., *c*.1940), p. 1.
75 WL, SA/FPA/A7/101, note from Holland, 10 January 1940.
76 Bowlby, *Carried Away*, pp. 35–7.
77 Peel, 'The manufacture and retailing of contraceptives', 123; Porter and Hall, *The Facts of Life*, p. 257.
78 Anderson and Berridge, 'The role of the community pharmacist', p. 64.
79 J. Hemingway, 'Sexual learning and the seaside: relocating the "dirty weekend" and teenage girls' sexuality', *Sex Education: Sexuality, Society and Learning*, 6:4 (2006), 433.
80 Rendell (uncatalogued papers), testimonials, no. 27, Mrs N., Earlsfield, 7 March 1927; no. 32, Mr J., Llanelly, 30 September 1929.

81 Borge, '"Wanting it Both Ways"', p. 164.
82 WL, PP/BED/B.2, letter by Reid to Dawson, 9 March 1933.
83 Xrayser II, 'Observations and reflections', *Chemist and Druggist* (6 December 1924), p. 819.
84 Hansard, 'Contraceptives (Slot Machine Sales)', HC vol. 468, cols. 990–3 (24 October 1949).
85 LMA, PC/SHO/1/048, Report, 5 October 1949; D. H. Chadwick, Inspector report, 3 November 1949.
86 WL, SA/FPA/A17/80, Contraceptive slot machines, 'Slot machine contraceptives: "boys of grammar school buy them"', *Bradford Telegraph* (20 October 1949).
87 London School of Economics and Political Science (LSE), Women's Library, 3AMS/B/09/06, '"Ban slot machines in public", women urge', *Evening Post* (20 October 1949).
88 WL, SA/FPA/A17/80, 'Rector Says we must ban these machines', *Birmingham Gazette* (17 October 1949).
89 WL, SA/FPA/A17/80, '100 indignant letters a day', *Sunday Pictorial* (23 October 1949).
90 LMA, PC/SHO/1/049, Shops Act – Sale of Contraceptives from Automatic Machines, Newspaper Cuttings, 1949–51, 'Hairdressers oppose slot machines, sale of contraceptives', *Hackney Gazette and the London Advertiser* (17 October 1949).
91 B. L. Q. Henriques and C. Colville, 'A temptation to youth', *The Times* (12 September 1949), p. 5. For more on Henriques, see K. Bradley, 'Juvenile delinquency, the juvenile courts and the Settlement Movement 1908–1950: Basil Henriques and Toynbee Hall', *Twentieth Century British History*, 19:2 (2008), 150.
92 LMA, PC/SHO/1/048, Slot machines, 11 and 12 January 1950. Those stolen included those at Newington Causeway, Grange Road SE1, two from Bethnal Green Road E2, Brick Lane, Tottenham Court Road, one from Forest Hill Station, Wandsworth Road SW8, Balham High Road SW12, Waterloo Road SE1, Newington Butts SE11.
93 LSE, Women's Library, 3AMS/B/09/06, 'Low Standards of Govt, protest by JP', *Daily Telegraph* (22 September 1949).
94 WL, SA/FPA/A17/80, 'York Convocation appeal to local council – Slot machines that "damage moral life"', *Yorkshire Post* (27 October 1949); 'Primate urges "vigorous" steps: enforcement of ban', *Daily Telegraph* (25 October 1949).
95 WL, SA/FPA/A17/80, 'Contraceptives from slot machines', *Christian World* (24 November 1949).
96 WL, PP/BED/B.2, letter by F. Webster to Chief Constable, Leeds City Police, 6 April 1933; LMA, PC/SHO/1/047, Correspondence

with Key Stone Automatics and Shopkeepers, Letter from Siger Products, 15 November 1949.
97 WL, SA/FPA/A17/80, 'Slot machines: a doctor braves the Bishop's wrath', *Reynolds* (16 October 1949); 'Slot machine protest', *Daily Telegraph* (31 October 1949).
98 J. H. D. Butler, 'Contraceptives and automatic machines', *Freethinker* (12 March 1950), p. 108.
99 Bingham, 'The British popular press and venereal disease', 1063.
100 LSE, Women's Library, 3AMS/B/09/06, *Sunday Pictorial* (25 September 1949).
101 WL, SA/FPA/A17/80, 'Favours slot machines', *Willesden Chronicle* (30 September 1949).
102 LMA, PC/SHO/1/047, Report by Chief Officer of the Public Control Dept, R. J. B. McDowell, 30 January 1950.
103 'Slot machines law protests – loopholes left say councils', *Daily Telegraph* (31 March 1950), p. 8.
104 WL, SA/FPA/A7/79, letter by Reid to Clifford Smith, 28 March 1960.
105 B. L. Q. Henriques, *Indiscretions of a Magistrate: Thoughts on the Work of the Juvenile Court* (London: Non-Fiction Book Club, 1950), p. 58.
106 WL, FPA, SA/FPA/A17/80, [Press cutting], Sale of Contraceptives, Medical Press, 9 November 1949; Borge, '"Wanting it Both Ways"', p. 171.
107 'Rendell's', *Chemist and Druggist* (25 January 1947), p. 7; Borge, '"Wanting it Both Ways"', p. 174.
108 LRC, *London Image: The Staff Magazine of the LRC Group* (Autumn/Winter 1964), p. 9; (Spring/Summer 1965), p. 14.
109 Peel, 'The manufacture and retailing of contraceptives', 123–4; Borge, '"Wanting it Both Ways"', p. 177.
110 Borge, '"Wanting it Both Ways"', p. 166.
111 Anderson and Berridge, 'The role of the community pharmacist', p. 65.
112 'Pharmaceutical Society's annual meeting', *Chemist and Druggist* (23 May 1953), p. 513.
113 Brownfield-Pope, 'From Chemist Shop to Community Pharmacy', p. 147.

Epilogue

As historical accounts of birth control in Britain before the contraceptive Pill have argued, rubber and chemical contraceptives played a role in the fertility decline, in female sexual emancipation and in shaping the dynamics of sexual relationships. But as this book has outlined, contraceptives were also important commodities produced, branded, advertised, distributed, sold and consumed alongside a variety of other goods. Contraceptive firms transformed their goods from disguised and niche semi-medical appliances to products more visibly marked out for their purpose of preventing pregnancy (and venereal disease for condoms); they did so within the more liberalised sexual culture of the interwar period through manual and mechanised production, branded and trademarked packaging, promotion in the press, mail order through catalogues and birth control tracts, distribution at birth control clinics and by doctors, and display, sale and promotion from chemists, surgical stores and slot machines. Yet, the need to balance profit with enduring consumer sensibilities, embarrassment and sexual ignorance in a culture that also remained private and moralistic was met through the continued use of euphemistic language on packaging and in printed advertising, the mail-order distribution of catalogues in plain brown envelopes and chemists' discreet display of contraceptives. This industry strategy made contraceptives both visible and invisible, appealing to a broad range of knowing consumers, including middle- and working-class married couples, soldiers, sailors, adolescents and bachelors about town, while maintaining the ignorant status of the unknowing.

By maintaining this disguised yet visible status, contraceptives and the commodification processes firms used to make them widely available aimed to communicate messages of authenticity, reliability and respectability. In retail, brands such as Rendell's 'Wife's Friend' soluble pessaries and LRC's 'Durex' latex condoms were able to create and maintain loyalty among end consumers, prompting retailers to stock them. In print, firms mimicked the tropes of the growing genre of birth control manuals, with surgical stores imitating both products and publications. But another important way in which companies communicated these messages was through forging relationships with those increasingly considered the gatekeepers of contraceptive knowledge. In the nineteenth century these gatekeepers were largely neo-Malthusians with a small middle-class following, but by the interwar period, birth control advocates and the medical profession took on this role and had much wider appeal. Lamberts was able to build its relationship with Marie Stopes in the 1920s due to its existing reputation in the trade, while all manufacturers competed to supply the clinics of the National Birth Control/Family Planning Association in the 1930s.

It is birth control campaigners, the medical profession and allied fields that historians have often depicted as the key (albeit indirect) agents of change in birth control in the interwar years and beyond. Indeed, the contraceptive Pill is often seen as a natural culmination of the medicalisation of birth control, and with it the development of ever more effective contraceptive technologies that first began to be produced on a significant scale in this period. But focusing solely on medical and charitable influence provides an incomplete picture of contraceptive development. Viewing contraceptives as commodities not only brings into focus the neglected labour of the manufacturers, distributors and retailers that had supplied contraceptives to consumers long before clinic doctors and nurses, but also highlights the importance of medicalisation as a form of rhetoric introduced by medical practitioners and birth controllers who sought legitimacy in a society that began to view medical science as an ultimate moderniser. Just as medical practitioners sought to transform maternity and infant welfare into a medical specialism, with the clinic and the hospital as key emblematic sites, practitioners also sought to control the mechanical means of reproduction.[1]

Unpicking the birth control rhetoric, we see that firms were often more knowledgeable about the technical details of contraceptives than practitioners; practitioners, chemists, nurses and consumers turned to firms for birth control information, as well as contraceptive supply, when there was no consensus on contraceptive reliability and efficacy. The National Birth Control Association's introduction of new definitions of reliable and efficient contraceptives through standardised laboratory and clinical testing in the mid-1930s was the profession's most obvious attempt at birth control domination. The Association's increasing rejection of forms of print that mentioned company or product names (as in the case of 'Michael Fielding'), along with the Royal Pharmaceutical Society's introduction of more stringent codes of conduct on contraceptive display, sought to subvert market control. But even after contraceptives failed new tests, practitioners and consumers alike continued to rely on such appliances into the 1950s because they had long used them and were loyal to brands, products and firms, demonstrating the limits of medical attempts at control. Chemists too, as the largest form of contraceptive retailer with quasi-medical status, largely chose whether to sell contraceptives and how they did so.

Viewing contraceptives as commodities then not only allows us to challenge medicalisation as an inevitable chronological process but also demonstrates how medicalisation, broadly, and the search for effective and reliable contraceptive methods, specifically, were an assertion of medical authority and represented the search for legitimacy in an arena in which the market had dominated. Indeed, consumer concerns about contraceptive efficacy and reliability were far from new with the establishment of birth control clinics, but were bound up with brand loyalty, price, ease of use and access. The shift to a medical meaning of efficacy and reliability under birth control advocates, doctors and nurses provided medicine with a new authority in birth control that was only partially successful. Durex did not become Britain's most popular condom brand by the end of the period solely because it was reliable, but because LRC had manipulated the market, its intermediaries and end consumers with low prices, free goods and aggressive marketing methods. We have to accept then that commerce had more of an impact on ideas and practices surrounding birth control than previously acknowledged, even if this impact was diffuse and nebulous.

The blurred boundaries between interwar charity, medicine and commerce highlight the need for historians of birth control to pay more attention to business and economic concerns, to take seriously the output of companies, ephemeral or otherwise, and to challenge the privileging of ideas and practices over materiality. Collaborations between charity, medicine and commerce were often far from smooth. The industry's dominance over contraceptive distribution and thus birth control knowledge led to tense negotiation in the interwar years, much of which remained unresolved in the post-Second World War era. Commercial and medical negotiation over birth control was most obvious within the clinic setting and extended into print and retail; but negotiation also extended beyond the medical arena and into the political, social and moral realm with the Contraceptives (Regulation) Bill. The Bill represented a 'moral panic' among social conservatives over the effects of expanded contraceptive visibility on ignorant women and unmarried adolescents; its most ardent supporters failed to see Neilans's distinction between birth control as a practice and its 'conscienceless commercialisation'. But the Bill failed because of a lack of consensus on how increased contraceptive commercialisation could enable voluntary family limitation among married couples while restricting access to adolescents without damaging the legitimate business of contraceptive firms.

There was also little way for either end consumers or intermediaries to distinguish between genuine and imitation products and publications or even between manufacturers and wholesalers or surgical stores and chemists. Stopes considered manufacturers like Lamberts, chemists and even slot machines as vital to the dissemination of contraceptives and associated knowledge to working-class consumers, but deplored the exposure that expanded contraceptive production gave to young women in the factory, was unable to distinguish between the published works of medical authors and surgical stores and was disillusioned with Lamberts' business practices. Members of the National Birth Control/Family Planning Association relied on Lamberts for its products, but deplored its Birth Control Advisory Bureau and found it difficult to overcome continual faults with its products. Lord Bertrand Dawson, royal physician and one of the first to conduct research into the contraceptive industry, found contraceptive manufacturing as respectable as in any other trade and uncovered only a limited amount of unsolicited distribution of advertising for birth control goods and visible display of such goods in chemists' windows; however, he argued that the mail-order trade could not be responsible for monitoring customer age and neither should the prohibition of the window display of contraceptives restrict embarrassed consumers from pointing out the products they required to a shop assistant. The trade then was as full of contradictions as commentators were of opinions.

But this book's focus on the continual debates and contradictions over overt contraceptive commercialisation and between commerce, medicine, and the respectable and non-respectable is not only important for uncovering the underexplored role of companies in struggles over birth control. It also forms a case study of the contradictions and tensions present in interwar Britain as a whole as it struggled to leave behind a reserved Victorianism and Edwardianism that rejected overt sexual cultures and sought to embrace a modern society based on science, technology and medicine. Indeed, those who grew up in sexual ignorance before the First World War went on to become protagonists of the birth control movement and commercialisation debates. Dawson, Haire, Himes, Neilans, Malleson, directors of the Lambert company and, most famously, Stopes in her public pronouncements of her unhappy first marriage to Reginald Ruggles Gates, were just a handful of historical actors who embodied these tensions. The tensions of this period provide historians of birth control, and indeed historians in general, with few clear answers, never mind a coherent narrative, but it is the battles between old and new that make this period interesting and encourage an alternative view of history as a straightforward chronology of change. Instead, this more intensive focus on the interwar period highlights continuities, as well as change. Indeed, contraceptives developed in the 1880s, such as Rendell's 'Wife's Friend', Higginson's syringe and Lambert's 'Malthusian' sheaths, crepe rubber manufacturing and discreet forms of advertising and contraceptive retail display sat alongside new latex condoms first made in 1932 and the more open print and retail promotion of contraceptives as birth control products. That said, the interwar period should not be seen as a discreet entity of time studied in isolation. In fact, the contradictory and clashing stances on birth control and contraceptive commercialisation in the interwar period interrupted by the Second World War quickly resumed thereafter, perhaps most notably represented by debates over slot machines and the introduction of the local byelaw to prohibit contraceptive sales via this means. While many interwar protagonists died before seeing the advent of the contraceptive Pill and the longer-term effects of contraceptive commercialisation on access to birth control, it did not mean the end of this first era in which contraceptive visibility, social anxieties around sex, and optimism based on scientific medicine were combined. Many of the interwar manuals of these authors continued to sell and were read into the 1960s.[2]

Acknowledging the importance of commerce in shaping professional and public perceptions of birth control and of contraceptives as interwar commodities not only extends existing historical narratives of Britain in this period but also has the potential to revise our understanding of Britain's economic and moral relationship with its empire and the rest of the world during these apex years through its contraceptive supply and associated forms of print.[3] Most obviously, much greater attention needs to be paid to the industry's reliance on rubber from Malay and its wider implications for imperial and colonial history, but so too is further study required of the effects of the exportation of British brands and the impact of international distribution agents of these brands on the British economy. For example, research by Sarah Hodges on South Indian interwar consumers and their access to a wide range of contraceptive products and publications, Joanne Richdale on the moral anxieties surrounding the import and availability of Rendell's pessaries and 'Pro-Race' caps in New Zealand and Alison Mackinnon on the impact contraceptive imports on professional women in Australia could be fruitfully extended.[4] Indeed, Lamberts, LRC, Prentif and Rendell successfully recruited and employed untold numbers of agents across the world, from Brazil to Madras.[5]

Further incorporation of the commercial perspective into birth control history also has the potential to enhance our understanding of subsequent changes in contraceptive supply and birth control behaviour. Negotiations over contraceptive availability continued into the arguably more socially conservative era of the 1950s, but the contradictions of the interwar period were not resolved by the introduction of the Pill in 1961 and its availability to the unmarried from 1968. Most historical studies of the Pill have emphasised that its tablet form was emblematic of medicine; its medical status made it a respectable method of birth control that separated sex from reproduction and allowed the medical profession to monopolise its distribution, alongside abortion provision following the Abortion Act 1967. But medicine did not dominate late twentieth-century contraceptive supply. While the Pill's availability through prescription may have created a divide in medical and commercial contraceptive methods in the public's consciousness, medicine and commerce continued to share the responsibility for contraceptive supply in the post-Pill period, just as some men and women continued to vary their birth control methods. Indeed, as broader recent histories of late twentieth-century sex and birth control acknowledge, the commercial supply of the condom, pessaries and spermicides increased amid the growth in Pill prescribing and within a culture that was more open to public discussions of sexual practices inside and outside marriage and increasingly dominated by mass consumerism.[6] Contraceptives were finally openly discussed in print as commodities and reviewed according to their efficacy, convenience, safety and price in the Consumers' Association's *Which?* magazine in 1963 and 1966.[7]

Historians beginning to address late twentieth-century contraceptive commercial supply have, however, only emphasised the condom. No doubt this was because the condom was the most popular contraceptive in 'the permissive society' among both men and women, married and single; users outnumbered those of the Pill three to two into the 1960s and overall sales were 100 million per year by 1963.[8] But the condom was also the contraceptive most clearly marked as a conspicuous commodity, albeit an embarrassing or 'unmentionable' one.[9] In addition to the *Which?* magazine review, the Consumers' Association's British Standard Kitemark also marked out the condom as a product tested for safety and efficiency like any other, as did its more open sale from slot machines placed in men's toilets, from retailers long associated with condom supply, including surgical stores, chemists' and barber's shops, as well as retailers new to the condom market like the self-service supermarket.[10]

LRC's late twentieth-century monopolising strategies also highlighted the condom, and particularly its world-leading 'Durex' brand, as worthy of attention. Having subsumed or outpriced most of its competitors, the firm controlled much of the condom market, both at home and abroad, and its profiteering resulted in unfavourable reports by the Monopolies and Mergers Commission. The Commission argued that LRC's pricing policy had long acted against the public interest because it had taken advantage of the fact that condom consumers had long associated quality with price and that it had 'felt entitled to high profits, a fair reward, including a return on the goodwill built up in the Durex brand name for operating in and developing successfully a market shunned by others'. The Commission recommended that the firm reduce its prices and establish a maximum retail price.[11] Extensive condom promotion by the State and chemists, State-set price controls on LRC's condoms and the emergence of Mates condoms as LRC's most serious competition during the AIDS crisis in the 1980s and 1990s again highlights the historical contingency of contraceptive markets and suggests that commerce had a demonstrable impact on late twentieth-century sexual health.[12] By 2018, net revenue for the health products of the Reckitt Benckiser Group PLC, of which Durex is a leading brand, totalled £7,762 million.[13]

But more attention needs to be paid to the condom as a late twentieth- and early twenty-first-century commodity within a larger global contraceptive market consisting of medical practitioners, researchers, universities, pharmaceutical companies and other contraceptive goods. What, for example, are the implications of the fact that W. J. Rendell's 'Wife's Friend' was not only a household name in Britain until at least the 1970s but also became an important import in the late twentieth-century contraceptive market in China too? At the time of writing, Rendell is still operating solely as a licenser of the brand to the Chinese market.[14] Amid the controversies over the safety of the Pill and intrauterine devices (IUDs), how and why did Lamberts' 'Prentif Cavity Rim Cervical Cap' become the only rubber cap approved by the Food and Drug Administration for general use in the United States from the late 1970s, and to what impact?[15] What commercial birth control cultures enabled slot machines vending Durex condoms to proliferate on the streets of cities across Europe? How did a national state-sponsored family planning service beginning in 1974 under National Health Service reorganisation navigate commercial supply?[16]

We also need to consider the longer-term moral implications of wider contraceptive use. MP Leo Abse indicated in a 1968 speech in the House of Commons that the Family Planning Act of 1967 – which allowed local authorities to supply contraceptives on social, rather than medical, grounds – was proof of the widespread acceptance of birth control in Britain.[17] Yet, contemporary concerns about making emergency hormonal contraception (the 'morning-after pill') available off-the-shelf demonstrate that fears of increased promiscuity resulting from the creation of greater access to birth control products are enduring.[18] Sex, birth control and contraceptive supply have long been moralised, medicalised and subject to complex negotiations, but it is only by paying attention to the beginnings of the open public discussion of birth control in the interwar period that we see where and how these negotiations over mass contraceptive consumption began.

Notes

1 See for example, I. Loudon, 'Childbirth', in I. Loudon (ed.), *Western Medicine: An Illustrated History* (Oxford: Oxford University Press, 1997), pp. 206–20.
2 Cook, 'Sex and the doctors', p. 202.
3 D. Heath, *Purifying Empire: Obscenity and the Politics of Moral Regulation in Britain, India and Australia* (Cambridge: Cambridge University Press, 2010).
4 S. Hodges, *Contraception, Colonialism and Commerce: Birth Control in South India, 1920–1940* (Aldershot: Ashgate, 2008), particularly ch. 4; Richdale, 'Ladies' and gentlemen's toilet and rubber requisites'; A. Mackinnon, *Love and Freedom: Professional Women and the Reshaping of Personal Life* (Cambridge: Cambridge University Press, 1997).
5 WL, SA/FPA/A7/66, Memo, 8 November 1939; SA/FPA/A7/71, list of agents for Durex Protectives and Paragons and Durol, 22 July 1938.
6 Borge, '"Wanting it Both Ways"'; Jobling, 'Playing safe'; Mechen, '"Closer together"'.
7 Consumers' Association, 'Contraceptives', *Which?* supplement (November 1963); 'Contraceptives', *Which?* supplement (June 1966).
8 Borge, '"Wanting it Both Ways"', p. 248.
9 A. Wilson and C. West, 'The marketing of unmentionables', *Harvard Business Review*, 59:1 (1981), 91–102.
10 Monopolies and Mergers Commission, *Contraceptive Sheaths* (1975), p. 24. By the 1970s, surgical shops maintained 12 per cent of the condom retail market, while barber's shops had 29 per cent. Hansard, 'Contraceptives Sales (Vending Machines)', HC vol. 693, col. 83 (16 April 1964).
11 Monopolies and Mergers Commission, *Contraceptive Sheaths* (1975), pp. 65, 74, 76.
12 Monopolies and Mergers Commission, *Contraceptive Sheaths: A Report on the Supply in the UK of Contraceptive Sheaths* (London: HMSO, 1994). For more on condom promotion during the AIDS pandemic, see B. Field and K. Wellings, *Stopping AIDS: AIDS/HIV Public Education and the Mass Media in Europe* (London: Longman, 1996); N. Vitellone, *Object Matters: Condoms, Adolescence and Time* (Manchester: Manchester University Press, 2008); V. Berridge, *AIDS in the UK: The Making of Policy 1981 to 1994* (Oxford: Oxford University Press; 1996).
13 Reckitt Benckiser, 'Annual report 2018', www.rb.com/investors/annual-report-2018/ [accessed 17 February 2020].
14 Pers. comm with Joe Ward, Rendell director, 20 May 2017.
15 Neushal, 'Marie C. Stopes', 271; R. Chalker, *The Complete Cervical Cap Guide* (New York: Harper and Row, 1987), pp. 2–5.

16 Leathard, *The Fight for Family Planning*, pp. 200, 227–9.
17 Hansard, 'Contraceptive Industry', HC vol. 765, col. 1192 (24 May 1968).
18 C. Murphy and V. Pooke, 'Emergency contraception in the UK – stigma as a key ingredient of a fundamental women's healthcare product', *Sexual and Reproductive Health Matters*, 27:3 (2019), 122–5, https://doi.org/10.1080/26410397.2019.1647399; G. Barrett, and R. Harper, 'Health professionals' attitudes to the deregulation of emergency contraception (or the problem of female sexuality)', *Sociology of Health and Illness*, 22:2 (2000), 197–216. Also, see Holz, *The Birth Control Clinic*, p. 151.

Appendix

Contraceptive catalogues

Catalogues are listed alphabetically by company name and date. Pseudonymous authors are also listed by company.

Abbreviations of catalogue location or reference

AO	Author's own
Bod	Bodleian Library, University of Oxford
BL	British Library
Cam	University of Cambridge
Fry	Fryer, *British Birth Control Ephemera* (1969)
Hac	Hackney Archives
Him	Himes, *Medical History of Contraception* (1963)
Job	Jobling, 'Playing safe' (1997)
KE	Keele University Library
M-O	Mass-Observation
MUVS	Museum of Contraception and Abortion, Vienna
Lei	University of Leicester
LSE	London School of Economics
Ren	W. J. Rendell, Hitchin
TMM	Thackray Medical Museum
WL	Wellcome Library

Allbutt, H. A., *The Wife's Handbook: How a Woman Should Order Herself During Pregnancy, in the Lying-In Room, and After Delivery*, 3rd edn (London: W. J. Ramsey, 1886). [BL]
—— *The Wife's Handbook* (Forder, 1887). [Bod, 4th edn; BL, 6th edn]
—— *The Wife's Handbook*, 10th, 11th, 12th edns (n.p., 1889). [BL]
—— *The Wife's Handbook*, 14th, 15th edns (n.p., 1890). [BL]

—— *The Wife's Handbook*, 16th edn (Forder, 1891). [Cam; Bod; LSE]
—— *The Wife's Handbook*, 18th edn (n.p., 1892). [LSE]
—— *The Wife's Handbook*, 23rd edn (n.p., 1894). [BL]
—— *The Wife's Handbook*, 25th edn (n.p., 1895). [Lei; LSE]
—— *The Wife's Handbook*, 31st edn (Forder, 1899). [LSE]
—— *The Wife's Handbook*, 32nd edn (London: F. Brett, 1900). [LSE]
—— *The Wife's Handbook*, 33rd edn (London: G. Standring, 1901). [LSE]
—— *The Wife's Handbook*, 35th edn (London: G. Standring, 1902). [BL]
—— *The Wife's Handbook*, 41st edn (London: G. Standring, 1907). [LSE]
—— *The Wife's Handbook*, 45th edn (London: G. Standring, 1913). [BL]
—— *The Wife's Handbook*, 46th edn (London: G. Standring, c.1917). [LSE]
—— *The Wife's Handbook*, 56th edn (London: Bentley, 1922). [BL]
Allen Surgical Hygienic Co. Ltd, *Heritage: Planned Parenthood is but a Mark of Advancing Civilisation* (n.p., 1950).
Anglo-American Pharmaceutical Products Corp Ltd, [*Catalogue*] (n.p., 1930). [Fry]
Anglo-Scottish Surgical Stores Ltd, *Revised Catalogue* (n.p., [1930s]). [WL]
Army and Navy Co-Operative Society, *Yesterday's Shopping: The Army and Navy Stores Catalogue, 1907* (London: David and Charles, 1969). [TMM]
—— *General Catalogue* (n.p., 1883). [TMM]
Blake's Medical Stores, [Wilson, C. F.], *Practical Birth Control and Instruction for Working Mothers* (Bristol: Blake's Medical Stores, [1926]). [Him]
—— *Surgical Rupture Appliances* (n.p., 1935). [TMM]
—— *Catalogue of Contraceptives and Medical Sundries* (n.p., 1958). [TMM]
Blanchard, P., *How to Limit Your Family: An Illustrated List of Surgical, Hygienic and Domestic Specialities* (n.p., 1926). [Job]
Charles and Company, *Price List of Surgical Appliances and Rubber Goods* (n.p., 1910). [TMM]
—— *Revised Price List* (n.p., c.1938). [M-O]
Constantine and Jackson, *Illustrated Catalogue of Ladies' and Gentlemen's India Rubber Surgical Rubber Appliances* (n.p., 1882). [WL]
—— *Manufacturers of Ladies' and Gentlemans' Supporting Belts* (n.p., c.1885). [BL]
—— [*Catalogue*] (n.p., 1890). [TMM]
Curtis's Surgical Store Ltd, *Revised Catalogue of Surgical Rubber Goods, Pro-Race Appliances and Medical Sundries* (n.p., 1925). [TMM]
Dawson, J. (i.e. Arthur Clements), *Price List of Domestic and Surgical Appliances, Rubber Good and Medical Works etc, issued by Arthur Clements trading as J Dawson 3 The Facade, Villiers Street, The Strand, London, WC2, London, J Dawson* (n.p., 1923). [Fry, LSE]

Dorsan and Co., *Rubber Goods & Surgical Appliances of Every Description* (n.p., 1900). [TMM]
—— *Rubber Goods & Surgical Appliances of Every Description* (n.p., 1910). [TMM]
—— *The Wife's Handbook and Family Medical Guide: A Clear and Practical Treatise of Great Value to Wives and Mothers on the Management of Their Own Health – Including Suggestions for the Effectual Treatment of Most Women's and Children's Ailments* (n.p., c.1929). [WL]
Davies, [*Catalogue*] (n.p., 1894). [TMM]
Duplex Novelty Co., *Dr Kelly's Expanding Douche* (n.p., c.1925). [LSE]
Evans and Wormull, *Catalogue of Surgical Instruments* (n.p., 1876). [WL]
Franklin, J. G., *Catalogue of Surgical Goods* (n.p., 1910). [TMM]
—— *Catalogue of Surgical Goods* (n.p., 1947). [TMM]
—— *Catalogue of Surgical Goods* (n.p., 1950). [Hac]
—— *Catalogue of Surgical Goods* (n.p., 1957). [TMM]
George, W., *Most Modern and Up-to-Date Special List of Domestic and Surgical Appliances* (n.p., 1912). [TMM]
—— *Special List of Domestic and Surgical Appliances* (n.p., 1915). [TMM]
—— *Contraceptive Methods and Appliances* (n.p., 1940). [TMM]
—— *Contraceptive Methods and Appliances* (n.p., c.1950). [WL]
—— *Contraceptive Methods and Appliances* (n.p., 1950). [WL]
Graham, M. V., *A Common-Sense Treatise on Birth Control* (London: Bale, 1926). [Him]
Greenwood, H. N., *Price List of Rubber Appliances* (n.p., 1897). [TMM]
Hancock and Co. Ltd, *The Shadow of the Stork: A Text Book of Birth Control Methods* (London: n.p., 1933). [LSE]
—— *Corrective Medicine pour les Dames* (n.p., 1933). [TMM]
—— *The Shadow of the Stork* (n.p., 1934). [TMM; WL]
—— *The Shadow of the Stork* (n.p., 1938). [TMM]
—— *The Shadow of the Stork* (n.p., 1945). [TMM]
Holmes, J. R., *True Morality or The Theory and Practice of Neo-Malthusianism* (Wantage, Berks: 1891). [TMM]
—— *True Morality* (n.p., 1892). [TMM]
—— *True Morality* (n.p., 1896). [LSE; TMM]
—— *Supplementary Price List of Neo-Malthusian and Hygienic Requisites* (May 1914). [LSE]
—— *An Illustrated Price List of Neo-Malthusian Appliances and Hygienic Requisites* (May 1914). [LSE]
—— *True Morality* (n.p., 1905). [LSE; TMM]
—— *True Morality* (n.p., 1912). [TMM]

APPENDIX

—— *True Morality* (n.p., 1914). [LSE; TMM]
—— *True Morality* (n.p., 1922). [LSE]
—— *A Descriptive Price List of Neo-Malthusian Appliances and Hygienic Requisites: To Which is Added a List of Books Recommended for Serious Reading* (Spring 1931). [LSE]
—— *A Short List of the More Important Articles in the Practice of Neo-Malthusian Commonly called Birth Control* (Spring 1936). [LSE]
Hooper, M. R. *The Voice of Experience* (London: The Birth Control Advisory Bureau, 1938, 1960). [WL]
Hygienic Stores Ltd, *The Popular Herbal Family Medical Guide and Husband's and Wife's Handbook* (London: The Hygienic Stores, [between 1910 and 1919?]). [WL]
—— *Illustrated Prorace Catalogue* (n.p., 1925). [TMM]
—— [Mann, O.], *Birth Control (The Husband and Wife's Handbook): Being a comprehensive handbook on the management of health and the wholesome treatment of birth control, pregnancy, labour etc: knowledge of which is of vital importance to every married man or woman* (London: The Hygienic Stores, 1926). [LSE]
—— [Mann, O.], *Birth Control (The Husband and Wife's Handbook)* (London: The Hygienic Stores, 1927). [AO]
—— [Payne, D. R.], *Private Word to Women: Containing Wisdom for Wives and Hygiene for Ladies* (London: The Hygienic Stores, 1927). [LSE]
—— *Revised Catalogue of High-Class Rubber, Medical, Surgical Goods and Domestic Appliances* (London: The Hygienic Stores, 1928). [LSE]
—— *Regulated Parenthood* (London: The Hygienic Stores, c.1930). [WL]
—— [Reynolds, T. H.], *Birth Control: Its Use and Abuse with special chapters for young men and women about to marry* (London: The Hygienic Stores, 1933). [LSE]
—— [Reynolds, T. H.], *Birth Control* (London: The Hygienic Stores, 1934). [Bod]
—— [Payne, D. R.], *Private Words to Women* (London: The Hygienic Stores, 1934). [AO]
—— [Mann, O.], *Birth Control (The Husband and Wife's Handbook)* (London: The Hygienic Stores, 1935). [Bod]
—— *Revised Catalogue of High-Class Rubber, Medical, Surgical Goods and Domestic Appliances* (London: n.p., c.1936). [LSE]
—— [Payne, D. R.], *Private Words to Women: Containing Wisdom for Wives* (London: The Hygienic Stores, 1937). [Fry]
—— [Reynolds, T. H.], *Birth Control* (London: The Hygienic Stores, 1937). [AO]

—— [Mann, O.], *Birth Control (The Husband and Wife's Handbook)* (London: The Hygienic Stores, 1938). [LSE]
—— *Revised Catalogue of Birth Control and Surgical Rubber Goods* (n.p., 1937). [TMM]
—— *Regulated Parenthood* (n.p., c.1950). [M-O]
Ingram, J. G., [*Catalogue*] (n.p., 1890). [TMM]
—— *Catalogue of Surgical India Rubber Goods* (n.p., 1947). [TMM]
Jackson, L., *Price List of Rubber Goods* (n.p., 1907). [TMM]
Kait Pharmacies Ltd, *An Open Book on the Mysteries of the Sex Life* (London: Kait Pharmacies, 1934). [TMM]
Kingsland Hygienic Co. Ltd, [Phelps, A.], *Birth Control and What it Means* (London: Kingsland Hygienic Co. Ltd, 1925). [LSE]
—— [Phelps, A.], *Methods of Birth Control* (London: Phelps (Contraceptives) Ltd, 1937). [TMM]
—— [Phelps, A.], *Birth Control and What it Means*, 52nd edition (London: Kingsland Hygienic Co. Ltd, 1940). [LSE]
—— [Phelps, A.], *Children by Desire* (London: Phelps (Contraceptives) Ltd, 1940). [TMM]
—— [Phelps, A.], *Children by Desire* (London, Phelps (Contraceptives) Ltd, 1948). [LSE]
Lambert, A. [Vimule and Co.], *A List of Surgical Belts, Accouchement Requisites* (n.p., 1901). [TMM]
—— [Vimule and Co.], *A List of Surgical Belts* (n.p., 1902). [WL]
—— [Warren, S.], *The Wife's Guide and Friend: being plain and practical advice to women on the management of themselves during pregnancy and confinement, and on other matters of importance that should be known by every wife and mother* (London: A. Lambert, 1904). [AO]
—— *A List of Surgical Appliances* (n.p., 1926). [TMM]
—— [Warren, S.], *The Wife's Guide and Friend*, 22nd edn (London: A Lambert and Co, 1927). [LSE]
—— *A List of Surgical Appliances* (n.p., 1927). [TMM]
—— A/E. J. Lambert, *The Wife's Adviser* (n.p., 1928).
—— *Modern Contraceptive Methods and Appliances* (n.p., 1932). [TMM]
—— *A List of Contraceptive Appliances* (n.p., 1949). [WL]
Lambert, E., and Son, [*Catalogue*] (n.p., 1891). [TMM]
—— [*Catalogue*] (n.p., 1897). [TMM]
—— *Special List of Domestic and Surgical Specialities* (n.p., 1900). [WL]
—— *Special List of Domestic & Surgical Specialties* (n.p., 1903). [TMM]
—— *Special List of Domestic & Surgical Specialties* (n.p., 1905). [TMM]
—— *Special List of Domestic & Surgical Specialties* (n.p., 1911). [TMM; LSE]

Lamberts (Dalston) Ltd, *Revised List of Up-to-Date Contraceptive Appliances* (n.p., 1941). [MUVS]
—— *Latest Price List of Approved Contraceptive Appliances* (n.p., c.1950). [WL]
—— *Latest Price List of Approved Contraceptive Appliances* (n.p., 1951). [WL]
Lamberts Prorace Ltd, *Revised Price List of Approved Contraceptive Appliances* (n.p., 1933). [TM]
—— *Revised Price List of Up-to-Date Contraceptive Appliances* (n.p., 1936). [TMM]
—— *Revised Price List of Up-to-Date Contraceptive Appliances* (n.p., 1937). [WL]
—— *Latest Price List of Approved Contraceptive Appliances* (n.p., 1941). [MUVS]
Le Brasseur Surgical Manufacturing Co., *Revised List of Medical Goods for 1919* (n.p., 1919). [TMM]
—— *Revised List of Medical Goods 1925: Catalogue "C"* (n.p., 1925). [WL]
—— *Revised List of Surgical Rubber Specialties* (n.p., 1931). [TMM]
—— [Neale, D.], *Guide for Husbands and Wives or a Manual of Wisdom* (Birmingham: Le Brasseur Surgical Manufacturing Co. Ltd, 1933). [TMM]
—— [Neale, D.], *Guide for Husbands and Wives* (Birmingham: Le Brasseur Surgical Manufacturing Co. Ltd, c.1935). [LSE]
—— *Revised List of Surgical Rubber Specialities and Pro-Race Goods* (n.p., 1936). [TMM]
—— *Revised List of Surgical Rubber Specialities and Pro-Race Goods as recommended by all leading authorities on birth control* (n.p., 1937). [LSE]
—— [St Clair Maurice], *Advice to Married Women: A Frank and Outspoken Talk to Serious Minded People and those about to marry on Birth Control and Practice* (London: The Medical and Surgical Supply Co., 1937). [LSE]
—— [Goodman, B.], *My Views on Birth Control* (London: Medical and Surgical Supply Co, 1937). [LSE]
—— [Neale, D.], *Guide for Husbands and Wives* (Birmingham: Le Brasseur Surgical Manufacturing Co. Ltd, 1937). [LSE]
—— [St Clair Maurice], *Advice to Married Women* (London: The Medical and Surgical Supply Co., 1938). [AO]
—— [Stewart, G.], *Wedlock and Birth Control: A Straightforward Talk on a Momentous and Delicate Subject* (London: The Medical and Surgical Supply Co., c.1939). [LSE]

APPENDIX

―― [Stewart, G.], *Wedlock and Birth Control* (London: The Medical and Surgical Supply Co., c.1941). [LSE; TMM]
―― *Modern Methods of Family Limitation* (n.p., 1947). [TMM]
―― [The London Medical Manufacturing Co. Ltd], *Price List of Rubber Specialities, Pro-Race Goods and Appliances* (n.p., 1948). [M-O]
―― [Stewart, G.], *Wedlock and Birth Control* (London: The London Medical Manufacturing Co., 1948). [M-O]
―― [Goodman, B.], *My Views on Birth Control* (London: The London Manufacturing Co. Catalogue, 1948). [M-O]
―― *Revised List* (n.p., 1950). [M-O]
―― *Revised List* (n.p., 1951). [TMM]
―― *Revised List* (n.p., 1954). [TMM]
―― *The Manual of Wisdom* (n.p., 1959). [TMM]
Leyland and Birmingham Rubber Co. Ltd, [*Catalogue*] (n.p., c.1939). [WL]
Liberator League, *Family Limitation or Methods of Birth Control* (n.p., 1919). [Fry]
―― *Family Limitation or Methods of Birth Control* (n.p., 1922). [Fry]
London Rubber Company, *Bircon* (n.p., c.1931). [WL]
―― *Price List* (London: n.p., 1934?). [WL]
―― *Planned Families* (Excel Surgical Supplies, c.1952). [TMM]
―― *Durex* (n.p., 1958). [TMM]
Martyn, L., *Illustrated Price List of Gold Medal Surgical, Hygienic and Domestic Specialities* (n.p., 1900). [TMM]
Marvel Co., [*Catalogue*] (London: Constantine and Jackson, 1882). [WL]
Ortho-Gynol, *Personal Instructions* (n.p., 1960). [TMM]
―― *Freedom from Care* (n.p., 1960). [TM]
Prentif, *Contraceptive Practice: A Quarterly Bulletin Dealing in Family Spacing and Allied Subjects*, 1 (November 1937). [WL]
―― *Contraceptive Practice*, 2 (February 1938). [WL]
―― *'Prentif': The Approved Standard in Contraceptives* (n.p., c.1940). [WL]
―― *'Prentif': The Approved Standard in Contraceptives* (n.p., c.1943). [WL]
Read, J., *A Vindication of Read's Patent Syringe* (London: W. Glendinning, 1826). [BL; Bod; Cam; WL]
Rendal's Surgical Store, [*Catalogue*] (n.p., [1935]). [TMM]
Rendell, W. J., [pamphlet] (n.p., 1890). [TMM]
―― *How to Limit your Family: The Manufacture of a Scientific Product* (n.p., 1930–39?). [WL]
―― *Birth Control and the Medical Practitioner* (n.p., c.1935). [Ren]
―― *Modern Birth Control* (n.p., c.1940). [Ren]
―― *Contraceptives in Medical Practice* (n.p., 1950). [WL]

Seymour, S., [An Eminent Physician], *A Practical Treatise on Birth Control* (London: S. Seymour, 1926). [Him]
—— *Catalogue* (n.p., c.1935). [MUVS]
Solidol Chemical Ltd., *Woman's Guide to Intimate Hygiene* (London: Solidol, 1930). [TMM]
Stockwell Hygienic Co. Ltd, [Willis, A.], *How to Limit Your Family* (London: Stockwell Hygienic Co. Ltd, 1930–9?). [WL]
—— *How to Limit your Family: A Manual of Birth Control* (n.p., 1940). [TMM]
—— [Willis, A.], *How to Limit Your Family* (London: Stockwell Hygienic Co. Ltd, 1940). [TMM]
—— *How to Limit your Family* (n.p., 1950). [TMM]
Walton Rubber Goods Co., *Revised Price List of Rubber Goods and Contraceptive Appliances* (n.p., 1937). [TMM]
Welton, C. J., *Marriage and Its Mysteries, Being an Enquiry into the Great Social Evil of Overpopulation* (Nottingham: C. J. Welton, 1900).
—— *Man: His Diseases, and How to Cure Them*, 9th edn (Nottingham: C. J. Welton, 1904). [KE]
—— *Marriage and Its Mysteries*, 30th edn (Nottingham: C. J. Welton, 1904). [WL]
—— *Marriage and Its Mysteries* (n.p., 1908). [LSE]
Winchester Manufacturing Co., *Catalogue of Surgical Appliances* (n.p., 1938). [TMM]
Wright, H., *A Catalogue of the Most Approved Surgical Instruments, Trusses, &c.* ([London]: 1834). [WL]

Bibliography

Manuscript sources

Boots Company PLC Records Centre, Nottingham:
  Company archives: WBA/BT
British Library, London:
  Marie C. Stopes papers: BL Add. MS 58638–41; 58567
Lambeth Palace Library:
  Archbishop of Canterbury archive: W. Temple 14, ff. 384–96, Contraception
London Metropolitan Archives:
  Public Morality Council: A/PMC
  Public Control Department, Shops Acts and Markets: PC/SHO
London School of Economics and Political Science Archives and Special Collections:
  Association of Moral and Social Hygiene archive: 3AMS
  British Birth control ephemera, 1870–1948: Vol 10. COLL MISC 0435/5–0435/12
Mass-Observation, University of Sussex:
  File report, 1494–5, November 1942, War Factory
  Survey, 12 1/B, November-December 1942, Venereal Disease
  Survey, A9 1929–50, Sex
  Topic Collection, A9 16/A, 'Advertising and Publications: Published Material on Sex'
  Topic Collection, 12 16/A, 'Contraceptives and surgical products'
  Topic Collection, 12 16/B, 'Publications on Sex'
  Topic Collection, 12 3/E, Chapter 4 'Birth Control'
National Archives, London:
  Home Office papers: HO45

Vestry House Local Studies Library, London:
  London Rubber Company photograph collection
W. J. Rendell, Ickleford Manor, Hitchin:
  Uncatalogued company papers, 1885–1950
Thackray Medical Museum Resource Centre, Leeds:
  Trade catalogue collection: 1880–1960
Archives and Manuscripts Collection at the Wellcome Library for the History and Understanding of Medicine, London:
  Family Planning Association Archives: SA/FPA
  Marie C. Stopes papers: PP/MCS
  Bertrand Edward Dawson papers: PP/BED
  Edward Fyfe Griffith papers: PP/EFG

Official publications

Contraceptives Bill, Parliament: House of Lords, no. 110 (London: The Stationary Office, 1934).

Contraceptives (Regulation) Bill, Parliament: House of Commons, no. 115 (London: The Stationery Office, 1938).

Lewis-Faning, E., 'Report on an enquiry into family limitation and its influence on human fertility during the past fifty years', Papers of the Royal Commission on Population, 1 (London: HMSO, 1949).

Medical Aspects of Contraception/being the report of the Medical Committee appointed by the National Council of Public Morals in connection with the investigations of the National Birth-Rate Commission (London: M. Hopkinson, 1927).

Monopolies and Mergers Commission, *Contraceptive Sheaths: A Report on the Supply of Contraceptive Sheaths in the United Kingdom* (London: HMSO, 1975).

Monopolies and Mergers Commission, *Contraceptive Sheaths: A Report on the Supply in the UK of Contraceptive Sheaths* (London: HMSO, 1994).

Post Office Directory (London, 1883).

Parliamentary papers

Hansard, 'Contraceptives Bill', HL vol. 90, cols. 804–39 (13 February 1934).
Hansard, 'Contraceptives Bill', HL vol. 90, cols. 952–96 (27 February 1934).
Hansard, 'Contraceptives (Regulation) Bill', HC vol. 342, cols. 2420–38 (16 December 1938).
Hansard, 'Contraceptives (Slot Machine Sales)', HC vol. 468, cols. 990–3 (24 October 1949).

Hansard, 'Contraceptives Sales (Vending Machines)', HC vol. 693, col. 83 (16 April 1964).
Hansard, 'Contraceptive Industry', HC vol. 765, cols. 1192–8 (24 May 1968).

Local, provincial and national newspapers, trade journals and magazines

Aberdeen Press and Journal
Ballet
Barking, East Ham and Ilford Advertiser
Birmingham Gazette
Bradford Telegraph
Brighton Gazette
British Medical Journal
Cambrian News
Cambridge Daily News
Cornish Telegraph
Chemist and Druggist
Christian World
Daily Herald
Daily Telegraph
Derbyshire Courier
Dorette Designs
Edinburgh Evening Dispatch
Evening Post
Freethinker
Hackney Gazette and the London Advertiser
Harrow Observer and Gazette
Health and Beauty
Home Fashions
Home Review
Householders
Illustrated London News
Illustrated Police News
Lancet
London Image: The Staff Magazine of the LRC Group
Lincoln Gazette
The Malthusian
The New Generation
New Knitting
Nursing Mirror

Nursing World
Parents
The Practitioner
Preston Herald
The Queen
Reports of Patent, Design and Trademark Cases
Sporting Times: Otherwise Known as the 'Pink 'Un'
Sunday Pictorial
The Times
Trade Mark Journal
Truth
Weldon's Home Dressmaker
Wharfedale and Airedale Observer
Willesden Chronicle
Woman and Home
Woman's Magazine
Woman's World
Yorkshire Post

Internet sources

'The Robilton Company: an exclusive agency for the supply of genuine contraceptives', http://de.muvs.org/bibliothek/artikel/1428?media_id=7502.

Blue glass condom mould for rubber or latex moulding, Durrant and Sons, Bristol, England, 1900–1920, The Science Museum, Object number 2014–380 http://collection.sciencemuseum.org.uk/objects/co8421629/blue-glass-condom-mould-for-rubber-or-latex-moulding-condom-mould.

Old Bailey Proceedings Online, www.oldbaileyonline.org, version 8.0.

Reckitt Benckiser Group PLC, 'Annual report 2018', www.rb.com/investors/annual-report-2018/.

Books, theses and articles

Alexander, S., *Becoming a Woman and Other Essays in 19th and 20th Century Feminist History* (London: Virago, 1994).

Aly, G., and M. Sontheimer, *Fromms: How Julius Fromm's Condom Empire Fell to the Nazis* (New York: Other Press, 2011).

Anderson, S., 'Community pharmacy and sexual health in twentieth century Britain,' *Pharmaceutical Journal*, 266:7129 (2001), 23–9.

Anderson, S., and V. Berridge, 'The role of the community pharmacist in health and welfare, 1911–1986', in J. Bornat, R. Perks, P. Thompson and

J. Walmsley (eds), *Oral History, Health and Welfare* (London: Routledge, 2000), pp. 48–74.
Appadurai, A. (ed.), *The Social Life of Things: Commodities in Cultural Perspective* (Cambridge: Cambridge University Press, 1986).
Bailey, P., 'Fats Waller meets Harry Champion: Americanization, national identity and sexual politics in inter-war British music hall', *Cultural and Social History*, 4:4 (2007), 495–509.
Baker, J. R., *The Chemical Control of Conception* (London: Chapman and Hill, 1935).
Banks, J., *Victorian Values: Secularism and the Size of Families* (Aldershot: Gregg Revivals, 1994).
Banks, J., and O. Banks, *Feminism and Family Planning in Victorian England* (New York: Shocken Books, 1977).
Barrett, G., and R. Harper, 'Health professionals' attitudes to the deregulation of emergency contraception (or the problem of female sexuality)', *Sociology of Health and Illness*, 22:2 (2000), 197–216.
Baudrillard, J., *System of Objects* (London: Verso, 2006).
Beier, L. M., *For Their Own Good: The Transformation of English Working-Class Health Culture, 1880–1970* (Columbus: Ohio State University Press, 2008).
Benson, J., *The Rise of Consumer Society, 1880–1980* (London: Longman, 1994).
Benson, J., and L. Ugolini, 'Introduction', in J. Benson and L. Ugolini (eds), *Cultures of Selling: Perspectives on Consumption and Society since 1700* (Abingdon: Ashgate, 2006), pp. 1–28.
Berger, J., and M. Ward, 'Subtle signals of inconspicuous consumption', *Journal of Consumer Research*, 37 (2010), 555–69.
Berridge, V., *AIDS in the UK: The Making of Policy 1981 to 1994* (Oxford: Oxford University Press; 1996).
Besant, A., *The Law of Population: Its Consequences, and Its Bearing upon Human Conduct and Morals* (London: Freethinker, 1889).
Bingham, A., 'The British popular press and venereal disease during the Second World War', *Historical Journal*, 48:4 (2005), 1055–76.
—— *Family Newspapers? Sex, Private Life, and the British Popular Press 1918–1978* (Oxford: Oxford University Press, 2009).
Black, L., '*Which?* craft in post-war Britain: the Consumers' Association and the politics of affluence', *Albion*, 36:1 (2004), 52–82.
Bloch, I., *The Sexual Life of Our Time, in Its Relations to Modern Civilisations* (London: Rebman, 1909).
Blundell, J., *Observations on Some of the More Important Diseases of Women* (Philadelphia: A. Waldie, 1837).

Booysen, C., 'Quinine as a contraceptive', *Marriage Hygiene*, 2:1 (1935).
Borell, M., 'Biologists and the promotion of birth control research, 1918–1938', *Journal of the History of Biology*, 20:1 (1987), 51–87.
Borge, J., '"Wanting it Both Ways": the London Rubber Company, the Condom and the Pill, 1915–1970' (PhD thesis, University of London, 2017).
—— *Protective Practices: A History of the London Rubber Company and the Condom Business, 1915–1965* (Montreal: McGill-Queen's University Press, forthcoming).
Bowlby, R., *Carried Away: The Invention of Modern Shopping* (New York: Columbia University Press, 2001).
Bradley, K., 'Juvenile delinquency, the juvenile courts and the Settlement Movement 1908–1950: Basil Henriques and Toynbee Hall', *Twentieth Century British History*, 19:2 (2008), 133–55.
Brake, L., and M. Demoor, *Dictionary of Nineteenth-Century Journalism in Great Britain and Ireland* (Ghent: Academia Press, 2009).
Branca, P., *Silent Sisterhood: Middle Class Women in the Victorian Home* (London: Croom Helm, 1975).
Brand, P., 'Birth Control Nursing in the Marie Stopes' Mothers' Clinics, 1921–1931' (PhD thesis, De Montfort University, 2007).
Bristow, E. J., *Vice and Vigilance: Purity Movements in Britain since 1700* (London: Gill and Macmillan, 1977).
Brown, P. S., 'Female pills and the reputation of iron as an abortifacient', *Medical History*, 21 (1977), 291–304.
Brownfield-Pope, A. M., 'From Chemist Shop to Community Pharmacy: An Industry Wide Study of Retailing Chemists and Druggists, *c*. 1880–1960' (PhD Dissertation, University of East Anglia, 2003).
Bruley, S., *Women in Britain since 1900* (Basingstoke: Palgrave, 1999).
Bull, S., 'Managing the "Obscene M.D.": medical publishing, the medical profession, and the changing definition of obscenity in mid-Victorian England', *Bulletin of the History of Medicine*, 91:4 (2017), 713–43.
Bullough, V. L., 'A brief note on rubber technology and contraception: the diaphragm and the condom', *Technology and Culture*, 22:1 (1981), 104–11.
Business Methods for Chemists (London: Retail Pharmacists' Union, 1932).
Campbell, C., *The Romantic Ethic and the Spirit of Modern Consumerism* (Oxford: Basil Blackwell, 1987).
Casson, H., *Twelve Tips on Window Display* (London: The Efficiency Magazine, 1924).
—— *Window Display Above All* (London: The Efficiency Magazine, [1934]).

Chalker, R., *The Complete Cervical Cap Guide* (New York: Harper and Row, 1987).
Charles, E., *The Practice of Birth Control* (London: Williams and Norgate, 1932).
Cocks, H. G., 'Saucy stories: pornography, sexology and the marketing of sexual knowledge in Britain, c. 1918–70', *Social History*, 29:4 (2004), 465–84.
—— '"The social picture of our own times": reading obscene magazines in mid-twentieth-century Britain', *Twentieth Century British History*, 27:2 (2016), 171–94.
Cohen, D. A., 'Private lives in public spaces: Marie Stopes, the Mothers' Clinics and the practice of contraception', *History Workshop Journal*, 35 (1993), 95–116.
Cohen, S., *Folk Devils and Moral Panics* (London: MacGibbon and Kee, 1972).
Consumers' Association, 'Contraceptives', *Which?* supplement (November 1963).
—— 'Contraceptives', *Which?* supplement (June 1966).
Cook, H., 'The Long Sexual Revolution: British Women, Sex and Contraception in the Twentieth Century' (D.Phil thesis, University of Sussex, 1999).
—— 'Sex and the doctors: the medicalization of sexuality as a two-way process in early to mid-twentieth-century Britain', in W. de Blécourt and C. Usborne (eds), *Cultural Approaches to the History of Medicine: Mediating Medicine in Early Modern and Modern Europe* (Basingstoke, Palgrave Macmillan, 2004), pp. 192–211.
—— *The Long Sexual Revolution: English Women, Sex and Contraception, 1800–1975* (Oxford: Oxford University Press, 2004).
—— 'The English sexual revolution: technology and social change', *History Workshop Journal*, 59:2 (2005), 109–28.
Cook, M., *London and the Culture of Homosexuality, 1885–1914* (Cambridge: Cambridge University Press, 2008).
Coopey, R., S. O'Connor and D. Porter, *Mail Order Retailing in Britain: A Business and Social History* (Oxford: Oxford University Press, 2005).
Cox, G. M., *Clinical Contraception* (London: Heinemann, 1933, 1937).
Creighton, C., 'The rise and decline of the "male breadwinner family" in Britain', *Cambridge Journal of Economics*, 23 (1999), 519–41.
D'Arcy, F., 'The Malthusian League and the resistance to birth control propaganda in late Victorian Britain', *Population Studies*, 31:3 (1977), 429–48.

Darnton, R., 'First steps towards a history of reading', *The Kiss of Lamourette: Reflections in Cultural History* (New York and London: W. W. Norton and Co., 1990).

Davey, C., 'Birth control in Britain during the interwar years', *Journal of Family History*, 13:3 (1988), 329–45.

Dawson, P., and T. R. Schidrowitz (eds), *History of the Rubber Industry* (London: W. Heffer, 1952).

Drehler, N. A., 'The virtuous and the verminous: turn-of-the-century moral panics in London's public parks', *Albion*, 29:2 (1997), 246–67.

Drew, M., *Hints on Nursing* (London: R. Forder, 1889).

Duguid, P., T. da Silva Lopes and J. Mercer, 'Reading registrations: an overview of 100 years of trademark registrations in France, the United Kingdom and the United States', in T. da Silva Lopes and P. Duguid (eds), *Trademarks, Brands and Competitiveness* (New York and London: Routledge, 2010), pp. 9–31.

Edgerton, D., *The Shock of the Old: Technology and Global History since 1900* (New York: Oxford University Press, 2007).

Edwards, B., 'Making the West End Modern: Space, Architecture and Shopping in 1930s London' (PhD thesis, University of the Arts, London, 2004).

—— 'West End Shopping with *Vogue*: 1930s Geographies of Metropolitan Consumption', in J. Benson and L. Ugolini (eds), *Cultures of Selling: Perspectives on Consumption and Society since 1700* (Abingdon: Ashgate, 2006), pp. 29–58.

Elderton, E., *Report on the English Birth-Rate: Part I, England North of the Humber* (London: Eugenics Laboratory Memoirs, 1914).

Evans, B., *Freedom to Choose: The Life and Work of Dr. Helena Wright, Pioneer of Contraception* (London: Bodley Head, 1984).

Feery, L. M., *Modern Window Display: A Practical Guide for the Shopkeeper* (London: Cassell's Business Handbooks, 1922).

Ferguson, M., *Forever Feminine: Women's Magazines and the Cult of Femininity* (Aldershot: Gower, 1983).

Field, B., and K. Wellings, *Stopping AIDS: AIDS/HIV Public Education and the Mass Media in Europe* (London: Longman, 1996).

Fielding, M., *Parenthood: Design or Accident? A Manual of Birth Control* (1934; London: Noel Douglas, 1928).

Finn, M., 'Sex and the city: metropolitan modernities in English history', *Victorian Studies*, 44 (2001/2), 25–32.

Fisher, K., 'An Oral History of Birth Control Practice c.1925–50: A Study of Oxford and Wales' (D.Phil. thesis, University of Oxford, 1997).

—— '"Clearing up misconceptions": the campaign to set up birth control clinics in South Wales between the wars', *Welsh History Review*, 19:1 (1998), 103–29.

—— '"She was quite satisfied with the arrangements I made": gender and birth control in Britain, 1920–1950', *Past and Present*, 169 (2000), 161–93.

—— *Birth Control, Sex, and Marriage in Britain, 1918–1960* (Oxford: Oxford University Press, 2006).

Fisher, K., and S. Szreter, '"They prefer withdrawal": the choice of birth control in Britain, 1918–50', *Journal of Interdisciplinary History*, 34 (2003), 265–91.

Florence, L. S., *Birth Control on Trial* (London: Allen and Unwin, 1930).

Fowler, D., *The First Teenagers: The Lifestyle of Young Wage-Earners in Interwar Britain* (London: The Woburn Press, 1995).

Fraser, W. Hamish, *The Coming of the Mass Market, 1850–1914* (London: Archon Books, 1981).

Freidson, E., *Profession of Medicine: A Study of the Sociology of Applied Knowledge* (Chicago: University of Chicago Press, 1988).

French, M., 'Commercials, careers, and culture: travelling salesmen in Britain, 1890s–1930s', *Economic History Review*, 58:2 (2005), 352–77.

Fryer, P., *The Birth Controllers* (London: Secker and Warburg, 1965).

—— *British Birth Control Ephemera, 1870–1947* (London: The Barracuda Press, 1969).

Gazeley, I., 'Women's pay in British industry during the Second World War', *Economic History Review*, 61:3 (2008), 651–71.

Geppert, A. C. T., 'Divine sex, happy marriage, regenerated nation: Marie Stopes's marital manual Married Love and the making of a best-seller, 1918–1955', *Journal of the History of Sexuality*, 8:3 (1998), 389–433.

Gittins, D., *Fair Sex: Family Size and Structure, 1900–1939* (London: Hutchinson, 1982).

Grier, J., 'Eugenics and birth control: contraceptive provision in North Wales, 1918–1939', *Social History of Medicine*, 11:3 (1998), 443–48.

Griffith, E. F., *Contraception in General Practice* (London: Eyre and Spottiswoode, 1936).

—— *Voluntary Parenthood* (London: Heinemann, 1937).

Gurney, P., '"Intersex" and "dirty girls": Mass-Observation and working-class sexuality in England in the 1930s', *Journal of the History of Sexuality*, 8:2 (1997), 256–90.

Haire, N., *Hygienic Methods of Family Limitation* (London: G. Standring, 1922).

—— *Birth Control Methods* (London: G. Allen and Unwin, 1936).

Hall, L. A., *Hidden Anxieties: Male Sexuality, 1900–1950* (Boston: Polity Press, 1991).
—— '"The subject is obscene: no lady would dream of alluding to it": Marie Stopes and her courtroom dramas', *Women's History Review*, 22:2 (2013), 253–66.
—— *Sex, Gender and Social Change in Britain since 1880* (Basingstoke: Palgrave Macmillan, 2013).
Hall, R. (ed.), *Dear Dr Stopes: Sex in the 1920s* (London: Penguin, 1978).
—— *Marie Stopes: A Biography* (London: Virago, 1978).
Heath, D., *Purifying Empire: Obscenity and the Politics of Moral Regulation in Britain, India and Australia* (Cambridge: Cambridge University Press, 2010).
Hemingway, J., 'Sexual learning and the seaside: relocating the "dirty weekend" and teenage girls' sexuality', *Sex Education: Sexuality, Society and Learning*, 6:4 (2006), 429–43.
Henriques, B. L. Q., *Indiscretions of a Magistrate: Thoughts on the Work of the Juvenile Court* (London: Non-Fiction Book Club, 1950).
Hilton, M., *Consumerism in 20th-Century Britain: The Search for a Historical Movement* (Cambridge: Cambridge University Press, 2003).
Himes, N. E., *Medical History of Contraception* (Baltimore: The Williams and Wilkins Company, 1936).
Hobbs, A., *A Fleet Street in Every Town: The Provincial Press in England, 1855–1900* (Cambridge: Open Book Publishers, 2018).
Hodges, S., *Contraception, Colonialism and Commerce: Birth Control in South India, 1920–1940* (Aldershot: Ashgate, 2008).
Hoggart, R., *Uses of Literacy: Aspects of Working-Class Life with Special and Entertainments* (Harmondsworth: Penguin, 1957).
Holz, R., *The Birth Control Clinic in a Marketplace World* (Rochester, NY: University of Rochester Press, 2012).
Horton, T., *The French Letter King* (Bloomington: Author House, 2014).
Houlbrook, M., *Queer London: Perils and Pleasures in the Sexual Metropolis, 1918–1957* (Chicago: University of Chicago Press, 2005).
Howsam, L., 'What is the historiography of books? Recent studies in authorship, publishing, and reading in modern Britain and North America', *Historical Journal*, 51:4 (2008), 1089–1101.
Humphries, S., *Secret World of Sex: Forbidden Fruit, the British Experience, 1900–1950* (London: Sidgwick and Jackson, 1988).
Illich, I., *Medical Nemesis: The Expropriation of Health* (London: Marion Boyars, 1974).
Ingram, J. G., *A Century of Progress, 1847–1947* (London: Ingram, 1947).

Ittmann, K., 'Family limitation and family economy in Bradford, West Yorkshire 1851–1881', *Journal of Social History*, 25:3 (1992), 547–73.
Jackson, P., M. Lowe, D. Miller and F. Mort, 'Introduction: transcending dualisms', in P. Jackson, M. Lowe, D. Miller and F. Mort (eds), *Commercial Cultures: Economies, Practices, Spaces* (Oxford and New York: Berg, 2000), pp. 1–4.
Jankowski, J., *Shelf Life: Modern Package Design 1920–1945* (San Francisco: Chronicle Books, 1992).
Jobling, P., 'Playing safe: the politics of pleasure and gender in the promotion of condoms in Britain, 1972–1982', *Design History*, 10:1 (1997), 53–70.
Jones, C., and R. Porter (eds), *Reassessing Foucault: Power, Medicine and the Body* (London: Routledge, 1994).
Jones, C. L., *The Medical Trade Catalogue in Britain, 1880–1914* (London: Pickering and Chatto, 2013).
—— 'Under the covers? Contraceptives, commerce and the household in Britain, 1880–1960', *Social History of Medicine*, 29:4 (2016), 734–56.
Jones, E. L., 'The establishment of voluntary family planning clinics in Liverpool and Bradford: a comparative study', *Social History of Medicine*, 24:2 (2011), 352–69.
Jones, S., *The Illustrated Police News: London's Court Cases and Sensational Stories* (Nottingham: Wicked Publications, 2002).
Jütte, R., *Contraception: A History* (London: Polity Press, 2008).
Knight, P., 'Women and abortion in Victorian and Edwardian England', *History Workshop Journal*, 4 (1977), 57–68.
Laite, J. A., 'The Association for Moral and Social Hygiene: abolitionism and prostitution law in Britain (1915–1959)', *Women's History Review*, 17:2 (2008), 207–23.
Latham, M., *Regulating Reproduction: A Century of Conflict in Britain and France* (Manchester: Manchester University Press, 2002).
Lawrence, C., and A. K. Mayer (eds), *Regenerating England: Science, Medicine and Culture in Inter-War Britain* (Amsterdam: Roldophi, 2000).
Leiss, W., S. Kline and S. Jhally, *Social Communication in Advertising: Persons, Products, and Images of Well-Being* (New York: Methuen Publications, 1986).
Leathard, A., *The Fight for Family Planning* (London: Palgrave Macmillan, 1980).
Loudon, I., 'Childbirth', in I. Loudon (ed.), *Western Medicine: An Illustrated History* (Oxford: Oxford University Press, 1997), pp. 206–20.
Löwy, I., '"Sexual chemistry" before the Pill: science, industry and chemical contraceptives, 1920–1960', *British Journal for the History of Science*, 44:2 (2011), 245–74.

Mackinnon, A., *Love and Freedom: Professional Women and the Reshaping of Personal Life* (Cambridge: Cambridge University Press, 1997).

MacNamara, T., *Birth Control and American Modernity: A History of Popular Ideas* (Cambridge: Cambridge University Press, 2018).

Malleson, J., *The Principles of Contraception* (London: V. Gollancz, 1935).

Marks, L., *Sexual Chemistry: A History of the Contraceptive Pill* (New Haven and London: Yale University Press, 2001).

Mass-Observation, *The Press and Its Readers* (London: Art and Technology, 1949).

Matthews, R., *The History of the Provincial Press in England* (London: Bloomsbury, 2017).

McIntosh, T., '"An abortionist city": maternal mortality, abortion, and birth control in Sheffield, 1920–1940', *Medical History*, 44 (2000), 75–96.

McKibbin, R., *Classes and Cultures, England 1918–1951* (Oxford: Oxford University Press, 1998).

McLaren, A., 'Women's work and regulation of family size', *History Workshop Journal*, 4:1 (1977), 70–81.

—— *Birth Control in Nineteenth-Century England* (London: Croom Helm, 1978).

—— *A History of Contraception: From Antiquity to the Present Day* (Blackwell, 1990).

Mechen, B., '"Closer together": Durex condoms and contraceptive consumerism in 1970s Britain', in J. Evans and C. Meehan (eds), *Perceptions of Pregnancy from the Seventeenth to the Twentieth Century* (Cham: Palgrave Macmillan, 2016), pp. 213–36.

Mold, A., *Making the Patient-consumer: Patient Organisations and Health Consumerism in Britain* (Manchester: Manchester University Press, 2016).

Mort, F., *Dangerous Sexualities: Medico-Moral Politics in England since 1830* (London: Routledge and Kegan Paul, 1987).

—— 'Paths to mass consumption: historical perspectives', in P. Jackson, M. Lowe, D. Miller and F. Mort (eds), *Commercial Cultures: Economies, Practices, Spaces* (Oxford and New York: Berg, 2000), pp. 7–14.

Murphy, C., and V. Pooke, 'Emergency contraception in the UK – stigma as a key ingredient of a fundamental women's healthcare product', *Sexual and Reproductive Health Matters*, 27:3 (2019), 122–5.

Murphy, J., *The Condom Industry in the United States* (London: McFarland, 1990).

Nava, M., and A. O'Shea (eds), *Modern Times: Reflections on a Century of English Modernity* (London: Routledge, 1996).

Nead, L., *Victorian Babylon: People, Streets and Images in Nineteenth-Century London* (New Haven and London: Yale University Press, 2005).

Neushul, P., 'Marie C. Stopes and the popularization of birth control technology', *Technology and Culture*, 39:2 (1998), 245–72.
Ogburn, M., *Spaces of Modernity: London's Geographies 1680–1780* (New York and London: Guilford Press, 1998).
Parker, K. W., 'Sign consumption in the 19th-century department store: an examination of visual merchandising in the grand emporiums (1846–1900)', *Journal of Sociology*, 39:4 (2003), 353–71.
Peel, J., 'The manufacture and retailing of contraceptives in England', *Population Studies*, 17 (1963), 113–25.
Peel, J., and M. Potts, *Textbook of Contraceptive Practice* (Cambridge: Cambridge University Press, 1969).
Peel, R.A. (ed.), *Marie Stopes, Eugenics and the English Birth Control Movement* (London: Galton Institute, 1996).
Perkin, H., *The Rise of Professional Society in England since 1880* (London: Routledge, 1989).
Porter, R., and L. Hall (eds), *The Facts of Life: The Creation of Sexual Knowledge in Britain, 1650–1950* (New Haven and London: Yale University Press, 1995).
Power, M., 'The wife's adviser(s): a literary note', *James Joyce Quarterly*, 32 (1995), 706–9.
Pugh, M., *We Danced All Night: A Social History of Britain between the Wars* (London: The Bodley Head, 2009).
Rappaport, E., 'Packaging China: foreign articles and dangerous tastes in the Mid-Victorian tea party', in F. Trentmann (ed.), *The Making of the Consumer: Knowledge, Power and Identity in the Modern World* (New York and Oxford: Berg, 2006), pp. 125–46.
—— *Shopping for Pleasure: Women in the Making of London's West End* (Princeton: Princeton University Press, 2000).
Richdale, J., 'Ladies' and gentlemen's toilet and rubber requisites: the development of New Zealand's commercial trade in contraceptives and birth control literature 1900s–1940', *Health and History*, 15:2 (2013), 72–92.
Roberts, E., 'Working wives and their families', in T. Barker and M. Drake (eds), *Population and Society in Britain, 1850–1980* (London: Batsford, 1982), pp. 140–71.
Roberts, R., *The Classic Slum: Salford Life in the First Quarter of the Century* (1971; Harmondsworth: Penguin, 1973).
Rose, Jo., *The Intellectual Life of the British Working Classes* (New Haven: Yale University Press, 2001).
Rose, Ju., *Marie Stopes and the Sexual Revolution* (London: Faber and Faber, 1992).

Rowntree, G., and R. M. Pierce, 'Birth control in practice: part one', *Population Studies*, 15:1 (1961), 3–31.

Rusterholz, C., 'English women doctors, contraception and family planning in transnational perspective (1930–1970)', *Medical History*, 63:2 (2019), 153–172.

Ryley Scott, G., *Scott's Encyclopaedia of Sex* (London: T. Warner Laurie Ltd, 1939).

Sachsenmaier, D., S. N. Eisenstadt and J. Riedel (eds), *Reflections on Multiple Modernities: European, Chinese and Other Interpretations* (Leiden: Brill, 2002).

Sarch, A., 'Those dirty ads! Birth control advertising in the 1920s and 1930s', *Critical Studies in Mass Communication*, 14:1 (1997), 31–48.

Schofield, M., *The Sexual Behaviour of Young People* (London: Longman, 1965).

Short, B., D. Gilbert and D. Matless, 'Historical geographies of British modernity', in D. Gilbert, D. Matless and B. Short (eds), *Geographies of British Modernity: Space and Society in the Twentieth Century* (Oxford: Blackwell, 2003), pp. 1–28.

Sigel, L. Z., 'Censorship in inter-war Britain: obscenity, spectacle, and the workings of the liberal state', *Journal of Social History*, 45:1 (2011), 61–83.

—— *Making Modern Love: Sexual Narratives and Identities in Interwar Britain* (Philadelphia: Temple University Press, 2012).

Slater, S. A., 'Containment: Managing street prostitution in London, 1918–1959', *Journal of British Studies*, 49:2 (2010), 332–57.

Sloan, D. G., 'The extent of contraceptive use and the social paradigm of modern demography', *Sociology*, 17:3 (1983), 380–7.

Smith, H., *Masculinity and Same-Sex Desire in Industrial England, 1895–1957* (Basingstoke: Palgrave Macmillan, 2015).

Smith, M. L., 'Inconspicuous consumption: non-display goods and identity formation', *Journal of Archaeological Method and Theory*, 14 (2007), 412–38.

Soloway, R., *Birth Control and the Population Question in England, 1870–1930* (Chapel Hill: University of North Carolina Press, 1982).

—— 'The "perfect" contraceptive: eugenics and birth control research in Britain and American in the interwar years', *Journal of Contemporary History*, 30 (1995), 637–64.

Stopes, M. C., *A Letter to Working Mothers: On How to Have Healthy Children and Avoid Weakening Pregnancies*, 5th edn (London: The Mother's Clinic for Constructive Birth Control, 1926).

Summerfield, P., *Women Workers in the Second World War* (London: Croom Helm, 1984).
Sutton, M., *We Didn't Know Aught: A Study of Women's Sexuality, Superstition and Death in Women's Lives in Lincolnshire during the 1930s, '40s and '50s* (Stamford: Paul Watkins, 1992).
Szreter, S., *Fertility, Class and Gender, 1860–1940* (Cambridge: Cambridge University Press, 1996).
Szreter, S., and K. Fisher, *Sex Before the Sexual Revolution: Intimate Life in England, 1918–1963* (Cambridge: Cambridge University Press, 2010).
Szuhan, N., 'Sex in the laboratory: the Family Planning Association and contraceptive science in Britain, 1929–1959', *British Journal for the History of Science*, 51:3 (2018), 487–510.
Taft, W. N., *Handbook of Window Display* (New York: McGraw-Hill, 1926).
Tebbut, M., *Women's Talk? A Social History of Gossip in Working-Class Neighbourhoods, 1860–1960* (Aldershot: Scolar Press, 1995).
Tilt, E. J., *A Handbook of Uterine Therapeutics* (New York: Wood, 1863).
Timmins, G. L., *Window Dressing: The Principles of 'Display'* (London, Sir I. Pitman and Sons, 1922).
Tinkler, P., *Constructing Girlhood: Popular Magazines for Girls Growing up in England, 1920–1950* (London: Taylor and Francis, 1995).
Tone, A., 'Contraceptive consumers: gender and the political economy of birth control in the 1930s', *Journal of Social History*, 29 (1996), 485–508.
—— *Devices and Desires: A History of Contraceptives in America* (New York: Hill and Wang, 2001).
—— 'Making room for rubbers: gender, technology, and birth control before the Pill', *History and Technology*, 18 (2002), 51–76.
—— 'Medicalizing reproduction: the Pill and home pregnancy tests', *Journal of Sex Research*, 49:4 (2012), 319–27.
Trentmann, F., 'The evolution of the consumer: meanings, identities, and political synapses before the age of affluence', in S. Garon and P. L. Maclachlan (eds), *The Ambivalent Consumer: Questioning Consumption in East Asia and the West* (Ithaca: Cornell University Press, 2006), pp. 37–42.
—— 'Knowing consumers – histories, identities, practices: an introduction', in F. Trentmann (ed.), *The Making of the Consumer: Knowledge, Power and Identity in the Modern World* (New York and Oxford: Berg, 2006).
—— *Empire of Things: How We Became Consumers from the Fifteenth Century to the Twenty-First* (London: Allen Lane, 2016).
Tully, J., *The Devil's Milk: A Social History of Rubber* (New York: Monthly Review Press, 2011).

Velde, T. van de, *Fertility and Sterility in Marriage: Their Voluntary Promotion and Limitation* (London: Heinemann, 1931).

Vitellone, N., *Object Matters: Condoms, Adolescence and Time* (Manchester: Manchester University Press, 2008).

Voge, C. I., *The Chemistry and Physics of Contraceptives* (London: Cape, 1933).

Walkowitz, J. R., *City of Dreadful Delight: Narratives of Sexual Danger in Late-Victorian London* (Chicago: Chicago University Press, 1992).

—— *Nights Out: Life in Cosmopolitan London* (New Haven and London: Yale University Press, 2012).

Wallis, P., 'Consumption, retailing and medicine in early modern London', *Economic History Review*, 61 (2008), 26–53.

Waters, C., 'Introduction: beyond "Americanization": rethinking Anglo-American cultural exchange between the wars', *Cultural and Social History*, 4:4 (2007), 451–59.

Watkins, S. C., and A. D. Danzi, 'Women's gossip and social change: childbirth and fertility control among Italian and Jewish women in the United States, 1920–1940', *Gender and Society*, 9:4 (1995), 469–90.

Webb, B., *The Discovery of the Consumer* (London: Benn, 1928).

Weeks, J., *Sex, Politics and Society: The Regulation of Sexuality since 1800* (Harlow: Longman, 1989).

Wilson, A., and C. West, 'The marketing of unmentionables', *Harvard Business Review*, 59:1 (1981), 91–102.

Wood, C., and B. Suitters, *The Fight for Acceptance: A History of Contraception* (Aylesbury: Medical and Technical Publishing Co. Ltd, 1970).

Woodruff, W., *The Rise of the British Rubber Industry during the Nineteenth Century* (Liverpool: Liverpool University Press, 1958).

Woycke, J., *Birth Control in Germany, 1871–1933* (London: Routledge, 1988).

Wyndham, D., *Norman Haire and the Study of Sex* (Sydney: Sydney University Press, 2012).

Index

Note: contraceptive brand names can be found under companies' names

abortifacients 4, 73, 80, 142
  see also female pills
abortion 5, 14, 21, 65, 106, 153, 183, 210
abstinence 5
adolescents 14–16, 23, 53, 120–2, 124, 172, 181–3, 186, 190–2, 194–5, 197, 205, 208
advertisements 16, 42, 71, 74, 78, 98–100, 103, 105–8, 110–13, 115–16, 120–4, 144, 178, 185, 188, 195
  see also books; print culture
Allbutt, Henry Arthur 38–9, 67–8, 73–4, 76, 77, 100, 102–3, 138
anti-Semitism 34, 80, 141
armed forces 48, 52–3, 56, 84, 88, 159–60
  see also soldiers; Royal Navy
Association of Moral and Social Hygiene 1, 17–18, 32
  see also moralists; Public Morality Council; social conservatives

bachelor 14, 105, 109
barbers 23, 73, 124, 178–9, 190, 195, 197–8
  see also hairdressers

Besant, Annie 35, 38–9, 66, 74, 77
Birth Control Advisory Bureau 143–4, 208
birth control clinics 1, 7, 10, 12, 15, 19–20, 22–3, 40, 44, 56, 70–2, 80, 82–3, 106, 111, 134–54, 157–8, 160–5, 173, 188–9, 205–7
birth controllers 9–10, 12, 21, 50, 56, 206
books 8, 14, 40–1, 71, 80, 101–3, 107–13, 117, 119, 122–3, 126, 173
  see also advertisements; print culture
booksellers 103, 108, 110, 173
Boots 88, 175, 196
brands 11, 21–2, 63–7, 71–3, 82–4, 87–90, 98, 103, 134, 177, 190–1, 206–7, 210
  see also intellectual property; packaging; trademarks
Brasseur Surgical Manufacturing Company, Le 76, 78–80, 111–6, 119, 123, 154

INDEX

cap 1, 32, 37–9, 41–2, 44, 48, 52, 56, 70–3, 76–7, 79–84, 88, 108, 137, 139–43, 145–9, 152–63, 175, 182, 212
  cervical 8, 22, 33–5, 64, 82, 161–5
  see also pessary, occlusive
  Dutch 34, 44, 82, 149–52, 155–9, 162
  see also diaphragm
  see also pessary
catalogue 14, 16, 22, 36, 42, 66, 72, 76–8, 81, 86–7, 98, 100–25, 138, 143, 145, 151, 162, 176–7, 182, 189, 205
  see also mail-order; price list
chemists 9, 10, 18, 22–4, 35–7, 48–9, 56, 65–6, 68–73, 79, 86, 88, 107, 110, 117, 122–3, 134, 136, 149, 157–9, 172–98, 205–8, 211
coitus interruptus 5
  see also withdrawal
condom 1, 3, 5, 7, 8, 15–16, 20–1, 31–3, 41–50, 53–6, 64, 72–6, 80, 83, 87–9, 108–9, 124, 139, 142, 148–61, 157, 164, 173, 178–98, 205–6, 209, 211–12
  see also latex; sheath
commercialisation 23–4, 31–2, 63, 135, 172–3, 179, 191, 208–9
commodification 21, 205
communication communities 50–1, 55, 57
Constantine and Jackson 41, 43, 76, 79–80, 103, 174
consumers 4, 6–8, 12–16, 19, 21–3, 31, 33–4, 36, 42–3, 50, 63–4, 69, 72, 75–7, 79, 82–5, 89–90, 98, 100, 108, 110, 115, 120, 123, 125, 135, 147, 173, 176, 179, 184, 191–4, 197–8, 206
end 8, 11–12, 14, 17–18, 87, 99, 149, 158, 176, 206–8

female 176
ignorant 63, 77
knowing 14, 65, 173–5, 181, 197, 107, 205
male 184
middle-class 38–9, 84, 105
modern 186
unknowing 22, 35–6, 107, 113, 125, 175, 181, 198
upper-class 38
working-class 38, 84, 175, 208
contraceptive Pill 3–5, 9, 19, 24, 65, 164–5, 205–6, 209–12
Contraceptives (Regulation) Bill 1–2, 16, 19, 31, 63, 75, 98, 120, 122, 124–5, 134–5, 172–3, 181–2, 185–6, 193, 197, 208
Cox, Gladys 84, 153–4, 157

Dawson, Bertrand 1, 2, 18, 23, 31–3, 48–9, 51, 56, 63, 106, 112, 122–3, 134–5, 181, 183–5, 188–91, 208–9
diaphragm 8, 32–4, 49, 55, 88, 137, 139, 149, 156, 161–4
  see also cap, Dutch; Mensinga, W. P. J.
doctors 7, 9, 36, 51, 73–4, 87, 107, 109, 116–17, 135, 138–40, 142, 149, 153–6, 159–60, 162, 189, 192, 205–7
  see also medical practitioners; medical profession

efficacy 4, 8–11, 19, 45, 82–3, 134–5, 146, 149, 152–3, 207, 211
Elderton, Ethel 36, 50, 100, 105, 121, 175
enema 1, 32, 35–6, 41, 48, 84, 175, 177
  see also syringe
eugenics 8, 36, 71, 111, 117, 141, 147

INDEX

euphemistic 14, 99, 105,107, 124–5, 205

Family Planning Association 16–18, 23, 52, 56, 82, 124–5, 135, 146, 151–2, 156, 159–61, 164–5, 189, 196, 206, 208
see also National Birth Control Association
female pills 21, 65, 100, 115
see also abortifacients
fertility 3, 5, 8, 11, 21, 35, 43, 50–1, 101, 106
decline 5, 205
First World War 1–2, 6, 19, 34, 39–40, 43, 73, 100, 105, 173, 175, 197, 209

gatekeepers 8–10, 135, 206
George, W. 43–5, 76, 103, 123, 146, 174, 185
Griffith, Edward F. 134, 150–2, 155–6

hairdressers 178, 187, 190–2, 195
see also barbers
Haire, Norman 44, 117–19, 122, 137–40, 153, 156, 162, 193, 209
Hancock of Fleet Street 86, 122–3, 146, 176, 185
Harrison, R. 155, 157–8, 163, 187
see also Prentif
Harrison, W. T. 43–4, 187
see also Prentif
Himes, Norman 10, 31–2, 39, 111, 115, 139, 145–6, 155, 209
hygiene 108, 110, 114
aids 75
appliances 175
feminine 107, 195
stores 187
see also rubber stores; surgical stores

industry 3, 6, 11, 24, 56–7, 64, 82, 89, 151, 154, 180, 183, 205, 208
textile 50
intellectual property 19, 63–5, 80, 83, 89, 98
see also brands; packaging; trademarks
intermediaries 7–9, 12, 17, 22, 99, 207–8

Jackson, Lionel A., 40–3, 80, 173
see also London Rubber Company; LRC

laboratory 88, 135, 149, 151, 153, 155, 163, 165, 207
tests 84, 90, 152, 154, 160
see also testing
Lambert, A. 86, 114
Lamberts (Dalston) Ltd 82, 84, 86, 109, 111, 114, 116–18, 121, 123, 137–65, 187–8, 191, 206, 208–10
Lambert, E., and Son 32, 34–42, 48–9, 52–3, 55–7, 65, 67, 69–81, 89, 100–3, 113, 115, 209
'Anti-Geniture' 69, 81, 121, 176
Chinosol 137, 140, 143, 149
'Lam-butt' 70, 74, 109, 116, 138–9, 144
'Malthusian' 14, 38–9, 65, 209
'Pro-Race' 22, 64, 70–82, 84, 89, 110, 112, 115, 121, 137–41, 144, 148, 161–2, 176, 181, 188, 191, 210
'Racial' 69, 72, 137, 140, 149, 161–2
latex 3, 16, 21, 31–3, 40–50, 53–7, 137, 152, 188
see also condom
London Rubber Company 3, 15, 41

London Rubber Company (*cont.*)
  see also Jackson, Lionel A.; LRC; Reid, Angus
LRC 21, 32–3, 40–51, 53–7, 64, 71–3, 76, 80, 88–90, 118, 124, 139, 148, 150, 152, 156–65, 173, 178, 181, 188–90, 195, 206–7, 210–11
  'Durex' 64, 76, 84, 88–9, 148–9, 160, 181, 184, 190, 206–7, 211–12
  see also Jackson, Lionel A.; London Rubber Company; Reid, Angus

mail-order 4, 18, 41, 81, 83, 90, 99–101, 105, 114, 118, 146, 176, 205, 208
  see also catalogue; price list
Malthusian League, The 35, 38–9, 56, 66–7, 75, 106, 137–8, 166
  see also Lambert, E. and Sons 'Malthusian'; Neo-Malthusian
Malleson, Joan 52, 145, 155, 162, 209
manufactory 37, 40–1, 45–56, 158
  see also manufacturers; production
manufacturers 2, 4, 6, 10, 13, 17, 21–2, 31, 33–4, 40, 44–5, 55–6, 64, 66, 68, 76–7, 79, 86, 89–90, 99, 107, 110–11, 120, 124–5, 135–7, 150–1, 154, 157, 163–5, 175–6, 178, 187–91, 195–6, 198, 206, 208
  see also manufactory; production
market 15–19, 22, 24, 32, 37, 42, 45–6, 48, 55, 64–7, 75, 77, 83, 85, 89–90, 101, 105, 107, 134–5, 148–9, 151, 160–1, 163, 173, 186, 188, 190–1, 197–8, 207, 211–12
marketplace 4, 6, 11, 24, 37, 65, 135–6, 185

marriage 2–3, 13, 18, 39, 43, 50–1, 107–8, 110–11, 114, 124, 144, 146, 209, 211
Mass-Observation 17, 85–6, 88, 99, 215, 223, 231, 234
medicalisation 9, 11, 135, 165, 206–7
medical practitioners 10–12, 19, 36, 39–40, 84, 110–11, 134–40, 143, 147–8, 150, 155–6, 159, 206, 212
  see also doctors; medical profession
medical profession 3, 8–11, 18, 21, 38, 43–4, 56, 98, 110–11, 114, 125, 136, 138–9, 141, 146, 149, 153, 164, 206, 210
  see also doctors; medical practitioners
Mensinga, W. P. J. 33–4
  see also cap, Dutch; diaphragm
pessary 36, 38, 67
modernity 6, 12, 24, 68
moralists 15, 18, 34, 44, 48, 51, 63, 75, 89, 98, 120, 182
  see also Association of Moral and Social Hygiene; Public Morality Council; social conservatives
morality 8, 24, 56, 120, 192

National Birth Control Association 21, 33, 42–5, 56, 72, 82, 111, 117, 119, 134–5, 137, 145, 147–51, 206–8
  see also Family Planning Association
Neilans, Alison 1, 2, 4, 7, 23, 31, 208–9
Neo-Malthusian 100–5, 121, 179, 206
  see also Lambert, E. and Sons 'Malthusian'; Malthusian League, The

INDEX   243

nurses 35, 71, 135, 137, 140–1,
    144–6, 206–7

packaging 18, 21, 63–5, 69, 72–3,
    77–9, 82, 89–90, 152, 158,
    172, 175, 185, 205, 235
  see also brands; intellectual
    property; trademarks
pessary 34, 36, 41, 65, 73–9, 83–8,
    108–9, 114–18, 140, 151, 154,
    156, 175–6, 187, 198, 211
  chemical 1, 48, 69, 71, 81–7,
    102, 108, 137, 163–4, 178
    see also spermicides
  occlusive 33, 78, 84, 116
    see also cap
  quinine 22, 52, 64–5, 77, 79,
    116, 122, 139–40, 149
pharmacists 68, 123, 158, 186–7,
    189, 191
pornography 41, 108, 111, 173,
    181, 229
pregnancy 4, 7–8, 20, 24, 108, 110,
    114, 135, 138, 205
Prentif 43–6, 48–9, 56, 72–3,
    83, 107, 111–12, 146, 149,
    151–63, 165, 187–9, 210,
    212
  see also Harrison, R.; Harrison,
    W. T.
price list 16, 73, 100, 151
  see also catalogue; mail-order
print culture 19, 22, 98, 105, 181,
    183
  see also advertisements; books
production 4, 19, 21, 23, 33, 35,
    37–9, 41–57, 66, 103, 112,
    154–5, 162, 163, 208
  cement process 16
  condom 31
  latex 6, 16, 32–3, 40–1, 46, 48–9,
    188
  mass 87
  mechanised 32, 205
  rubber 32, 34, 40, 43, 137

sheath 37
  see also manufactory;
    manufacturers
promiscuity 2, 7, 13, 51, 53, 56,
    190, 194, 212
prostitution 15, 42, 99, 173, 179,
    183
Public Morality Council 17–18,
    181, 183, 186, 188, 192, 194,
    197
  see also Association of Moral and
    Social Hygiene; moralists;
    social conservatives

Reid, Angus 4, 89, 124, 158, 164,
    189–91
  see also Jackson, Lionel A.;
    London Rubber Company;
    LRC
reliability 4, 7, 8, 10–11, 14, 22,
    44–5, 64, 67, 72, 77–8, 83, 85,
    89–90, 98, 135, 147, 151, 165,
    205, 207
Rendell, W. J. 21–2, 52–3, 64–7,
    69, 71–90, 107, 117, 138, 146,
    175–6, 187, 195, 210, 212
  pessary 21–2, 64–9, 76, 79, 139,
    190, 206, 210
  'Wife Friend, The' 21–2, 64–9,
    72–6, 83–9 100, 122, 149,
    191, 206, 209
retail 19, 22–3, 40–5, 68–70, 75,
    83, 86, 90, 106, 142, 145,
    148–50, 163, 172–8, 185–91,
    195–8, 206, 208–9, 211
retailers 1, 4, 6, 7, 12, 15–16, 34,
    37, 72, 76, 78, 100, 102, 118,
    138, 206–7
respectability 10, 12, 19, 31, 33,
    56–7, 89–90, 106, 118, 175,
    190–1, 196, 206
Royal Navy 43, 56, 76, 194
  see also armed forces; soldiers
Royal Pharmaceutical Society 18,
    123, 184–6, 191, 196–7

rubber stores 40, 64, 75, 88,
117–18, 155
see also hygiene stores; surgical
stores

Second World War 2, 4, 9, 11,
19, 33, 40, 48, 64, 79, 86, 88,
122, 124, 135, 137, 152, 191,
208–9
sheath 1, 5, 15, 20, 32–4, 37–42,
45, 49–50, 65, 69, 72, 75, 84,
108–10, 114, 116, 148–51,
158, 160, 163–4, 173–9, 183,
209
see also condom
shop displays 175, 181, 184, 195,
198
slot machines 14, 23, 73, 124, 134,
178–83, 186, 190–8, 205,
208–9, 211–12
social conservatives 16, 19, 21–3,
56, 208
see also Association of Moral and
Social Hygiene; moralists;
Public Morality Council
Society for Constructive Birth
Control and Racial Progress 8,
17, 22, 70, 72, 139, 141, 143,
145, 148
Society for the Provision of Birth
Control Clinics 139, 145
Soho 43, 76, 173–4, 176–9, 185,
197
soldiers 14, 43, 160, 205
see also armed forces; Royal Navy
spermicides 8, 52, 84, 109, 147,
162
standardisation 9, 43, 69, 147,
165

Stopes, Marie Carmichael 3, 8,
17–18, 22, 34, 37, 39, 42, 52,
56, 70–82, 86–9, 99, 105–6,
109–13, 115–22, 125, 135,
137–46, 148–52, 155, 161–2,
166, 174–5, 177, 183–4, 187,
206, 208–9
surgical stores 21, 23, 45, 73,
75–82, 89–90, 107, 111–16,
118–25, 138, 146, 157,
173–4, 176, 178–9, 182–3,
185, 190–1, 193, 195, 197–8,
205–6, 208, 211
see also hygiene stores; rubber
stores
syringe 35–9, 42, 48, 67, 84, 108,
139, 175, 177, 209
see also enema

testing 44–7, 54–5, 109, 135, 137,
144, 149–53, 155, 157, 160,
163, 165, 207
see also laboratory, tests
tobacconists 173, 178–9, 190–1,
197
trademarks 21–2, 63–5, 69–70,
75–9, 82–3, 89–90
see also brands; intellectual
property; packaging

venereal disease 7, 13, 20–1, 40,
42–3, 51–3, 88, 99, 106, 194,
205
vulcanisation 32–4, 37, 40

window display 18, 23, 176, 178,
181, 184, 192, 197, 208
withdrawal 5, 36, 85
see also coitus interruptus

EU authorised representative for GPSR:
Easy Access System Europe, Mustamäe tee 50,
10621 Tallinn, Estonia
gpsr.requests@easproject.com